Comprehensive Orton-Gillingham Plus Teacher Guide

Comprehensive OG Plus Scope & Sequence
Phonics Lessons for Early Elementary and Intervention

First Grade (Student Book B)

IMSE's Comprehensive Orton-Gillingham Plus Teacher Guide

Phonics Lessons for Early Elementary and Intervention

Acknowledgments

Teachers, we listened, researched, and delivered. IMSE will continue to provide you with the best instruction and up-to-date research so you can concentrate on what you do best: teach!

I would like to express special thanks and gratitude to Janice Kohler who worked tirelessly to write and provide IMSE and teachers around the world with effective teacher guides to implement IMSE's structured literacy program.

In addition Kimberley Collins, our inside editor, we couldn't have done it without you. Your dedication and keen vision of the edits and content has been undeniably excellent.

I would also like to extend my thanks to Amy Gulley for her support and contributions to the teacher guides as well as all the various Instructors of IMSE who provided feedback, experience, and knowledge to provide state-of-the-art instruction in literacy.

Michael A. Satina, thank you for your design and partnership in the production of IMSE Impact.

Jeanne M. Jeup
IMSE Co-founder

The Institute for Multi-Sensory Education
24800 Denso Dr., Suite 202
Southfield, MI 48033
Phone 800-646-9788
Fax 248-735-2927
E-mail: info@imse.com
www.imse.com

To learn more about implementing the content in this book with fidelity, register to take IMSE's Comprehensive Orton-Gillingham Plus Training by visiting the website www.imse.com. IMSE is committed to providing quality professional development training in accredited structured literacy programs. Our instructors must meet the highest of standards and complete rigorous training to acquire qualifying credentials. Additional training and certification in IMSE's methodology, not included in this Teacher Guide, are required to become an IMSE Instructor. If you are interested in training fellow teachers in your district, please contact IMSE at 800-646-9788 for more information on how to become a district trainer.

COMPREHENSIVE
SCOPE AND SEQUENCE

Kindergarten

Concept #	Concept	Red Words		Card Pack #	Decodable Reader #
		Spell & Read	Read Only		
1	Mm /m/ (marshmallow)	the		1	
2	Aa /ă/ (apple)	was		2	
3	Ll /l/ (log)	is		3	
4	Oo /ŏ/ (octopus)	a		4	
5	Hh /h/ (hammer)	on		5	
6	Gg /g/ (goat)	and		6	
7	Cc /k/ (cat)	to		7	
8	Dd /d/ (dog)	for		8	
9	Tt /t/ (turtle)	go	orange, white	9	1
10	Ii /ĭ/ (igloo)	I, like	brown, stop	10	2
11	Jj /j/ (jam)	of, will	said	11	3
12	Kk /k/ (kite)	get, no	red, see	12	4
13	Pp /p/ (pig)	want, with	yellow	13	5
14	Uu /ŭ/ (umbrella)	said, you		14	6
15	Bb /b/ (bat)	in, put	bus	15	7
16	Rr /r/ (raccoon)	see, stop	blue, eek	16	8
17	Ff /f/ (fish)	from, off	sun	17	9
18	Nn /n/ (nose)	he, has	ouch	18	10
19	Ee /ĕ/ (edge)	have, me	pink	19	11
20	Ss /s/ (sun)	his, as	green	20	12
21	Ww /w/ (wagon)	my, into		21	13
22	Yy /y/ (yo-yo)	now, new		22	14
23	Vv /v/ (violin)	give	black	23	15
24	Xx /ks/ (box)	or, by	look	24	16
25	Zz /z/ (zebra)	went		25	17
26	qu /kw/ (queen)	do, are	good	26	18
27	Long vowels: /ā/, /ē/, /ī/, /ō/, /yōō/ (me, no, hi, mu/sic, ra/ven)	they, any	fish	2, 4, 10, 14, 19	19
28	Digraph: ch /ch/ (chin)	½ color list	help	27	20

Concept #	Concept	Red Words		Card Pack #	Decodable Reader #
		Spell & Read	Read Only		
29	Digraph: sh /sh/ (shoe)	½ color list		28	21
30	Digraph: th /TH/ (voiced) (feather)	one, two (could teach the whole number list)	three, four, five, seven, eight, nine	29	22
31	Digraph: th /th/ (unvoiced) (thumb)	come	her	29	23
32	Digraph: wh /w/ or /hw/ (whistle)	who, what, where, why		30	24
	Optional: Two-Syllable Closed/Open Decodable Reader		play, ball		25

First Grade

Concept #	Concept	Red Words		Card Pack #	Decodable Reader #
		Spell & Read	Read Only		
33	ss, ll, ff, zz (Sammy Loves Friendly Zebras) 1-1-1 Rule (kiss, bell, huff, jazz)	were, does	our	31	26
34	Compound Words (sunset)	some, good		None	27
35	Closed/Open Syllables with VC/CV and V/CV (ra/ven, Ve/nus, si/lo, hel/lo, mu/sic)	there, done	help (review)	2, 4, 10, 14, 19	28
36	Two-Consonant Beginning R Blends (truck)	her, here		32	29
37	Two-Consonant Beginning L Blends (sled)	under, down		33	30
38	Two-Consonant Beginning S Blends (snail)	onto, people	oven	34	31
39	Two-Consonant Beginning W Blends (swing)	saw, both	park	35	32

Concept #	Concept	Red Words		Card Pack #	Decodable Reader #
		Spell & Read	Read Only		
40	Ending T Blends (left)	should, could, would, over		36	33
41	Ending L Blends (milk)	love, live, out		37	34
42	Remaining Ending Blends (jump) and syllabication of 3 or more syllables (hob/gob/lin)	day, too, eye		38	35
43	y as a vowel /ī/ (cry)	all, again		39	36
44	-ng/-nk /ŋ/ (sang, sink)	boy, girl, sign	play	40	37
45	-ck /k/ (rock) 1-1-1 Rule	your, which, look	way	41	38
46	-tch /ch/ (match) 1-1-1 Rule	also, use		42	39
47	-dge /j/ (fudge) 1-1-1 Rule	today, yesterday	chair	43	40
48	3rd Syllable Type and 3rd Syllable Pattern: Magic E and VC/V (bike, fixate)	first, around, going		44	41
49	y as a vowel /ē/ (baby)	walk		39	42
50	Soft c /s/ and g /j/ (city, giraffe)	say, their	center	6 and 7 Plus 45	43
51	-ed /id/, /d/, /t/ (folded, soared, crashed)	how, once		46	44
52	-s /s/ or /z/, -es /iz/ (cats, dogs, dishes)	another		47	45
53	4th Syllable Type: Vowel Team: ea/ee /ē/ (treat, bee)	pull, wash		48	46
54	Vowel Team: ai/ay /ā/ (sail, clay)	every, everyone	school, tractor	49	47
55	Vowel Team: oa/oe /ō/ (boat, toe)	know, knew		50	48
56	-ing (walking)	friend		51	49
57	Contractions with am, is, are, has, not (I'm, he's, we're, isn't)	been, our, other		None	50

Second Grade

Concept #	Concept	Red Words		Card Pack #	Decodable Reader #
		Spell & Read	Read Only		
58	Three-Consonant Blends and Blends with Digraphs (scr, shr, spl, spr, squ, str, thr) (scream, shrimp, splash, spring, squid, street, thread)	away, after		52	51
59	Schwa (bacon)	few, many		None	52
60	5th Syllable Type: Bossy R: er (fern)	call, room, ball	swollen	53	53
61	Bossy R: ir (birth)	water, watch		54	54
62	Bossy R: ur (fur)	far, goes	pizza	55	55
63	Diphthongs: oi, oy (oil, boy) and 4th Syllable Pattern: V/V (poem, employee)	because, very		56	56
64	Diphthongs: ou, ow (out, brown)	door, car		57	57
65	igh (light)	great, though		58	58
66	3 Great Rules: Doubling (zapped)	don't, little		None	59
67	3 Great Rules: Drop (liked)	through		None	60
68	3 Great Rules: Change (cried)	always, hour		None	61
69	6th Syllable Type: Consonant-le (saddle)	sure, buy		59	62
70	Kind Old Words (kind, old, wild, colt, post)			None	63
71	Bossy R: ar (farm)	only		60	64
72	Bossy R: or (torn)	these, those, took		61	65
73	/aw/ spelled au and aw (August, fawn)	work, word, world		62	66

Concept #	Concept	Red Words		Card Pack #	Decodable Reader #
		Spell & Read	Read Only		
74	Contractions with have, would, will (they've, she'd, we'll)	touch	house	None	67
75	Other uses for silent e (house, love, face, huge, nose)			None	68
76	y as a vowel /ĭ/ (gym)	hall		39	69
77	ph /f/, gh /f/ (phone, cough)	enough, laugh, read		63 and 64	70
78	ch /k/ and /sh/ (echo, chef)	often		27	71
79	/o͞o/ spelled oo and ew (scoop, stew)	heard, thought		65 and 66	72
80	/o͞o/ spelled oo and u (took, put)	together		65 and 14	73
81	Other Bossy R Combinations: /air/ ar, ear, er (bear) /ar/ ear (heart) /er/ or, ar, ear, our (earth) /or/ ar, our (ward)	different		None	74
82	Silent Letters (Could also discuss Greek unusual spellings) (ghost, gnat, knife, lamb, scent, write, castle)	move		None	75
83	Homophones (to, two, too, there, their, they're)			None	76

Notes:

_____

_____

_____

_____

_____

_____

_____

_____

_____

_____

_____

_____

_____

_____

_____

_____

_____

_____

_____

About IMSE

The Institute for Multi-Sensory Education (IMSE) was founded in 1996 by educators Jeanne Jeup and Bronwyn Hain and is headquartered in Southeast Michigan. Just as many educators have experienced frustration in not feeling adequately prepared to teach reading after teacher preparatory programs, Jeanne and Bronwyn felt the same. In an effort to increase literacy proficiency, they made it their life's work to prepare educators to teach all students to read using a structured approach.

Based on the Orton-Gillingham approach, IMSE's explicit, sequential, systematic, multi-sensory instruction is imperative to student success. IMSE's IDA Accredited Structured Literacy courses include a literacy trifecta. *IMSE's Phonological Awareness Course* focuses on the importance of orthographic mapping, phonological awareness, and phonemic awareness. It is designed for teachers who teach all ages. *IMSE's Comprehensive Orton-Gillingham Plus Course* focuses on phonics and orthography. It is geared toward general education grades K-2 and teachers whose students require intervention in phonics and orthography. *IMSE's Morphology Plus Course* focuses on morphology, fluency, vocabulary, comprehension, and written expression. It is geared toward general education grades 3-5 and teachers whose students require intervention in those areas.

What is Structured Literacy™ and the Science of Reading?

Structured Literacy is supported by research (known as the Science of Reading) and is explicit, systematic, and cumulative. It also integrates listening, speaking, reading, and writing. Structured Literacy emphasizes the structure of language across all components, including phonology, orthography, syntax, morphology, semantics, and discourse. The key features of any Structured Literacy program include explicit, systematic, sequential instruction; cumulative practice and ongoing review; a high level of student-teacher interaction; use of examples and non-examples; decodable text; and prompt, corrective feedback (Spear-Swerling, 2018). Educators should also optimize academic learning time (ALT) by being prepared and on time, using a routine, decreasing transition times, avoiding digressions, utilizing small groups, increasing time spent in critical content, and making sure the materials are not too difficult or too easy (Archer & Hughes, 2011). To read more on the elements of Structured Literacy, visit IDA at https://dyslexiaida.org/effective-reading-instruction/.

The term Science of Reading is often misinterpreted as a specific teaching program. Therefore, to help eliminate confusion, a team of top literacy experts came together to define the Science of Reading. This definition was released on February 3, 2021, at The Reading League's Winter Symposium. The definition reads:

> The Science of Reading is a vast, interdisciplinary body of scientifically-based research about reading and issues related to reading and writing. This research has been conducted over the last five decades across the world, and it is derived from thousands of studies conducted in multiple languages. The science of reading has culminated in a preponderance of evidence to inform how proficient reading and writing develop;

why some have difficulty; and how we can most effectively assess and teach and, therefore, improve student outcomes through prevention of and intervention for reading difficulties. The Science of Reading is derived from researchers from multiple fields, including cognitive psychology, communication sciences, developmental psychology, education, implementation science, linguistics, neuroscience, and school psychology.

To join the Science of Reading movement and to learn more, visit https://www.whatisthescienceofreading.org/.

IMSE and the Science of Reading

The basis of IMSE's foundational approach to teaching reading can be tied to Jeanne Chall's *Learning to Read: The Great Debate* (1967). During Chall's three years of observing classrooms, studying textbooks, and analyzing research studies on how children learn to read, the determination was made that instruction to beginning or emergent readers supported the skill of decoding. The study found that early decoding produced better word recognition and spelling and made it easier for the child to read with understanding. The study also found that the knowledge of symbols (letters) and sounds had more of an influence on a child's reading achievement than that child's IQ, or mental ability.

IMSE's trainings provide educators with the skills needed to integrate research-based, explicit, systematic, and multi-sensory instruction into their current curriculum. The Theoretical Models of Reading (Gough and Tunmer's Simple View of Reading; Hollis Scarborough's The Reading Rope; Linnea Ehri's The Four Phases of Word Reading; and Seidenberg and McClelland's The Four-Part Processing Model for Word Recognition) are the backbone of IMSE's training programs. In addition, IMSE follows and abides by *The Knowledge and Practice Standards for Teachers of Reading* (International Dyslexia Association [IDA], 2018). The Science of Reading research supports the approach IMSE uses in their training courses.

The multi-sensory approach to teaching reading is supported by studies conducted on reading. In one such study, Joshi et al. (2002) concluded:

> The results of this study showed that first-grade children taught with the multisensory teaching approach based on Orton-Gillingham principles performed better on tests of phonological awareness, decoding and reading comprehension than the control groups. It may, therefore, be concluded that the higher scores for children from the treatment groups may be attributed to the multisensory approach used in this study. (pp. 237-238)

To learn more about the Science of Reading and the research indicated, consider taking an IMSE course.

About This Teacher Guide

IMSE's Comprehensive Orton-Gillingham Plus Teacher Guide was written as the scope and sequence that correlates with the 30-hour *IMSE Comprehensive Orton-Gillingham Plus Course.* There is no common, standard scope and sequence utilized throughout the field of reading. Grade-level skills are approximated and will vary based on student achievement. IMSE's systematic scope and sequence was selected based on a number of factors. These factors include the frequency of the concept, the type of sound, and the similarities in the written features of the grapheme. The concepts gradually go from simple to more complex. The scope and sequence also includes two vowels within the first four lessons so that words can be read and spelled. Sentences can be read and written after the first nine concepts are taught.

Routines are provided for the concepts taught in *IMSE's Comprehensive Orton-Gillingham Plus Course,* including the Three-Part Drill, Teaching a New Concept with the Application of the New Concept, Red Words, and Syllabication. General education classroom teachers in grades K-2 can begin with the appropriate grade level. Teachers who wish to use this scope and sequence as an intervention should give IMSE's Level 1 Initial Assessment to determine where to begin instruction. This assessment is taught in *IMSE's Comprehensive Orton-Gillingham Plus* 30-hour course.

Instruction in phonological awareness is also imperative in grades K-2 (and beyond for struggling readers). Consider taking the *IMSE Phonological Awareness Course* to learn more about assessment and skills in this area. Assess students using the PAST to determine a starting point for instruction in phonological awareness. IMSE recommends *Equipped for Reading Success,* by Dr. David Kilpatrick, and/or *Interventions for All: Phonological Awareness* by Yvette Zgonc. Teachers should implement these strategies into daily lesson plans.

Instruction in fluency, vocabulary, and comprehension is also imperative for all students. Incorporate fluency into your literacy lessons daily/weekly (minimum 30 minutes per week) by using Rapid Word Charts, *IMSE Decodable Readers,* words and sentences, Acadience Reading K-6 or DIBELS 8th Edition, repeated reading, and other activities.

Incorporate vocabulary into your literacy lessons daily/weekly (minimum 50 minutes per week) by choosing 3-5 appropriate tier two words (can pull from rich literature or decodable readers). Teach the words through explicit, direct instruction using student-friendly definitions, word webs, vocabulary charts, illustrations, and other activities.

In grades K-2, the focus for comprehension should be on language comprehension. Incorporate oral language comprehension into your literacy lessons daily/weekly (approximately 100 minutes per week). Comprehension instruction should be explicit, direct instruction that includes teacher modeling, guided practice, and independent practice. Plan ahead to build on students' background knowledge, language structures, verbal reasoning, and literacy knowledge.

Building a shared-knowledge classroom and school opens the ability to communicate with one another and share a common language. Building background knowledge for all students is essential in helping disadvantaged students "catch up." According to Hirsch (2020):

> There is only one kind of school that accomplishes that double goal of quality and equality. It is the shared-knowledge school. Such a school transforms each classroom into a speech community. . . . because all genuine learning requires the possession of shared, unspoken knowledge that enables accurate comprehension. (pp. 58-59)

Core Knowledge provides a free literacy curriculum for preschool through eighth grade. This can be used as the language comprehension piece of your literacy block. This curriculum provides read-aloud books on topics that spread both horizontally (across different classrooms within the same grade) and vertically (across grade levels). This curriculum includes a teacher's guide to help lead discussions on the topics and is highly recommended by IMSE. You can find the free downloads at https://www.coreknowledge.org/curriculum/download-curriculum/.

To learn more about morphology, fluency, vocabulary, and comprehension, consider taking *IMSE's Morphology Plus Course*. Participants in the course also receive the *IMSE Writing and Grammar* video course.

EL Considerations for Teaching a New Concept

Alliteration & New Card: Briefly discuss the differences and similarities between the English sound for a new concept and the native languages represented in your classroom, if applicable. Highlight what your articulators are doing to produce proper pronunciation of the new concept. If the new concept is a sound that does not exist in an EL's native language, this explicit instruction on how to form the new sound will be needed.

Object & Brainstorm: If necessary, provide a guided brainstorm activity for your ELs to help them contribute to the brainstorming list. Teacher-directed brainstorming can be done by providing images of words with the target initial sound and a quick translation into the ELs' native language to help build meaning and vocabulary.

Letter Formation: Teachers must be aware of whether a student's native language uses alphabetic print. Even if ELs have no instruction in the native language, environmental exposure to a different writing system can affect how they recognize and reproduce written letters in the English alphabet. Provide students with an explanation of how letters in the English alphabet are formed with straight lines, circles, and curved lines. Repeat the letter formation practice regularly as needed.

Word & Sentence Dictation: Dictate known words and phrases for ELs. In addition to using the word in a sentence to create meaning, provide a translation of the word and sentence when possible to help students make connections to background knowledge with the target word or phrase and make connections to their native language.

Decodable Reader: If you are using the booklet version of the decodable reader, engage in a quick picture walk to provide a context for the story. Provide students with native language translation of unknown content words to help build an understanding of the story before reading.

First Grade Teacher Guide

SCOPE AND SEQUENCE

It is recommended that *general education* teachers assess students prior to instruction. The PAST assessment and IMSE's Level 1 Initial Assessment can help guide instruction and provide a benchmark for students. First-grade teachers can administer IMSE's Level 1 Midterm at midyear and Level 1 Final at the end of the year.

Teachers using the guide for *intervention* should assess to determine a starting point. The PAST assessment, IMSE's Beginning Reading Skills Assessment, and IMSE's Level 1 Initial are recommended. (Please note that most intervention students older than kindergarten can begin IMSE's assessments with Level 1 Initial. However, struggling or emergent readers who struggle significantly with Level 1 Initial can be administered IMSE's Beginning Reading Skills Assessment.) After assessment, provide intervention for missed concepts, reassess to ensure mastery, and then continue assessing at the next level. Repeat the same pattern (teach missed concepts, assess for mastery, move forward and assess at the next level).

Teachers who have completed *IMSE's Comprehensive Orton-Gillingham Plus* 30-hour course should follow the Blue Flip Chart and refer to the *IMSE Comprehensive Orton-Gillingham Plus Teacher Training Manual* for the *why* and *how* of instruction.

Student workbooks for word and sentence dictation practice are available from IMSE's website. The workbooks have prepared visual cues aligned with the words and sentences included in this guide. Five phonetic words for dictation are included within each lesson for Days 1-3. Dictation for some concepts may include pseudowords or review words from previous lessons. A practice spelling test is recommended for Day 4, and a regular spelling test is recommended for Day 5. For these assessments, students are not provided visual cues. Words for Days 4 and 5 may be selected from Days 1-3, any additional words that may be listed with Days 4-5, or words from previous lessons.

The dictation sentences included in this guide are aligned with the student workbooks as follows: Sentences #1 and #2 are for Day 1; sentences #3 and #4 are for Day 2; and sentences #5 and #6 are for Day 3. The remaining sentences may be used for additional practice or for the assessment on Days 4 and 5.

Beginning with Concept #35, multisyllabic words are included for dictation. For additional multisyllabic words and sentences containing multisyllabic words to be used for dictation, reading, or syllable division, refer to the *IMSE Syllable Division Word Book*.

Please note that children need repeated reading opportunities to apply learned phonics skills. In addition to dictation practice, the words and sentences in this guide can be used for reading practice. Those words, along with *IMSE Decodable Readers*, provide valuable opportunities to develop decoding skills through controlled text.

The following lessons are meant to be completed on a weekly basis but can be individualized for students as needed.

See the sample weekly lesson plans on the following pages: Sample Weekly Lesson and Closed/Open Syllables Lesson.

Guidelines for Lessons (advanced)

Below are guidelines for implementing IMSE's approach for 90 minutes or 30 minutes, depending on whether it is being used as the curriculum or as a supplement to a current curriculum. If used as supplemental, it is important to regularly incorporate the Three-Part Drill (review), decodable readers, and practice with spelling phonetic and irregular words. In addition, it is imperative to include phonological awareness each day in grades K-2 and beyond if necessary.

When implementing this approach as an intervention, the time spent in each area will depend on the student's individual goals, Individualized Education Program (IEP), or area of weakness.

Sample Weekly Lesson (advanced) for a minimum of 90 min. of literacy instruction (Some literacy blocks are up to 120 minutes.)

Component	Monday	Tuesday	Wednesday	Thursday	Friday
Three-Part Drill	Three-Part Drill (10)	Optional: Three-Part Drill (10)	Three-Part Drill (10)	Optional: Three-Part Drill (10)	Three-Part Drill (10)
Phonological Awareness	PA Direct Instruction (10) • Activity in Zgonc's PA book • One-Minute Activity in Kilpatrick's *Equipped* (Incorporate additional One-Minute Activities 5-10x/day in various time periods.)	Kilpatrick's One-Minute PA Activity (1-10) (Incorporate additional One-Minute Activities 5-10x/day in various time periods.)	PA Direct Instruction (10) • Activity in Zgonc's PA book • One-Minute Activity in Kilpatrick's *Equipped* (Incorporate additional One-Minute Activities 5-10x/day in various time periods.)	Kilpatrick's One-Minute PA Activity (1-10) (Incorporate additional One-Minute Activities 5-10x/day in various time periods.)	Kilpatrick's One-Minute PA Activity and/or Direct Instruction (10) • One-Minute Activity in Kilpatrick's *Equipped* (Incorporate additional One-Minute Activities 5-10x/day in various time periods.)
Teaching a New Concept (phonics, spelling rules, etc.) **and Syllable Division**	Multi-Sensory Experience (25) • card • object • literature	Optional: Review New Concept (centers)	Syllabication (10) • Select words and sentences from *The Syllable Division Word Book* or *IMSE's Comprehensive OG Plus Teacher's Guide.*	Syllabication (10) • Select words and sentences from *The Syllable Division Word Book* or *IMSE's Comprehensive OG Plus Teacher's Guide.*	Optional: Syllabication or review (centers)
Word and Sentence Dictation	Application of Words and Sentences (10) • Select words and sentences for dictation from *IMSE's Comprehensive OG Plus Teacher Guide.*	Application of Words and Sentences (10) • Select words and sentences for dictation from *IMSE's Comprehensive OG Plus Teacher Guide.*	Application of Words and Sentences (10) • Select words and sentences for dictation from *IMSE's Comprehensive OG Plus Teacher Guide.*	Concept and Red Word Practice Test (15) • Select concept words and sentences as well as Red Words from *IMSE's Comprehensive OG Plus Teacher Guide.*	Concept and Red Word Test (15) • Select concept words and sentences as well as Red Words from *IMSE's Comprehensive OG Plus Teacher Guide.*
Red Words	Optional: Review from last week's words	Teach 1-5 New Red Words (25+)	Review (10)	Review (10)	Assess (see above)
Decodable Reader	IMSE Book (15) • Highlight concept words in green and read. • Underline Red Words in red and read.	IMSE Book (15) • Read pages. Students should read without errors. If there is an error, correct and have them reread the sentence.	IMSE Book (15) • Read pages. Students should read without errors. If there is an error, correct and have them reread the sentence.	IMSE Book (15) • Read pages. Students should read without errors. If there is an error, correct and have them reread the sentence.	IMSE Book (15) • Use a clean copy without pictures for students to read. Can combine this with fluency. • Comprehension questions

Component	Monday	Tuesday	Wednesday	Thursday	Friday
Fluency (CBM, decodable reader, words/sentences, Rapid Word Chart)	Optional: • Cold read decodable for repeated reading throughout the week. • Rapid Word Chart	Rapid Word Charts (10)	Optional: • Rapid Word Charts • IMSE Practice Book • Can assign either of these for homework	Rapid Word Charts (10) • IMSE Practice Book	• Progress Monitor & Practice (10) • Read clean copy of decodable reader. • Progress Monitor with CBM.
Language Comprehension (background knowledge, language structures, verbal reasoning, vocabulary, literacy knowledge)	Total Time: (20) Read rich literature to students. • Identify concept words. Vocabulary (3-5, Tier 2 words from decodable readers or rich literature) Comprehension • Discussion questions	Total Time: (20) Vocabulary (3-5, Tier 2 words from decodable readers or rich literature) Comprehension • Discussion questions	Total Time: (25) Vocabulary (3-5, Tier 2 words from decodable readers or rich literature) Comprehension • Discussion questions	Total Time: (20) Vocabulary (3-5, Tier 2 words from decodable readers or rich literature) Comprehension • Discussion questions	Total Time: (30) Vocabulary (3-5, Tier 2 words from decodable readers or rich literature) • Assess Comprehension • Reread the story for deeper understanding.
Written Expression	Optional: • Daily journal writing or other skills (sentence writing, paragraph writing, etc.)	Activity (10) • Select one of the oral language comprehension questions and have students write a written response in their journals.	Optional: • Daily journal writing or other skills (sentence writing, paragraph writing, etc.)	Activity (10) • Incorporate writing activity that correlates with the decodable reader.	Optional: • Daily journal writing or other skills (sentence writing, paragraph writing, etc.)
Homework Options	Rapid Word Chart, Decodable Reader, Study Weekly Red Words	Rapid Word Chart, Decodable Reader, Study Weekly Red Words	Rapid Word Chart, Decodable Reader, Study Weekly Red Words	Rapid Word Chart, Decodable Reader, Study Weekly Red Words	Rapid Word Chart, Decodable Reader, Study Weekly Red Words

Sample Weekly Lesson (advanced) for a minimum of 30 min. of supplemental literacy instruction

Component	Monday	Tuesday	Wednesday	Thursday	Friday
Three-Part Drill	Three-Part Drill (10)		Three-Part Drill (5-10)		Three-Part Drill (10)
Phonological Awareness		Kilpatrick's One-Minute PA Activity (1)	Kilpatrick's One-Minute PA Activity (1)	Kilpatrick's One-Minute PA Activity (1)	Kilpatrick's One-Minute PA Activity (1)
Teaching a New Concept (phonics, spelling rules, etc.) **and Syllable Division**	Multi-Sensory Experience (15)		Syllabication (10)		
Word and Sentence Dictation	Application of Words and Sentences (5)	Application of Words and Sentences (10)	Application of Words and Sentences (5)	Concept and Red Word Review and Pretest (e.g., activities, sentence dictation) (20)	Concept and Red Word Test (10)
Red Words		Teach 1-5 New Red Words (10)	Review New Red Words (5)		
Decodable Reader		IMSE Book (10)	Optional: IMSE Book (5)	IMSE Book (10)	IMSE Book (10)
Homework Options	Rapid Word Chart, Decodable Reader, Study Weekly Red Words	Rapid Word Chart, Decodable Reader, Study Weekly Red Words	Rapid Word Chart, Decodable Reader, Study Weekly Red Words	Rapid Word Chart, Decodable Reader, Study Weekly Red Words	Rapid Word Chart, Decodable Reader, Study Weekly Red Words

Closed and Open (Long Vowels) Weekly Lesson

Sample Weekly Lesson (open/closed) for a minimum of 90 min. of literacy instruction (Some literacy blocks are up to 120 minutes.)

Component	Monday	Tuesday	Wednesday	Thursday	Friday
Three-Part Drill	Three-Part Drill (10) • m through -ss, -ll, -ff, -zz	Optional: Three-Part Drill (10)	Three-Part Drill (10) • m–open syllables (long vowels)	Optional: Three-Part Drill (10)	Three-Part Drill (10) • m–open syllables (long vowels)
Phonological Awareness	PA Direct Instruction (10) • P. 104 "I'll Sing a Little Word" in Zgonc's PA book • F1.1 in Kilpatrick's *Equipped* • (Incorporate additional One-Minute Activities 5-10x/day in various time periods.)	Kilpatrick's One-Minute PA Activity (1-10) • F1.2 in Kilpatrick's *Equipped* (Incorporate additional One-Minute Activities 5-10x/day in various time periods.)	PA Direct Instruction (10) • P. 107 "The Forest Animals' Surprise" in Zgonc's PA book • F1.3 in Kilpatrick's *Equipped* (Incorporate additional One-Minute Activities 5-10x/day in various time periods.)	Kilpatrick's One-Minute PA Activity (1-10) • F1.4 in Kilpatrick's *Equipped* (Incorporate additional One-Minute Activities 5-10x/day in various time periods.)	Kilpatrick's One-Minute PA Activity and/or Direct Instruction (10) • F1.5 in Kilpatrick's *Equipped* (Incorporate additional One-Minute Activities 5-10x/day in various time periods.)
Teaching a New Concept (phonics, spelling rules, etc.) **and Syllable Division**	Multi-Sensory Experience (25) • a, e, i, o, u cards (#2, 4, 10, 14, 19) • house • *Abiyoyo* by Pete Seeger	Optional: Review New Concept (centers)	Syllabication (10) • upset, basin, submit, cupid, ego	Syllabication (10) • napkin, rabbit, robot, halo, tempo	Optional: Syllabication or review (centers)
Word and Sentence Dictation	Application of Words and Sentences (10) • pp. 30-31 in *IMSE's Comprehensive OG Plus Teacher Guide* • alto, banjo, veto, combo, even 1. Give the rabbit a bit of catnip. 2. The hero was at the hotel.	Application of Words and Sentences (10) • pp. 30-31 in *IMSE's Comprehensive OG Plus Teacher Guide* • ditto, unit, goblin, iris, open 1. Polo is not as fun as tennis. 2. Dennis will get the banjo.	Application of Words and Sentences (10) • pp. 30-31 in *IMSE's Comprehensive OG Plus Teacher Guide* • zero, velvet, hippo, jumbo, humid 1. Do not dip the napkin in there. 2. The muffin is done.	Concept and Red Word Practice Test (15) • Red Words: there, done, some, good, does • Concept Words pp. 30-31 in *IMSE's Comprehensive OG Plus Teacher Guide* • limbo, mascot, gumbo, polo, tennis, candid, motto, jello, combat, hello 1. A robot does not have an ego. 2. Tom will submit the bill. Read: help	Concept and Red Word Test (15) • Red Words: there, done, some good, does • Concept Words pp. 30-31 in *IMSE's Comprehensive OG Plus Teacher Guide* • raven, thesis, gusto, muffin, latex, hiccup, banjo, lasso, basin, robot 1. Do not omit the goblin. 2. The shot upset the bobcat. Read: help

Component	Monday	Tuesday	Wednesday	Thursday	Friday
Red Words	Optional: Review from last week's words	Teach 1-5 New Red Words (25+) • there, done • Read-only: help	Review: (10) • there, done • Read-only: help	Review: (10) • there, done • Read-only: help	Assess (see above)
Decodable Reader	IMSE Book #28 (15) • Highlight concept words in green and read. • Underline Red Words in red and read.	IMSE Book #28 (15) • Read pages. Students should read without errors. If there is an error, correct and have them reread the sentence.	IMSE Book #28 (15) • Read pages. Students should read without errors. If there is an error, correct and have them reread the sentence.	IMSE Book #28 (15) • Read pages. Students should read without errors. If there is an error, correct and have them reread the sentence.	IMSE Book #28 (15) • Use a clean copy without pictures for students to read. Can combine this with fluency. • Comprehension questions
Fluency (CBM, decodable reader, words/sentences, Rapid Word Chart)	Optional: • Cold read decodable for repeated reading throughout the week. • Rapid Word Chart	Rapid Word Charts: (10) • even, halo, humid, latex, open • there, done, help, some, good	Optional: • Rapid Word Charts • IMSE Practice Book • Can assign either of these for homework	• Rapid Word Charts (10) • IMSE Practice Book	Progress Monitor & Practice (10) • Read clean copy of decodable reader. • Progress Monitor with CBM.

Component	Monday	Tuesday	Wednesday	Thursday	Friday
Language Comprehension (background knowledge, language structures, verbal reasoning, vocabulary, literacy knowledge)	Total Time: (20) Read rich literature to students. • *Abiyoyo* by Pete Seeger • Identify concept words. Vocabulary (3-5, Tier 2 words from decodable readers or rich literature) • ukulele, wand, ostracized, staggered Comprehension • Background knowledge of African lullabies • Clarify: Why were the father and son ostracized? Who is Abiyoyo? • Predict: Do you think the town will let them come back? • Summarize: The father and son were sent out of the town for being annoying. They were allowed back in the town after they saved the day from Abiyoyo.	Total Time: (20) Vocabulary (3-5, Tier 2 words from decodable readers or rich literature) • ukulele, wand, ostracized, staggered • synonyms: guitar, stick, left out, started to fall Comprehension • How might you feel if you were ostracized? • Have you ever felt left out? What happened? • Discuss narrative elements. • Moral: Everyone has value. Find the good in everyone.	Total Time: (25) Vocabulary (3-5, Tier 2 words from decodable readers or rich literature) • ukulele, wand, ostracized, staggered • Word Web Comprehension • Clarify ostracized. • What is a folktale or lullaby? • Why were the father and son asked to leave? • Why were they allowed to come back? • Who is Abiyoyo?	Total Time: (20) Vocabulary (3-5, Tier 2 words from decodable readers or rich literature) • ukulele, wand, ostracized, staggered • Act out the words. Comprehension • Have you ever ostracized someone? If so, why? How does that feel? • Moral: Find the good in everyone. Everyone has value.	Total Time: (30) Vocabulary (3-5, Tier 2 words from decodable readers or rich literature) Assess • ukulele, wand, ostracized, staggered • Use the words in sentences (orally). Comprehension • Reread the story for deeper understanding.
Written Expression	Optional: • Daily journal writing or other skills (sentence writing, paragraph writing, etc.)	Activity (10) • Select one of the oral language comprehension questions and have students write a written response in their journals.	Optional: • Daily journal writing or other skills (sentence writing, paragraph writing, etc.)	Activity (10) • Write about a time when you baked something. If you have never baked anything, what would you want to bake if you could? (correlates with the decodable reader)	Optional: • Daily journal writing or other skills (sentence writing, paragraph writing, etc.)

Table of Contents
First Grade

Concept #	Concept	Red Words Spell & Read	Red Words Read Only	Card Pack #	Decodable Reader #	Page #
47	-dge /j/ (fudge) 1-1-1 Rule	today, yesterday	chair	43	40	143
48	3rd Syllable Type and 3rd Syllable Pattern: Magic E and VC/V (bike, fixate)	first, around, going		44	41	151
49	y as a vowel /ē/ (baby)	walk		39	42	163
50	Soft c /s/ and g /j/ (city, giraffe)	say, their	center	6 and 7 Plus 45	43	173
Review for Concepts m–soft c and g						183
51	-ed /id/, /d/, /t/ (folded, soared, crashed)	how, once		46	44	185
52	-s /s/ or /z/, -es /iz/ (cats, dogs, dishes)	another		47	45	197
53	4th Syllable Type: Vowel Team: ea/ee /ē/ (treat, bee)	pull, wash		48	46	207
54	Vowel Team: ai/ay /ā/ (sail, clay)	every, everyone	school, tractor	49	47	219
55	Vowel Team: oa/oe /ō/ (boat, toe)	know, knew		50	48	229
56	-ing (walking)	friend		51	49	239
57**	Contractions with am, is, are, has, not (I'm, he's, we're, isn't)	been, our, other		None	50	249
Review for Concepts m–contractions with am, is, are, has, not						258

* The Level 1 Midterm assessment, which includes concepts m–ng/nk, can be administered after this lesson.

** The Level 1 Final assessment, which includes concepts m–basic contractions, can be administered after this lesson.

Sammy Rule: -ss, -ll, -ff, -zz

(kiss, bell, huff, jazz)   (1-1-1 Rule)

Card Pack #31 Decodable Reader #26	
Object Ideas:	**Literature Ideas:**
Hershey's Kiss®, bell, fizz, fuzz, jazz, Little Debbie® Zebra Cake, puffcorn	▪ *The Great Fuzz Frenzy* by Janet Stevens and Susan Stevens Crummel ▪ *Noisy Poems* by Jill Bennett ▪ *The Doorbell Rang* by Pat Hutchins ▪ *The Kissing Hand* by Audrey Penn ▪ *Full, Full, Full of Love* by Trish Cooke ▪ *Jazz Baby* by Lisa Wheeler ▪ *The Fiesta Dress: A Quinceañera Tale* by Caren McNelly McCormack ▪ *The Three Little Pigs* (The wolf will huff and puff.)

Notes

- Use the Comprehensive Flip Chart for the steps on how to teach each part of IMSE's Lesson Plan.
  - Use the Advanced Lesson Plan for all remaining lessons.
- Use www.etymonline.com to help establish why a word might not follow the expected rules or patterns.
- This is a 1-1-1 rule: If a word has one syllable, one short vowel, and ends with one consonant sound made by s, l, f, or z, double the final consonant.
- There is no extra visual cue for word dictation. Because this is a spelling rule, students should know the rule.
- Display the Sammy poster as a reminder for students. (A color copy is located in the Masters.)
- In the Auditory/Kinesthetic Drill, students will know two ways to spell /f/ (f, -ff), /l/ (l, -ll), /s/ (s, -ss), and /z/ (z, -zz).
- Place these cards at the end of the blending board and only with short vowel sounds.
- Be careful with "all" words (e.g., mall, ball) and "oll" words (e.g., poll, toll). Teach those units as word families.

Sammy – ss
Loves – ll
Friendly – ff
Zebras – zz

I love you

Phonological Awareness:

Materials Needed:
tokens, sound boxes, one-minute activities, or Zgonc PA book

Use the PAST assessment to determine a starting point for instruction. Incorporate daily phonological awareness activities by using Zgonc's tiered activities and/or Kilpatrick's One-Minute Activities in *Equipped for Reading Success*.

Phonemic awareness warm-up: Use tokens (or letter tiles once concepts have been taught) and sound boxes to do a quick phonemic awareness activity that ties in with the new concept, if appropriate.

 ## Three-Part Drill

Materials Needed:
review cards, sand, blending board, vowel tents or sticks

Do this at least 3x per week. Use the Flip Chart for steps. Include the new concept after Day 1.

- Vowel Intensive: Use the Flip Chart for steps.
  - Do the Vowel Intensive with all 5 vowels.

V	VC	CVC
a	ag, ap, ab	lat, cad, zan
e	et, en, eb	zeg, ren, med
i	ig, ib, im	lin, hib, fid
o	ob, ot, oz	rom, hob, cog
u	un, ud, ub	sup, pum, dut

  - **NOTE:** If students are doing well with the Vowel Intensive, (T) give an assessment with 20 CVC syllables (not real words). If students pass with 80% accuracy or better, discontinue the Vowel Intensive.
- Below is a sample script. Remember to use review concepts only.

---

1. **Visual:**
   (T) Tell me the sounds you know for these letters.
   (S) /m/, /l/, etc.
2. **Auditory/Kinesthetic:**
   (T) You know two ways to spell this. (S) split trays. (T) Eyes on me.
   Spell /k/. Repeat.
   (S) /k/ c says /k/; k says /k/

---

3. **Blending:**
   (T) Tell me the sound for each letter as I point. Then blend the sounds together to read the word or syllable. Give me a thumbs up if it is a real word.
   (S) /mmm/ /ŏŏŏ/ /mmm/ *mom* (thumbs up)
   Alternative:
   (T) Watch me first. /mmm/ /ŏŏŏ/ /mmm/ *mom*
   (T) Do it with me. (T&S) /mmm/ /ŏŏŏ/ /mmm/ *mom*
   (T) Your turn. (S) /mmm/ /ŏŏŏ/ /mmm/ *mom* (thumbs up)

Vowel Intensive: Model the visual cue while calling out the sound. Students will do the visual cue as they repeat the sound. Students will then hold up the vowel tent while stating the letter name and sound.
- (T): Eyes on me. The sound is /ă/. Repeat.
- (S): /ă/ a says /ă/

Teaching a New Concept

Materials Needed:
concept card, screen, green crayon, object, sand, decodable readers, literature, P/G chart

Introduce on Monday, and practice daily.

1. (T) Shows the new concept card(s).
   a. (T) Tells students that they will learn another way to spell the /s/, /l/, /f/, and /z/ sounds.
   b. (T) States "-ss" says /s/. (S) Repeat. Continue with the other 3 sounds.
   c. (T) Teaches students the rule.
   d. (T) Shows the Sammy poster.

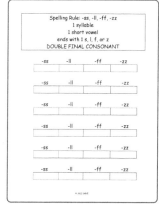

2. (T) Shows an object.
   a. (T) Allows students to manipulate the object and discuss prior knowledge. Reminds (S) that the object has the target sound(s) spelled with the target letter(s).

3. (S) Brainstorm to help establish a spelling rule, if applicable.
   a. Brainstorm words that have the target sound(s) or rule. The brainstorming can be a teacher-directed activity if students need extra support.

4. (T) Teaches Letter Formation, if needed. Can teach cursive handwriting.
   a. Use the steps for teaching letter formation on the Flip Chart.
   b. Use house paper to teach lowercase letters.
   c. Teach capital letters throughout the week. Capital letters go outside the house.

5. (T) Dictates target sound(s). (S) Practice all known spellings in the sand or other medium.

6. (T) Connects with literature.
   a. Read for language comprehension.
   b. Continue to work on language comprehension with rich literature throughout the week.

7. (S) Use decodable readers to practice the concepts learned.
  a. (S) Highlight words with the new concept. Read those words.
  b. (S) Highlight Red Words. Read those words.
  c. (S) Start reading the decodable reader.
  d. (S) Continue reading throughout the week.
  e. (S) Read a clean copy on Friday.
8. (T&S) Mark the Phoneme/Grapheme (P/G) chart by highlighting the target sound(s).

 ## Word Dictation

Materials Needed:
fingertapping hand, dictation paper, pencil

Practice daily. Use the Flip Chart to follow the steps for word dictation.

Day 1:	1. huff	2. fizz	3. mass	4. will	5. less
Day 2:	1. hiss	2. Jeff	3. pass	4. hill	5. jazz
Day 3:	1. boss	2. chill	3. puff	4. fuzz	5. off
Days 4-5:	Review prior words. Optional additional words: bill, buff, buzz, cuff, dill, doll, dull, fuss, gull, ill, lass, loss, mess, mill, miss, moss, pill, quill, razz, Ross, sass, sill, toss				

- Below is a sample script for word dictation.

  1. (T) States word: *boss*. Uses it in a sentence: My *boss* is kind and fair. (Pounds) *boss*. (T) Models fingertapping if needed: /b/ /ŏ/ /s/. (Pounds) *boss*.
  2. (S) State while pounding: *boss*. (Fingertap) /b/ /ŏ/ /s/. (Pound) *boss*. Write the letters known for the sounds.
  3. (T) When yours looks like mine, rewrite the word.
  4. (S) Rewrite.
  5. Repeat the process for each word.
  6. (S) Read the list of words multiple times to build automaticity.

 ## Sentence Dictation

Red Words are underlined. Students can fingertap the green words. Use the Flip Chart to follow the steps for sentence dictation.

1. Bill will fuss <u>and</u> yell.
2. I will sell <u>the</u> bell <u>and</u> <u>the</u> shell.
3. Will he buff <u>the</u> van <u>and</u> then chill?
4. I can go <u>to</u> <u>the</u> mill with Bill.
5. <u>The</u> dog fell in <u>the</u> well.
6. Did Chad <u>see</u> <u>the</u> big mess?

7. Were Dan and Nan at the shell?
8. I will pass the dill in the cup.
9. Does that cat hiss at you?
10. Bob will razz Jon with the bell, and then he will run.
11. The lass was ill and had a pill.
12. The gull will sit by a shell.

- Below is a sample script for sentence dictation.

1. (T): Listen to the sentence. *Bill will fuss and yell.*
2. (T): Listen while I pound the syllables. *Bill will fuss and yell.*
3. (T): Pound it with me. (T&S): *Bill will fuss and yell.*
4. (T): You pound the sentence. (S): *Bill will fuss and yell.*
5. (T): Watch me as I point to the lines while stating the sentence. *Bill will fuss and yell.*
6. (T): You point to the lines while stating the sentence.
7. (S): *Bill will fuss and yell.*
8. (T): Now write the sentence. Fingertap if needed.

- Below is a sample script to check CUPS.*

1. (T): C stands for capitalization. Did you remember a capital letter at the beginning of your sentence? It's also a name. *Bill* would always be capitalized. If you forgot, fix it. If you remembered, put a tally mark above the capital letter. Add a mark in the box for C.
2. (T): U stands for understanding. Is your sentence neat? Reread it to yourself. Does it make sense? Could someone else understand it? If not, fix it. Add a mark in the box for U.
3. (T): P stands for punctuation. Did you remember a period at the end? If not, fix it. If you remembered, put a tally mark above the period. Add a mark in the box for P.
4. (T): S stands for spelling. Did you spell your words correctly? Check them. Now, check yours with mine (shows the teacher's copy). Fix any words you spelled incorrectly. Put a tally mark above the words you spelled correctly. Add a mark in the box for S.
5. (T): Rewrite your sentence with all of the corrections.
6. (T): Check for CUPS again. Put another mark in the boxes.
7. (T): Let's read the sentences.
8. (S) Read the sentences for fluency and automaticity.

***Please note:** Once students understand how to use CUPS, transition to letting them check their sentence independently before showing the teacher's copy.

Weekly Red Words

Materials Needed:
screen, red crayon, red word paper

Introduce on Tuesday, and practice daily. Use the Flip Chart for steps on how to teach a Red Word.

New:	Review:	New Read-Only:	Review Read-Only:
were, does	*(From K List)* the, was, is, a, and, to, for, like, of, want, said, you, put, see, stop, from, has, have, his, as, my, into, now, new, give, or, by, went, do, are, they, any, black, blue, brown, gray, green, orange, pink, purple, white, yellow, one, two, come, who, what, where, why	our	*(From K List)* stop, eek, ouch, look, good, help, three, four, five, seven eight, nine, her

Steps for Teaching a New Red Word:

1. (T) States the word. (*were*)
2. (T&S) Use tokens to determine how many sounds are in the word. (/w/ /er/; 2)
3. (T&S) Discuss how we would expect to spell each sound as the teacher writes the grapheme(s) correctly. Identify what is unexpected or irregular about the spelling of the word. It could also be expected, but the concept hasn't been taught yet.
4. (T&S) Discuss the etymology of the word, if appropriate (lexical words). Visit www.etymonline.com for more information on the word.
5. (T) Defines the word, and writes a sentence using the word.
6. (T) Writes the word on Red Word paper with the screen underneath, using red crayon.
7. (S) Write the word on Red Word paper with the screen underneath, using red crayon. (S) Show the word to the teacher.
   (**NOTE:** The teacher should have students chunk the word if it has more than four letters.)

8. (T&S) Stand up, holding the Red Word in the nondominant hand. Armtap word while naming each letter. Then "underline" the word by sweeping left to right while stating the word, 3x. (**NOTE:** Left-handed students will place their left hand on their right wrist. They tap to their right shoulder. Underline from wrist to shoulder. Right-handed students place their right hand on their left shoulder. They tap to their left wrist. Underline shoulder to wrist.)

9. (T&S) Trace crayon bumps with the pointer finger while naming the letters, 3x.

10. (T&S) Place the screen over the paper and trace the word with the pointer finger while naming the letters, 3x.

11. (S) Turn paper over. With red crayon, write the word without the screen one time, and hold up the word for the teacher to check. (S) Write the word two more times.

12. (S) Write an original sentence in pencil and underline the Red Word with a red crayon. (**NOTE:** The sentence can also be dictated by the teacher while the student writes or dictated by the student while the teacher writes it.)

13. Repeat the steps for *does*. (/d/ /ŭ/ /z/; 3)

Review Ideas for Red Words:

- Sculpt the word using red Play-Doh or clay. Have students spell the word as they smash each letter.
- Print flashcards from IOG, and practice reading.
- Armtap the word to review.
- Cross-clap the word to review.
- Stomp the letters to review.
- Use a voice jar with popsicle sticks that have a different voice (e.g., robot, baby, cheerleader, monster) listed on each stick. Have a student draw a stick from the jar. The class armtaps the word using the voice selected. (Another option is to have an electronic spinning wheel with the voices listed on the wheel.)

Fluency, Vocabulary, and Comprehension

- Incorporate fluency into your literacy lessons daily/weekly (minimum 30 min/week) by using Rapid Word Charts, IMSE Decodable Readers, words and sentences, Acadience Reading K-6 or DIBELS 8th Edition, repeated reading, and other activities.
- Incorporate vocabulary into your literacy lessons daily/weekly (minimum 50 min/week) by choosing 3-5 appropriate tier two words (can pull from rich literature or decodable readers). Teach the words through explicit, direct instruction using student-friendly definitions, word webs, vocabulary charts, illustrations, and other activities.
- Incorporate oral language comprehension into your literacy lessons daily/weekly (approximately 100 min/week). Comprehension instruction should be explicit, direct instruction that includes teacher modeling, guided practice, and independent practice. Plan ahead to build on students' background knowledge, language structures, verbal reasoning, and literacy knowledge.

Extension Activity Ideas

- Create a foldable for this rule to add to an Interactive Notebook. Begin with a square piece of paper. Fold in each corner so that the points meet in the middle. On the outside flaps, write -ss on one corner, -ff on another, -ll, and then -zz. Open up the flaps. On the flat middle section, write out the 1-1-1 rule. Fold the corners back in. Lift up the -ss corner, and brainstorm words that meet the rule. Write them on the back of the -ss flap. Continue with each of the other letters.

Jeff will pass Buzz.

-ff, -ll, -ss, -zz

- Bring a stuffed zebra. Have students wear a "Sammy" nametag and hold the stuffed zebra. Have them stand under several paper hearts. Take a picture as each student hugs the zebra. Add it to a bulletin board titled: Sammy Loves Friendly Zebras.

- As a fun variation, you could do Sammy Loves Fried Zebra Cakes. You can have students wear a chef's hat with an "S" on it (for Sammy). Have them hold a frying pan with a Little Debbie Zebra Cake in the pan. Add this to a bulletin board titled: Sammy Loves Fried Zebra Cakes.

Sammy Loves Flying Zebras

- See alternative posters to Sammy Loves Friendly Zebras in the margin. (A color copy of these posters is in the Masters.)
- Visit IMSE's Orton-Gillingham's Pinterest page for more ideas.

Weekly Lesson Reminders

- Daily practice with writing the weekly Red Word(s)
- Kilpatrick's "One-Minute Activities" for daily phonological awareness practice
- Zgonc's phonological awareness activities
- Listen to rich literature to work on oral language comprehension.
- Target concept practice sheets from IMSE's practice books
- Practice test on Thursday and test on Friday

Compound Words (sunset)

Card Pack #None Decodable Reader #27	
Object Ideas:	**Literature Ideas:**
backpack, sunset, starfish, baseball, basketball, football, seashell, bathtub, birdhouse	▪ *If You Were a Compound Word* by Trisha Speed Shaskan ▪ *Once There Was a Bull...(Frog)* by Rick Walton ▪ *Shortcut* by Donald Crews ▪ *Teammates* by Peter Golenbock ▪ *Cloudy With a Chance of Meatballs* by Judi Barrett

Notes

- Use the Comprehensive Flip Chart for the steps on how to teach each part of IMSE's Lesson Plan.
- Use www.etymonline.com to help establish why a word might not follow the expected rules or patterns.
- This is a "bridge" lesson into multisyllabic words.
- Teach students that a compound word is a word that has 2 one-syllable words put together to form a new word. The meaning of the compound word relates back to each of the one-syllable words (e.g., bathtub, football).

Phonological Awareness:

Materials Needed:
tokens, sound boxes, one-minute activities, or Zgonc PA book

Use the PAST assessment to determine a starting point for instruction. Incorporate daily phonological awareness activities by using Zgonc's tiered activities and/or Kilpatrick's One-Minute Activities in *Equipped for Reading Success.*

Phonemic awareness warm-up: Use tokens (or letter tiles once concepts have been taught) and sound boxes to do a quick phonemic awareness activity that ties in with the new concept, if appropriate.

Three-Part Drill

Materials Needed:
review cards, sand, blending board, vowel tents or sticks

Do this at least 3x per week. Use the Flip Chart for steps.

- Vowel Intensive: Use the Flip Chart for steps.

- Do the Vowel Intensive with all 5 vowels.

V	VC	CVC
a	ag, ap, ab	lat, cad, zan
e	et, en, eb	zeg, ren, med
i	ig, ib, im	lin, hib, fid
o	ob, ot, oz	rom, hob, cog
u	un, ud, ub	sup, pum, dut

- **NOTE:** If students are doing well with the Vowel Intensive, (T) give an assessment with 20 CVC syllables (not real words). If students pass with 80% accuracy or better, discontinue the Vowel Intensive.

▪ Below is a sample script. Remember to use review concepts only.

1. **Visual:**
   (T) Tell me the sounds you know for these letters.
   (S) /m/, /l/, etc.

2. **Auditory/Kinesthetic:**
   (T) You know two ways to spell this. (S) split trays. (T) Eyes on me.
   Spell /k/. Repeat.
   (S) /k/ c says /k/; k says /k/

3. **Blending:**
   (T) Tell me the sound for each letter as I point. Then blend the sounds together to read the word or syllable. Give me a thumbs up if it is a real word.
   (S) /mmm/ /ŏŏŏ/ /mmm/ *mom* (thumbs up)
   Alternative:
   (T) Watch me first. /mmm/ /ŏŏŏ/ /mmm/ *mom*
   (T) Do it with me. (T&S) /mmm/ /ŏŏŏ/ /mmm/ *mom*
   (T) Your turn. (S) /mmm/ /ŏŏŏ/ /mmm/ *mom* (thumbs up)

   *Vowel Intensive: Model the visual cue while calling out the sound. Students will do the visual cue as they repeat the sound. Students will then hold up the vowel tent while stating the letter name and sound.
   - (T): Eyes on me. The sound is /ă/. Repeat.
   - (S): /ă/ a says /ă/

 ## Teaching a New Concept

Materials Needed:
concept card, screen, green crayon, object, sand, decodable readers, literature, P/G chart

Introduce on Monday, and practice daily.

1. (T) Tells students that they will learn about compound words.
   a. (T) Tells students that a compound word is made up of two smaller words. This creates a new word with a combined meaning of each smaller word.

    b. (T) States an example, such as *bath* and *tub*. When we combine these words, it creates *bathtub*, a tub where we take a bath.

2. (T) Shows an object.
    a. (T) Allows students to manipulate the object and discuss prior knowledge. Reminds (S) that the object represents the target concept.

3. (S) Brainstorm to help establish a spelling rule, if applicable.
    a. Brainstorm words that have the target concept. The brainstorming can be a teacher-directed activity if students need extra support.
    b. (S) Can use puzzle pieces with one word on each piece. When the pieces combine, they create a compound word (e.g., *mail* on one piece and *box* on another to combine for *mailbox*).

4. (T) Connects with literature.
    a. Read for language comprehension.
    b. Continue to work on language comprehension with rich literature throughout the week.

5. (S) Use decodable readers to practice the concepts learned.
    a. (S) Highlight words with the new concept. Read those words.
    b. (S) Highlight Red Words. Read those words.
    c. (S) Start reading the decodable reader.
    d. (S) Continue reading throughout the week.
    e. (S) Read a clean copy on Friday.

6. (T&S) Mark the Phoneme/Grapheme (P/G) chart by highlighting the target sound(s). (**NOTE:** For compound words, nothing will need to be marked on the P/G chart.)

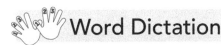 ## Word Dictation

Materials Needed:
fingertapping hand, dictation paper, pencil

Practice daily. Use the Flip Chart to follow the steps for word dictation.

Day 1:	1. bobcat	2. cashbox	3. pigpen	4. sunfish	5. hatbox
Day 2:	1. catfish	2. Batman	3. sunset	4. bedbug	5. pigpen
Day 3:	1. dishpan	2. humbug	3. suntan	4. bathtub	5. upset
Days 4-5:	Review prior words. Optional additional words: catnip, hotbed, hotdog, midship, within				

- Below is a sample script:

> 1. (T) States word: *bathtub*. Uses it in a sentence: Clean out the *bathtub*. (Pounds each syllable) *bath/tub*.
> 2. (S) State while pounding each syllable: *bath/tub*.
> 3. (T) Models fingertapping, if needed. First syllable: (Pounds) *bath*. (Fingertaps) /b/ /ă/ /th/. (Pounds) *bath*.

4. (S) State first syllable while pounding: *bath*. (Fingertap) /b/ /ă/ /th/. (Pound) *bath*. Write the letters known for the sounds.

5. (T) Second syllable: (Pounds) *tub*. (Fingertaps) /t/ /ŭ/ /b/. (Pounds) *tub*.

6. (S) State second syllable while pounding: *tub*. (Fingertap) /t/ /ŭ/ /b/. (Pound) *tub*. Write the letters known for the sounds.

7. (T) When yours looks like mine, rewrite the word.

8. (S) Rewrite.

9. Repeat the process for each word.

10. (S) Read the list of words multiple times to build automaticity.

Sentence Dictation

Red Words are underlined. Students can fingertap the green words. Use the Flip Chart to follow the steps for sentence dictation.

1. The bedbug bit Pam.
2. Did Jed get the bobcat?
3. Do not put the cat in the bathtub!
4. The dishpan was wet.
5. He got his pet some catnip.
6. The bathtub was hot!
7. Sam did not get a good suntan.
8. Did you see the sunfish at sunset?
9. The cat got some catnip.
10. Sam and Tom sat in the pigpen.
11. Mom is upset with the mess!

- Below is a sample script for sentence dictation.

1. (T): Listen to the sentence. *The bedbug bit Pam.*
2. (T): Listen while I pound the syllables. *The bedbug bit Pam.* (Make sure to pound *bedbug* twice because it has two syllables.)
3. (T): Pound it with me. (T&S): *The bedbug bit Pam.*
4. (T): You pound the sentence. (S): *The bedbug bit Pam.*
5. (T): Watch me as I point to the lines while stating the sentence. (Tap the line for *bedbug* twice because it has two syllables.) *The bedbug bit Pam.*
6. (T): You point to the lines while stating the sentence.
7. (S): *The bedbug bit Pam.*
8. (T): Now write the sentence. Fingertap if needed.

■ Below is a sample script to check CUPS.*

1. (T): C stands for capitalization. Did you remember a capital letter at the beginning of your sentence? Did you remember a capital letter for *Pam*? It is a name. If you forgot, fix it. If you remembered, put a tally mark above each capital letter. Add a mark in the box for C.

2. (T): U stands for understanding. Is your sentence neat? Reread it to yourself. Does it make sense? Could someone else understand it? If not, fix it. Add a mark in the box for U.

3. (T): P stands for punctuation. Did you remember a period at the end? If not, fix it. If you remembered, put a tally mark above the period. Add a mark in the box for P.

4. (T): S stands for spelling. Did you spell your words correctly? Check them. Now, check yours with mine (shows the teacher's copy). Fix any words you spelled incorrectly. Put a tally mark above the words you spelled correctly. Add a mark in the box for S.

5. (T): Rewrite your sentence with all of the corrections.

6. (T): Check for CUPS again. Put another mark in the boxes.

7. (T): Let's read the sentences.

8. (S) Read the sentences for fluency and automaticity.

***Please note:** Once students understand how to use CUPS, transition to letting them check their sentence independently before showing the teacher's copy.

Weekly Red Words

Materials Needed:
screen, red crayon, red word paper

Introduce on Tuesday, and practice daily. Use the Flip Chart for steps.

New:	Review:	New Read-Only:	Review Read-Only:
some, good	were, does		our

Steps for Teaching a New Red Word:

1. (T) States the word. (*some*)
2. (T&S) Use tokens to determine how many sounds are in the word. (/s/ /ŭ/ /m/; 3)
3. (T&S) Discuss how we would expect to spell each sound as the teacher writes the grapheme(s) correctly. Identify what is unexpected or irregular about the spelling of the word. It could also be expected, but the concept hasn't been taught yet.
4. (T&S) Discuss the etymology of the word, if appropriate (lexical words). Visit www.etymonline.com for more information on the word.
5. (T) Defines the word, and writes a sentence using the word.

6. (T) Writes the word on Red Word paper with the screen underneath, using red crayon.

7. (S) Write the word on Red Word paper with the screen underneath, using red crayon. (S) Show the word to the teacher.
   (**NOTE:** The teacher should have students chunk the word if it has more than four letters.)

8. (T&S) Stand up, holding the Red Word in the nondominant hand. Armtap word while naming each letter. Then "underline" the word by sweeping left to right while stating the word, 3x. (**NOTE:** Left-handed students will place their left hand on their right wrist. They tap to their right shoulder. Underline from wrist to shoulder. Right-handed students place their right hand on their left shoulder. They tap to their left wrist. Underline shoulder to wrist.)

9. (T&S) Trace crayon bumps with the pointer finger while naming the letters, 3x.

10. (T&S) Place the screen over the paper and trace the word with the pointer finger while naming the letters, 3x.

11. (S) Turn paper over. With red crayon, write the word without the screen one time, and hold up the word for the teacher to check. (S) Write the word two more times.

12. (S) Write an original sentence in pencil and underline the Red Word with a red crayon. (**NOTE:** The sentence can also be dictated by the teacher while the student writes or dictated by the student while the teacher writes it.)

13. Repeat the steps for *good*. (/g/ /o͞o/ /d/; 3)

Review Ideas for Red Words:

- Sculpt the word using red Play-Doh or clay. Have students spell the word as they smash each letter.
- Print flashcards from IOG, and practice reading.
- Armtap the word to review.
- Cross-clap the word to review.
- Stomp the letters to review.
- Use a voice jar with popsicle sticks that have a different voice (e.g., robot, baby, cheerleader, monster) listed on each stick. Have a student draw a stick from the jar. The class armtaps the word using the voice selected. (Another option is to have an electronic spinning wheel with the voices listed on the wheel.)

Fluency, Vocabulary, and Comprehension

- Incorporate fluency into your literacy lessons daily/weekly (minimum 30 min/ week) by using Rapid Word Charts, IMSE Decodable Readers, words and sentences, Acadience Reading K-6 or DIBELS 8th Edition, repeated reading, and other activities.
- Incorporate vocabulary into your literacy lessons daily/weekly (minimum 50 min/ week) by choosing 3-5 appropriate tier two words (can pull from rich literature or decodable readers). Teach the words through explicit, direct instruction using student-friendly definitions, word webs, vocabulary charts, illustrations, and other activities.

- Incorporate oral language comprehension into your literacy lessons daily/weekly (approximately 100 min/week). Comprehension instruction should be explicit, direct instruction that includes teacher modeling, guided practice, and independent practice. Plan ahead to build on students' background knowledge, language structures, verbal reasoning, and literacy knowledge.

Extension Activity Ideas

- Create a foldable for this concept to add to an Interactive Notebook. Begin with strips of paper. Fold each end into the middle to create a book. On the first flap, write a one-syllable word (e.g., cat). Draw a picture of the word. On the second flap, write another one-syllable word (e.g., fish). Draw a picture of that word. Open the flaps and write the compound word combining the two one-syllable words (e.g., catfish). Draw a picture of the new word. Use real compound words.

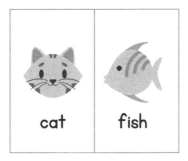
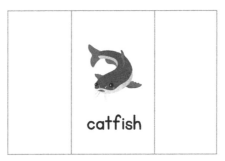

- Use puzzle pieces to put together compound words. You can also use plastic Easter eggs, blocks, etc.

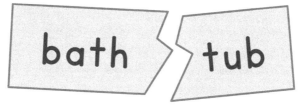

- Visit IMSE's Orton-Gillingham's Pinterest page for more ideas.

Weekly Lesson Reminders

- Daily practice with writing the weekly Red Word(s)
- Kilpatrick's "One-Minute Activities" for daily phonological awareness practice
- Zgonc's phonological awareness activities
- Listen to rich literature to work on oral language comprehension.
- Target concept practice sheets from IMSE's practice books
- Practice test on Thursday and test on Friday

Long Vowels: Closed/Open Syllable Types I & 2 (Cl/O)

VC/CV and V/CV Syllable Patterns I & 2 (ra/ven, Ve/nus, si/lo, hel/lo, mu/sic)

Card Pack #2, 4, 10, 14, 19	Decodable Reader #28
Object Ideas:	**Literature Ideas:**
house with door from Masters or IOG	<ul><li>*Aesop's Fables*</li><li>*No, David!* by David Shannon</li><li>*Go, Dog. Go!* by P. D. Eastman</li><li>Olivia series by Ian Falconer</li><li>*Lon Po Po: A Red-Riding Hood Story From China* by Ed Young</li><li>*Abiyoyo* by Pete Seeger</li><li>*Separate Is Never Equal: Sylvia Mendez and Her Family's Fight for Desegregation* by Duncan Tonatiuh</li></ul>

Notes

- Use the Comprehensive Flip Chart for the steps on how to teach each part of IMSE's Lesson Plan.
- This was taught in kindergarten, but it should be reviewed in 1st grade or with older students.
- Reminder: Students should state both sounds they know for the vowels during the Visual part of the Three-Part Drill. They should state the short sound first, and then state the long sound. The teacher can provide the visual cue of a bent left arm (to represent a closed door) and then an extended left arm (to represent an open door).
- In the Auditory/Kinesthetic part of the drill, students only know one way to spell each of the long vowel sounds.
- In the Blending part of the drill, be sure to occasionally remove the final consonant to open up the vowel sound and practice an open syllable (long vowel).
- Pull out the 5 vowel cards: #2, #4, #10, #14, and #19.
- The Vowel Intensive is only for short vowel sounds; do not include long vowels in that drill.

- Take note of the sounds of /ōō/ and /yōō/. Start with /yōō/. Then teach /ōō/ as students begin to encounter words with that sound. When the "u" card comes up in the Visual Drill, students say: /ŭ/ /yōō/ /ōō/.

- Syllabication starts this week.

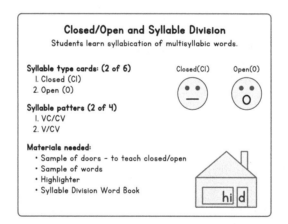

 # Phonological Awareness:

Materials Needed:
tokens, sound boxes, one-minute activities, or Zgonc PA book

Use the PAST assessment to determine a starting point for instruction. Incorporate daily phonological awareness activities by using Zgonc's tiered activities and/or Kilpatrick's One-Minute Activities in *Equipped for Reading Success*.

Phonemic awareness warm-up: Use tokens (or letter tiles once concepts have been taught) and sound boxes to do a quick phonemic awareness activity that ties in with the new concept, if appropriate.

Three-Part Drill

Materials Needed:
review cards, sand, blending board, vowel tents or sticks

Do this at least 3x per week. Use the Flip Chart for steps. Include the new concept after Day 1.

- Vowel Intensive: Use the Flip Chart for steps.
  - Do the Vowel Intensive with all 5 vowels.

V	VC	CVC
a	ag, ap, ab	lat, cad, zan
e	et, en, eb	zeg, ren, med
i	ig, ib, im	lin, hib, fid
o	ob, ot, oz	rom, hob, cog
u	un, ud, ub	sup, pum, dut

  - **NOTE:** If students are doing well with the Vowel Intensive, (T) give an assessment with 20 CVC syllables (not real words). If students pass with 80% accuracy or better, discontinue the Vowel Intensive.

- Below is a sample script. Remember to use review concepts only.

1. **Visual:**
   (T) Tell me the sounds you know for these letters.
   (S) /m/, /l/, etc.

2. **Auditory/Kinesthetic:**
   (T) You know two ways to spell this. (S) split trays. (T) Eyes on me.
   Spell /k/. Repeat.
   (S) /k/ c says /k/; k says /k/

3. **Blending:**
   (T) Tell me the sound for each letter as I point. Then blend the sounds together to read the word or syllable. Give me a thumbs up if it is a real word.
   (S) /mmm/ /ŏŏŏ/ /mmm/ *mom* (thumbs up)
   Alternative:
   (T) Watch me first. /mmm/ /ŏŏŏ/ /mmm/ *mom*
   (T) Do it with me. (T&S) /mmm/ /ŏŏŏ/ /mmm/ *mom*
   (T) Your turn. (S) /mmm/ /ŏŏŏ/ /mmm/ *mom* (thumbs up)

   *Vowel Intensive:** Model the visual cue while calling out the sound. Students will do the visual cue as they repeat the sound. Students will then hold up the vowel tent while stating the letter name and sound.
   - (T): Eyes on me. The sound is /ă/. Repeat.
   - (S): /ă/ a says /ă/

Teaching a New Concept

Materials Needed:
concept card, screen, green crayon, object, sand, decodable readers, literature, P/G chart

Introduce on Monday, and practice daily.

1. (T) Shows the new concept card(s).
   a. (T) Shows all 5 vowel cards.
      i. Remind students of the sounds they know for these letters. Review each of the short vowels while doing the hand gestures.
      ii. Inform students that today they are going to learn (or review) another sound for these letters. Sometimes these letters say their name. Sometimes "a" just says /ā/, "e" says /ē/, "i" says /ī/, "o" says /ō/, and "u" says /yo͞o/. (S) Repeat each sound.
      iii. Tell students that today they will learn when to make the short sound and when to make the long sound (where the vowel just says its name).
   b. (T) Reminds students that vowels are voiced sounds.
   c. (T) Reminds students where to find the vowels in the alphabet.
   d. (T) Uses mirrors to discuss the mouth, tongue, and teeth placement.
2. (T) Shows an object.
   a. Show a house (IOG) with the word *bed* written on it. The "d' should be on the door. Have students read the word on the house. Ask if the door is closed or open. (closed) Tell students that the consonant "d" is closing in the vowel. This is called a closed syllable.
   b. Now open the door. The consonant is gone, and the vowel is free to say its own name (extend your left arm). Now the word says *be*. Is the door closed or open? (open) Tell students that this is an open syllable.
   c. (T) Allows students to manipulate the object and discuss prior knowledge. Reminds (S) that the object has the target sound(s) spelled with the target letter(s).
3. (S) Brainstorm.
   a. Continue to brainstorm words together using paper houses (made from IOG or copied from the *Masters*).
4. (T) Teaches Letter Formation, *if needed*. Students could begin to learn cursive.
   a. Use the steps for teaching letter formation on the Flip Chart.
   b. Use house paper to teach lowercase letters.
   c. Teach capital letters throughout the week. Capital letters go outside the house.
5. (T) Dictates target sound(s). (S) Practice all known spellings in the sand or other medium.
6. (T) Connects with literature.
   a. Read for language comprehension.
   b. Continue to work on language comprehension with rich literature throughout the week.

7. (S) Use decodable readers to practice the concepts learned.

   a. (S) Highlight words with the new concept. Read those words.

   b. (S) Highlight Red Words. Read those words.

   c. (S) Start reading the decodable reader.

   d. (S) Continue reading throughout the week.

   e. (S) Read a clean copy on Friday.

8. (T&S) Mark the Phoneme/Grapheme (P/G) chart by highlighting the target sound(s).

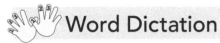
Word Dictation

Materials Needed:
fingertapping hand, dictation paper, pencil

Practice daily. Use the Flip Chart to follow the steps for word dictation.

Day 1:	1. alto	2. banjo	3. veto	4. combo	5. even
Day 2:	1. ditto	2. unit	3. goblin	4. iris	5. open
Day 3:	1. zero	2. velvet	3. hippo	4. jumbo	5. humid
Days 4-5:	Review prior words. Optional additional words: basin, candid, combat, cupid, ego, gumbo, gusto, halo, hello, hiccup, jello, lasso, latex, limbo, mascot, motto, muffin, napkin, omen, polo, rabbit, raven, robot, submit, tempo, tennis, thesis, upset				

- Below is a sample script for word dictation.

1. (T) States word: *bathtub*. Uses it in a sentence: Clean out the *bathtub*. (Pounds each syllable) *bath/tub*.

2. (S) State while pounding each syllable: *bath/tub*.

3. (T) Models fingertapping, if needed. First syllable: (Pounds) *bath*. (Fingertaps) */b/ /ă/ /th/*. (Pounds) *bath*.

4. (S) State first syllable while pounding: *bath*. (Fingertap) */b/ /ă/ /th/*. (Pound) *bath*. Write the letters known for the sounds.

5. (T) Second syllable: (Pounds) *tub*. (Fingertaps) */t/ /ŭ/ /b/*. (Pounds) *tub*.

6. (S) State second syllable while pounding: *tub*. (Fingertap) */t/ /ŭ/ /b/*. (Pound) *tub*. Write the letters known for the sounds.

7. (T) When yours looks like mine, rewrite the word.

8. (S) Rewrite.

9. Repeat the process for each word.

10. (S) Read the list of words multiple times to build automaticity.

Sentence Dictation

Red Words are underlined. Students can fingertap the green words. Use the Flip Chart to follow the steps for sentence dictation.

1. Give the rabbit a bit of catnip.
2. The hero was at the hotel.
3. Polo is not as fun as tennis.
4. Dennis will get the banjo.
5. Do not dip the napkin in there.
6. The muffin is done.
7. Tom will submit the bill.
8. The shot upset the bobcat.
9. Is the man in the quintet Irish?
10. Do not omit the goblin.
11. The rabbit sat on the hippo.
12. A robot does not have an ego.

- Below is a sample script for sentence dictation.

> 1. (T): Listen to the sentence. *The bedbug bit Pam.*
> 2. (T): Listen while I pound the syllables. *The bedbug bit Pam.* (Make sure to pound *bedbug* twice because it has two syllables.)
> 3. (T): Pound it with me. (T&S): *The bedbug bit Pam.*
> 4. (T): You pound the sentence. (S): *The bedbug bit Pam.*
> 5. (T): Watch me as I point to the lines while stating the sentence. (Tap the line for *bedbug* twice because it has two syllables.) *The bedbug bit Pam.*
> 6. (T): You point to the lines while stating the sentence.
> 7. (S): *The bedbug bit Pam.*
> 8. (T): Now write the sentence. Fingertap if needed.

- Below is a sample script to check CUPS.*

> 1. (T): C stands for capitalization. Did you remember a capital letter at the beginning of your sentence? Did you remember a capital letter for *Pam*? It is a name. If you forgot, fix it. If you remembered, put a tally mark above each capital letter. Add a mark in the box for C.
> 2. (T): U stands for understanding. Is your sentence neat? Reread it to yourself. Does it make sense? Could someone else understand it? If not, fix it. Add a mark in the box for U.
> 3. (T): P stands for punctuation. Did you remember a period at the end? If not, fix it. If you remembered, put a tally mark above the period. Add a mark in the box for P.

4. (T): S stands for spelling. Did you spell your words correctly? Check them. Now, check yours with mine (shows the teacher's copy). Fix any words you spelled incorrectly. Put a tally mark above the words you spelled correctly. Add a mark in the box for S.

5. (T): Rewrite your sentence with all of the corrections.

6. (T): Check for CUPS again. Put another mark in the boxes.

7. (T): Let's read the sentences.

8. (S) Read the sentences for fluency and automaticity.

*Please note:** Once students understand how to use CUPS, transition to letting them check their sentence independently before showing the teacher's copy.

Weekly Red Words

Materials Needed:
screen, red crayon, red word paper

Introduce on Tuesday, and practice daily. Use the Flip Chart for steps.

New:	Review:	New Read-Only:	Review Read-Only:
there, done	were, does, some, good	help	our

Steps for Teaching a New Red Word:

1. (T) States the word. (*there*)

2. (T&S) Use tokens to determine how many sounds are in the word. (/TH/ /ā/ /r/; 3)

3. (T&S) Discuss how we would expect to spell each sound as the teacher writes the grapheme(s) correctly. Identify what is unexpected or irregular about the spelling of the word. It could also be expected, but the concept hasn't been taught yet.

4. (T&S) Discuss the etymology of the word, if appropriate (lexical words). Visit www.etymonline.com for more information on the word.

5. (T) Defines the word, and writes a sentence using the word.

6. (T) Writes the word on Red Word paper with the screen underneath, using red crayon.

7. (S) Write the word on Red Word paper with the screen underneath, using red crayon. (S) Show the word to the teacher.
(**NOTE:** The teacher should have students chunk the word if it has more than four letters.)

8. (T&S) Stand up, holding the Red Word in the nondominant hand. Armtap word while naming each letter. Then "underline" the word by sweeping left to right while stating the word, 3x. (**NOTE:** Left-handed students will place their left hand on their right wrist. They tap to their right shoulder. Underline from wrist to shoulder. Right-handed students place their right hand on their left shoulder. They tap to their left wrist. Underline shoulder to wrist.)

9. (T&S) Trace crayon bumps with the pointer finger while naming the letters, 3x.

10. (T&S) Place the screen over the paper and trace the word with the pointer finger while naming the letters, 3x.

11. (S) Turn paper over. With red crayon, write the word without the screen one time, and hold up the word for the teacher to check. (S) Write the word two more times.

12. (S) Write an original sentence in pencil and underline the Red Word with a red crayon. (**NOTE:** The sentence can also be dictated by the teacher while the student writes or dictated by the student while the teacher writes it.)

13. Repeat the steps for *done*. (/d/ /ŭ/ /n/; 3)

Review Ideas for Red Words:

- Sculpt the word using red Play-Doh or clay. Have students spell the word as they smash each letter.
- Print flashcards from IOG, and practice reading.
- Armtap the word to review.
- Cross-clap the word to review.
- Stomp the letters to review.
- Use a voice jar with popsicle sticks that have a different voice (e.g., robot, baby, cheerleader, monster) listed on each stick. Have a student draw a stick from the jar. The class armtaps the word using the voice selected. (Another option is to have an electronic spinning wheel with the voices listed on the wheel.)

Syllabication (Decoding)

Materials Needed:
Strips of paper with words prewritten, Pencil, Highlighter, Syllable Division Posters

Introduce on Wednesday with the new concept. Practice regularly. This will be your students' first experience with syllabication. Therefore, it is important to walk through these steps explicitly. Before walking through these steps, give the Closed/Open quiz to ensure students know the difference between closed and open syllables. Have students label the syllables as Cl (closed) or O (open). Then have them read each syllable.

- Syllable Division Posters (Only show the first two syllable patterns by placing a sticky note over the other patterns. Show the posters for the first two syllable types [Closed and Open].)

Syllable Division Patterns	1. Closed Syllable (Cl) short vowel sound	2. Open Syllable (O) long vowel sound
1. vc|cv	mag|net	ra|ven
2. v|cv	ten|nis	I|rish
3. vc|v	tip|top	o|pen
4. v|v	tom|tom	e|ven
	up|set	hu|mid
		ju|do

- Below is a sample script for syllabication.

  1. Present the word *admit* on a strip of paper. (Only the teacher has it to model. After modeling, then the teacher and students will walk through the steps together several times. Then the students will have independent practice.)

  2. (T): What are the first two vowel sounds you see? (S): a and i.
     (T): Correct. I am going to underline the "a" and label it with a V for vowel. I am going to underline the "i" and label it with a V for vowel. Now, I'm going to draw a line connecting the bottom of the Vs.

  3. (T) Now I will look above the "bridge." How many consonants do you see above the bridge? (S): Two...d and m. (T): Correct. I will underline each one and mark those with a C for consonant.

  4. (T) Now I will look at our syllable patterns 1 and 2. Which pattern is this? (S): Pattern #1. (T): Correct. VC/CV is like pattern #1. I will draw the syllable wall between the consonants. I am going to really saturate the syllable wall with the highlighter.

  5. (T) Now I will carefully split the word into two syllables by tearing it apart along the syllable wall. Next, I will label my syllables. (Point to the first syllable.) What type of syllable is this, closed or open? (S): Closed. (T): Correct. I will label it Cl (closed). What is the second syllable type? (S): Closed. (T): I will label it Cl for closed.

  6. (T) Now I can read the first syllable. Let's do it together.
     (T&S): /a/ /d/, ad. (T): Let's read the second syllable. (T&S): /m/ /i/ /t/, mit.

  7. (T): Let's put the syllables together. What is the word? (S): admit. (T): Is that a real word? (S): Yes.

8. Go through the same process with *veto*, *sunset*, and *unit*, as well as nonsense words, such as *kippish*, *fithmid*, and *rafib*. (See the Masters for a copy of the page shown here.) Have students do the steps with you while working through these words. Find more words in the *IMSE Syllable Division Word Book*.

NOTE: Allow students to practice this skill independently with constructive feedback.

Fluency, Vocabulary, and Comprehension

- Incorporate fluency into your literacy lessons daily/weekly (minimum 30 min/week) by using Rapid Word Charts, IMSE Decodable Readers, words and sentences, Acadience Reading K-6 or DIBELS 8th Edition, repeated reading, and other activities.

- Incorporate vocabulary into your literacy lessons daily/weekly (minimum 50 min/week) by choosing 3-5 appropriate tier two words (can pull from rich literature or decodable readers). Teach the words through explicit, direct instruction using student-friendly definitions, word webs, vocabulary charts, illustrations, and other activities.

- Incorporate oral language comprehension into your literacy lessons daily/weekly (approximately 100 min/week). Comprehension instruction should be explicit, direct instruction that includes teacher modeling, guided practice, and independent practice. Plan ahead to build on students' background knowledge, language structures, verbal reasoning, and literacy knowledge.

Extension Activity Ideas

- Create multiple "houses" for students' Interactive Notebooks.
- Create a syllabication center.
- Visit IMSE's Orton-Gillingham's Pinterest page for more ideas.

Weekly Lesson Reminders

- Daily practice with writing the weekly Red Word(s)
- Kilpatrick's "One-Minute Activities" for daily phonological awareness practice
- Zgonc's phonological awareness activities
- Listen to rich literature to work on oral language comprehension.
- Target concept practice sheets from IMSE's practice books
- Practice test on Thursday and test on Friday

Two-Consonant Beginning R Blends (truck)

Card Pack #32 Decodable Reader #29	
Object Ideas:	**Literature Ideas:**
trail mix consisting of items that begin with R Blends (brown & green M&M's®, Craisins®, pretzels, etc.), freeze pop, grape, fruit, fraction, Froot Loops™  **Trail Blend Recipe** • Handful of granola • Handful of dried fruit (grapes, cranberries, and Craisins™) • Handful of pretzels • M&Ms™: green and brown (A color copy of this recipe is located in the Masters.)	▪ *Gravity* by Jason Chin ▪ *Drum Dream Girl: How One Girl's Courage Changed Music* by Margarita Engle ▪ *Brown Sugar Babe* by Charlotte Watson Sherman ▪ *Frida* by Jonah Winter ▪ *Henry's Freedom Box: A True Story From the Underground Railroad* by Ellen Levine ▪ *Brave Irene* by William Steig ▪ *Crickwing* by Janell Cannon ▪ *The Giving Tree* by Shel Silverstein ▪ Franklin the Turtle series by Paulette Bourgeois ▪ *Bread and Jam for Frances* by Russell Hoban ▪ *Two Friends: Susan B. Anthony and Frederick Douglass* by Dean Robbins ▪ *The Great Kapok Tree* by Lynne Cherry ▪ *Growing Vegetable Soup* by Lois Ehlert ▪ *Amazing Grace* by Mary Hoffman ▪ *Harold and the Purple Crayon* by Crockett Johnson ▪ *Our Tree Named Steve* by Alan Zweibel ▪ *Dreamers* by Yuyi Morales ▪ *Crown: An Ode to the Fresh Cut* by Derrick Barnes ▪ *We Are Grateful: Otsaliheliga* by Traci Sorell ▪ *Drawn Together* by Minh Le

 Notes

- Use the Comprehensive Flip Chart for the steps on how to teach each part of IMSE's Lesson Plan.
- Use www.etymonline.com to help establish why a word might not follow the expected rules or patterns.
- A blend consists of 2 or more consonants that blend together when speaking and reading.

- Each sound is heard in a blend. However, with coarticulation, sounds may change slightly (e.g., dr- may sound like /jr/ as in *drip*, tr- may sound like /chr/ as in *truck*).
- Use mini sound lines as an extra visual cue for word dictation. This reminds students that we still hear two sounds, but we give the blend one fingertap (to allow for coarticulation).

- If students struggle with these combinations, use tokens to first represent each sound. Then, use one finger to tap each sound in the blend. Build up to giving the blend one fingertap.

Phonological Awareness:

Materials Needed:
tokens, sound boxes, one-minute activities, or Zgonc PA book

Use the PAST assessment to determine a starting point for instruction. Incorporate daily phonological awareness activities by using Zgonc's tiered activities and/or Kilpatrick's One-Minute Activities in *Equipped for Reading Success*.

Phonemic awareness warm-up: Use tokens (or letter tiles once concepts have been taught) and sound boxes to do a quick phonemic awareness activity that ties in with the new concept, if appropriate.

Three-Part Drill

Materials Needed:
review cards, sand, blending board, vowel tents or sticks

Do this at least 3x per week. Use the Flip Chart for steps. Include the new concept after Day 1.

- Vowel Intensive: Use the Flip Chart for steps.
  - Do the Vowel Intensive with all 5 vowels.

V	VC	CVC
a	ag, ap, ab	lat, cad, zan
e	et, en, eb	zeg, ren, med
i	ig, ib, im	lin, hib, fid
o	ob, ot, oz	rom, hob, cog
u	un, ud, ub	sup, pum, dut

  - **NOTE:** If students are doing well with the Vowel Intensive, (T) give an assessment with 20 CVC syllables (not real words). If students pass with 80% accuracy or better, discontinue the Vowel Intensive.

- Below is a sample script. Remember to use review concepts only.

1. **Visual:**
   (T) Tell me the sounds you know for these letters.
   (S) /m/, /l/, etc.

2. **Auditory/Kinesthetic:**
   (T) You know two ways to spell this. (S) split trays. (T) Eyes on me.
   Spell /k/. Repeat.
   (S) /k/ c says /k/; k says /k/

3. **Blending:**
   (T) Tell me the sound for each letter as I point. Then blend the sounds together to read the word or syllable. Give me a thumbs up if it is a real word.
   (S) /mmm/ /ŏŏŏ/ /mmm/ *mom* (thumbs up)
   Alternative:
   (T) Watch me first. /mmm/ /ŏŏŏ/ /mmm/ *mom*
   (T) Do it with me. (T&S) /mmm/ /ŏŏŏ/ /mmm/ *mom*
   (T) Your turn. (S) /mmm/ /ŏŏŏ/ /mmm/ *mom* (thumbs up)

   Vowel Intensive: Model the visual cue while calling out the sound. Students will do the visual cue as they repeat the sound. Students will then hold up the vowel tent while stating the letter name and sound.
   - (T): Eyes on me. The sound is /ă/. Repeat.
   - (S): /ă/ a says /ă/

 ## Teaching a New Concept

Materials Needed:
concept card, screen, green crayon, object, sand, decodable readers, literature, P/G chart

Introduce on Monday, and practice daily.

1. (T) Shows the new concept card(s).
   a. (T) Tells students that we will learn a new concept today: beginning R Blends.
   b. (T) Tells students that they already know the sounds for these letters. When the letters live next to each other, sometimes the sounds become blended together. That's why we call them blends.
   c. (T) States "br-" says /br/. (S) Repeat. Continue with the other blends: cr, dr, fr, gr, pr, tr. Reminds students that the blends still make two sounds.

2. (T) Shows an object.
   a. (T) Allows students to manipulate the object and discuss prior knowledge. Reminds (S) that the object has the target sound(s) spelled with the target letter(s).

3. (S) Brainstorm to help establish a spelling rule, if applicable.
   a. Brainstorm words that have the target sound(s) or rule. The brainstorming can be a teacher-directed activity if students need extra support.

4. (T) Teaches Letter Formation, if needed. Can teach cursive writing.
   a. Use the steps for teaching letter formation on the Flip Chart.

b. Use house paper to teach lowercase letters.

c. Teach capital letters throughout the week. Capital letters go outside the house.

5. (T) Dictates target sound(s). (S) Practice all known spellings in the sand or other medium.

6. (T) Connects with literature.

a. Read for language comprehension.

b. Continue to work on language comprehension with rich literature throughout the week.

7. (S) Use decodable readers to practice the concepts learned.

a. (S) Highlight words with the new concept. Read those words.

b. (S) Highlight Red Words. Read those words.

c. (S) Start reading the decodable reader.

d. (S) Continue reading throughout the week.

e. (S) Read a clean copy on Friday.

8. (T&S) Mark the Phoneme/Grapheme (P/G) chart by highlighting the target sound(s).

 # Word Dictation

Materials Needed:
fingertapping hand, dictation paper, pencil

Practice daily. Use the Flip Chart to follow the steps for word dictation.

Day 1:	1. brag	2. drip	3. trash	4. Crisco	5. hundred
Day 2:	1. grass	2. brim	3. frog	4. tantrum	5. presto
Day 3:	1. grill	2. drag	3. trumpet	4. gremlin	5. crib
Days 4-5:	Review prior words. Optional additional words: address, Alfred, Brad, bran, brass, brat, crab, cram, crop, crud, culprit, drab, drum, express, Fran, Fred, grad, Greg, grim, grin, grit, grub, prep, prim, prom, prop, trap, trip, tripod, trot				

- Below is a sample script for one-syllable word dictation.

1. (T) States word: *boss*. Uses it in a sentence: My *boss* is kind and fair. (Pounds) *boss*. (T) Models fingertapping if needed: /b/ /ŏ/ /s/. (Pounds) *boss*.

2. (S) State while pounding: *boss*. (Fingertap) /b/ /ŏ/ /s/. (Pound) *boss*. Write the letters known for the sounds.

3. (T) When yours looks like mine, rewrite the word.

4. (S) Rewrite.

5. Repeat the process for each word.

6. (S) Read the list of words multiple times to build automaticity.

■ Below is a sample script for multisyllabic word dictation.

1. (T) States word: *bathtub*. Uses it in a sentence: Clean out the *bathtub*. (Pounds each syllable) *bath/tub*.

2. (S) State while pounding each syllable: *bath/tub*.

3. (T) Models fingertapping, if needed. First syllable: (Pounds) *bath*. (Fingertaps) /b/ /ă/ /th/. (Pounds) *bath*.

4. (S) State first syllable while pounding: *bath*. (Fingertap) /b/ /ă/ /th/. (Pound) *bath*. Write the letters known for the sounds.

5. (T) Second syllable: (Pounds) *tub*. (Fingertaps) /t/ /ŭ/ /b/. (Pounds) *tub*.

6. (S) State second syllable while pounding: *tub*. (Fingertap) /t/ /ŭ/ /b/. (Pound) *tub*. Write the letters known for the sounds.

7. (T) When yours looks like mine, rewrite the word.

8. (S) Rewrite.

9. Repeat the process for each word.

10. (S) Read the list of words multiple times to build automaticity.

Note: For blends, if students need to tap out each sound, use one finger to tap each sound of the blend. For example, when tapping out the word *brag*, the standard method is to tap /br/ /ă/ /g/. The following alternative can be used for students who need additional support: /b/ /r/ (2 taps with the same finger) /ă/ /g/. IMSE gives blends one fingertap to help with coarticulation.
Reminder: Fingertaps do not always equal the number of sounds.

C U P S Sentence Dictation

Red Words are underlined. Students can fingertap the green words. Use the Flip Chart to follow the steps for sentence dictation.

1. A dog and cat can trot.
2. The grill was hot, so I put it in the trash.
3. Did she trip on the grass?
4. A frog can hop and sit on the log.
5. Tell her to brush the big cat.
6. Sam had to get the grub here.
7. The drum was in the trash.
8. Put the fish on the grill.
9. The trumpet sat by the trash can.
10. Greg will go to the prom.
11. Pat will fix the trumpet.
12. The velvet dress was for Fran.
13. Brad did brag but was not bad.
14. Ben did nap in the crib with the pup.
15. She is so prim.

- Below is a sample script for sentence dictation.

  1. (T): Listen to the sentence. *The bedbug bit Pam.*
  2. (T): Listen while I pound the syllables. *The bedbug bit Pam.* (Make sure to pound *bedbug* twice because it has two syllables.)
  3. (T): Pound it with me. (T&S): *The bedbug bit Pam.*
  4. (T): You pound the sentence. (S): *The bedbug bit Pam.*
  5. (T): Watch me as I point to the lines while stating the sentence. (Tap the line for *bedbug* twice because it has two syllables.) *The bedbug bit Pam.*
  6. (T): You point to the lines while stating the sentence.
  7. (S): *The bedbug bit Pam.*
  8. (T): Now write the sentence. Fingertap if needed.

- Below is a sample script to check CUPS.*

  1. (T): C stands for capitalization. Did you remember a capital letter at the beginning of your sentence? Did you remember a capital letter for *Pam*? It is a name. If you forgot, fix it. If you remembered, put a tally mark above each capital letter. Add a mark in the box for C.
  2. (T): U stands for understanding. Is your sentence neat? Reread it to yourself. Does it make sense? Could someone else understand it? If not, fix it. Add a mark in the box for U.
  3. (T): P stands for punctuation. Did you remember a period at the end? If not, fix it. If you remembered, put a tally mark above the period. Add a mark in the box for P.
  4. (T): S stands for spelling. Did you spell your words correctly? Check them. Now, check yours with mine (shows the teacher's copy). Fix any words you spelled incorrectly. Put a tally mark above the words you spelled correctly. Add a mark in the box for S.
  5. (T): Rewrite your sentence with all of the corrections.
  6. (T): Check for CUPS again. Put another mark in the boxes.
  7. (T): Let's read the sentences.
  8. (S) Read the sentences for fluency and automaticity.

  *Please note: Once students understand how to use CUPS, transition to letting them check their sentence independently before showing the teacher's copy.

© IMSE 2022

Weekly Red Words

Materials Needed:
screen, red crayon, red word paper

Introduce on Tuesday, and practice daily. Use the Flip Chart for steps.

New:	Review:	New Read-Only:	Review Read-Only:
her, here	were, does, some, good, there, done		our, help

Steps for Teaching a New Red Word:

1. (T) States the word. (*her*)
2. (T&S) Use tokens to determine how many sounds are in the word. (/h/ /er/; 2)
3. (T&S) Discuss how we would expect to spell each sound as the teacher writes the grapheme(s) correctly. Identify what is unexpected or irregular about the spelling of the word. It could also be expected, but the concept hasn't been taught yet.
4. (T&S) Discuss the etymology of the word, if appropriate (lexical words). Visit www.etymonline.com for more information on the word.
5. (T) Defines the word, and writes a sentence using the word.
6. (T) Writes the word on Red Word paper with the screen underneath, using red crayon.
7. (S) Write the word on Red Word paper with the screen underneath, using red crayon. (S) Show the word to the teacher.
   (**NOTE:** The teacher should have students chunk the word if it has more than four letters.)
8. (T&S) Stand up, holding the Red Word in the nondominant hand. Armtap word while naming each letter. Then "underline" the word by sweeping left to right while stating the word, 3x. (**NOTE:** Left-handed students will place their left hand on their right wrist. They tap to their right shoulder. Underline from wrist to shoulder. Right-handed students place their right hand on their left shoulder. They tap to their left wrist. Underline shoulder to wrist.)
9. (T&S) Trace crayon bumps with the pointer finger while naming the letters, 3x.
10. (T&S) Place the screen over the paper and trace the word with the pointer finger while naming the letters, 3x.
11. (S) Turn paper over. With red crayon, write the word without the screen one time, and hold up the word for the teacher to check. (S) Write the word two more times.
12. (S) Write an original sentence in pencil and underline the Red Word with a red crayon. (**NOTE:** The sentence can also be dictated by the teacher while the student writes or dictated by the student while the teacher writes it.)
13. Repeat the steps for *here*. (/h/ /ē/ /r/; 3)

Review Ideas for Red Words:

- Sculpt the word using red Play-Doh or clay. Have students spell the word as they smash each letter.
- Print flashcards from IOG, and practice reading.
- Armtap the word to review.
- Cross-clap the word to review.
- Stomp the letters to review.
- Use a voice jar with popsicle sticks that have a different voice (e.g., robot, baby, cheerleader, monster) listed on each stick. Have a student draw a stick from the jar. The class armtaps the word using the voice selected. (Another option is to have an electronic spinning wheel with the voices listed on the wheel.)

Syllabication (Decoding)

Materials Needed:
IMSE Syllable Division Word Book, Pencil, Highlighter, Syllable Division Posters

Introduce on Wednesday with the new concept. Practice regularly.

- Choose 6 or more words with the new concept in the *IMSE Syllable Division Word Book* for syllabication.
- Use the steps on the Flip Chart and the Syllable Division Posters.

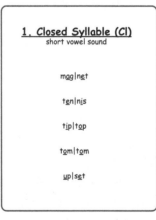

- Below is a sample script for syllabication.

1. Find the first two vowels or vowel units. Underline and label with a "v."
2. Draw the bridge. Underline the consonants or consonant units and label with a "c."
3. Find the pattern and divide the word.
4. Is there another vowel (other than an "e" at the end)? If so, repeat steps 1-3. If not, go to step 5.
5. Label each syllable.
6. Read the word.

> **NOTE:** If there are two consonants in the middle of a word, split the word between the two consonants. (Exception: If the two consonants are a digraph [sh, ch, th] they cannot be split.) If there are three or more consonants, some letters go together as one consonant unit (look for known digraphs or blends).

Fluency, Vocabulary, and Comprehension

- Incorporate fluency into your literacy lessons daily/weekly (minimum 30 min/week) by using Rapid Word Charts, IMSE Decodable Readers, words and sentences, Acadience Reading K-6 or DIBELS 8th Edition, repeated reading, and other activities.
- Incorporate vocabulary into your literacy lessons daily/weekly (minimum 50 min/week) by choosing 3-5 appropriate tier two words (can pull from rich literature or decodable readers). Teach the words through explicit, direct instruction using student-friendly definitions, word webs, vocabulary charts, illustrations, and other activities.
- Incorporate oral language comprehension into your literacy lessons daily/weekly (approximately 100 min/week). Comprehension instruction should be explicit, direct instruction that includes teacher modeling, guided practice, and independent practice. Plan ahead to build on students' background knowledge, language structures, verbal reasoning, and literacy knowledge.

Extension Activity Ideas

- Set up a center with a recording of words with blends. Have students use tokens and sound boxes to indicate how many sounds are in each word.
- Have an image of a blender. Have students brainstorm words that have blends.
- Visit IMSE's Orton-Gillingham's Pinterest page for more ideas.

Weekly Lesson Reminders

- Daily practice with writing the weekly Red Word(s)
- Kilpatrick's "One-Minute Activities" for daily phonological awareness practice
- Zgonc's phonological awareness activities
- Listen to rich literature to work on oral language comprehension.
- Target concept practice sheets from IMSE's practice books
- Practice test on Thursday and test on Friday

Notes:

_____

_____

_____

_____

_____

_____

_____

_____

_____

_____

_____

_____

_____

_____

_____

_____

_____

_____

Two-Consonant Beginning L Blends (sled)

Card Pack #33 Decodable Reader #30	
Object Ideas:	**Literature Ideas:**
flip-flop, blueberry, flour, glue, flower, plastic, cloud	▪ *Blueberries for Sal* by Robert McCloskey ▪ *Click, Clack, Moo: Cows That Type* by Doreen Cronin ▪ Clifford series by Norman Bridwell ▪ *Lilly's Purple Plastic Purse* by Kevin Henkes ▪ Flat Stanley series by Jeff Brown ▪ *Flip Flop!* by Dana Meachen Rau ▪ *Flour Girl* by David Michael Slater ▪ *A Sliver of Liver for Me Please?* by Jill Lyn Michaels ▪ *Little Cloud* by Eric Carle ▪ *Black, White, Just Right!* by Marguerite Davol ▪ *My Two Blankets* by Irena Kobald ▪ *Black Is a Rainbow Color* by Angela Joy

Notes

- Use the Comprehensive Flip Chart for the steps on how to teach each part of IMSE's Lesson Plan.
- Use www.etymonline.com to help establish why a word might not follow the expected rules or patterns.
- A blend consists of 2 or more consonants that blend together when speaking and reading.
- Each sound is heard in a blend. However, with coarticulation, sounds may change slightly (e.g., dr- may sound like /jr/ as in *drip*, tr- may sound like /chr/ as in *truck*).
- Use mini sound lines as an extra visual cue for word dictation. This reminds students that we still hear two sounds, but we give the blend one fingertap (to allow for coarticulation).

- If students struggle with these combinations, use tokens to first represent each sound. Then, use one finger to tap each sound in the blend. Build up to giving the blend one fingertap.

Phonological Awareness:

Materials Needed:
tokens, sound boxes, one-minute activities, or Zgonc PA book

Use the PAST assessment to determine a starting point for instruction. Incorporate daily phonological awareness activities by using Zgonc's tiered activities and/or Kilpatrick's One-Minute Activities in *Equipped for Reading Success*.

Phonemic awareness warm-up: Use tokens (or letter tiles once concepts have been taught) and sound boxes to do a quick phonemic awareness activity that ties in with the new concept, if appropriate.

Three-Part Drill

Materials Needed:
review cards, sand, blending board, vowel tents or sticks

Do this at least 3x per week. Use the Flip Chart for steps. Include the new concept after Day 1.

- Vowel Intensive: Use the Flip Chart for steps.
  - Do the Vowel Intensive with all 5 vowels.

V	VC	CVC
a	ag, ap, ab	lat, cad, zan
e	et, en, eb	zeg, ren, med
i	ig, ib, im	lin, hib, fid
o	ob, ot, oz	rom, hob, cog
u	un, ud, ub	sup, pum, dut

  - **NOTE:** If students are doing well with the Vowel Intensive, (T) give an assessment with 20 CVC syllables (not real words). If students pass with 80% accuracy or better, discontinue the Vowel Intensive.
- Below is a sample script. Remember to use review concepts only.

---

1. **Visual:**
   (T) Tell me the sounds you know for these letters.
   (S) /m/, /l/, etc.
2. **Auditory/Kinesthetic:**
   (T) You know two ways to spell this. (S) split trays. (T) Eyes on me.
   Spell /k/. Repeat.
   (S) /k/ c says /k/; k says /k/

---

3. **Blending:**
   (T) Tell me the sound for each letter as I point. Then blend the sounds together to read the word or syllable. Give me a thumbs up if it is a real word.
   (S) /mmm/ /ŏŏŏ/ /mmm/ *mom* (thumbs up)
   Alternative:
   (T) Watch me first. /mmm/ /ŏŏŏ/ /mmm/ *mom*
   (T) Do it with me. (T&S) /mmm/ /ŏŏŏ/ /mmm/ *mom*
   (T) Your turn. (S) /mmm/ /ŏŏŏ/ /mmm/ *mom* (thumbs up)

*Vowel Intensive: Model the visual cue while calling out the sound. Students will do the visual cue as they repeat the sound. Students will then hold up the vowel tent while stating the letter name and sound.
   - (T): Eyes on me. The sound is /ă/. Repeat.
   - (S): /ă/ a says /ă/

Teaching a New Concept

Materials Needed:
concept card, screen, green crayon, object, sand, decodable readers, literature, P/G chart

Introduce on Monday, and practice daily.
1. (T) Shows the new concept card(s).
   a. (T) Tells students that we will learn a new concept today: beginning L Blends.
   b. (T) Tells students that they already know the sounds for these letters. When the letters live next to each other, sometimes the sounds become blended together. That's why we call them *blends*.
   c. (T) States "bl-" says /bl/. (S) Repeat. Continue with the other blends: cl-, fl-, gl-, pl-, sl-. Reminds students that the blends still make two sounds.
2. (T) Shows an object.
   a. (T) Allows students to manipulate the object and discuss prior knowledge. Reminds (S) that the object has the target sound(s) spelled with the target letter(s).
3. (S) Brainstorm to help establish a spelling rule, if applicable.
   a. Brainstorm words that have the target sound(s) or rule. The brainstorming can be a teacher-directed activity if students need extra support.
4. (T) Teaches Letter Formation, if needed. Can teach cursive writing.
   a. Use the steps for teaching letter formation on the Flip Chart.
   b. Use house paper to teach lowercase letters.
   c. Teach capital letters throughout the week. Capital letters go outside the house.
5. (T) Dictates target sound(s). (S) Practice all known spellings in the sand or other medium.
6. (T) Connects with literature.
   a. Read for language comprehension.
   b. Continue to work on language comprehension with rich literature throughout the week.

7. (S) Use decodable readers to practice the concepts learned.

   a. (S) Highlight words with the new concept. Read those words.

   b. (S) Highlight Red Words. Read those words.

   c. (S) Start reading the decodable reader.

   d. (S) Continue reading throughout the week.

   e. (S) Read a clean copy on Friday.

8. (T&S) Mark the Phoneme/Grapheme (P/G) chart by highlighting the target sound(s).

 # Word Dictation

Materials Needed:
fingertapping hand, dictation paper, pencil

Practice daily. Use the Flip Chart to follow the steps for word dictation.

Day 1:	1. bled	2. plan	3. glob	4. dishcloth	5. influx
Day 2:	1. flip	2. clam	3. dogsled	4. gladness	5. plug
Day 3:	1. flag	2. classic	3. sled	4. ripplet	5. club
Days 4-5:	Review prior words. Optional additional words: blab, blip, blot, bobsled, clan, clap, clip, clog, clop, complex, flab, flap, flat, fled, flit, flop, glad, glib, glum, plastic, plod, plum, plus, slam, slap, slat, slid, slip, slit, slog, slop, slug				

- Below is a sample script for one-syllable word dictation.

  1. (T) States word: *boss*. Uses it in a sentence: My *boss* is kind and fair. (Pounds) *boss*. (T) Models fingertapping if needed: /b/ /ŏ/ /s/. (Pounds) *boss*.
  2. (S) State while pounding: *boss*. (Fingertap) /b/ /ŏ/ /s/. (Pound) *boss*. Write the letters known for the sounds.
  3. (T) When yours looks like mine, rewrite the word.
  4. (S) Rewrite.
  5. Repeat the process for each word.
  6. (S) Read the list of words multiple times to build automaticity.

- Below is a sample script for multisyllabic word dictation.

  1. (T) States word: *bathtub*. Uses it in a sentence: Clean out the *bathtub*. (Pounds each syllable) *bath/tub*.
  2. (S) State while pounding each syllable: *bath/tub*.
  3. (T) Models fingertapping, if needed. First syllable: (Pounds) *bath*. (Fingertaps) /b/ /ă/ /th/. (Pounds) *bath*.
  4. (S) State first syllable while pounding: *bath*. (Fingertap) /b/ /ă/ /th/. (Pound) *bath*. Write the letters known for the sounds.

© IMSE 2022

5. (T) Second syllable: (Pounds) *tub*. (Fingertaps) /t/ /ŭ/ /b/. (Pounds) *tub*.

6. (S) State second syllable while pounding: *tub*. (Fingertap) /t/ /ŭ/ /b/. (Pound) *tub*. Write the letters known for the sounds.

7. (T) When yours looks like mine, rewrite the word.

8. (S) Rewrite.

9. Repeat the process for each word.

10. (S) Read the list of words multiple times to build automaticity.

Note: For blends, if students need to tap out each sound, use one finger to tap each sound of the blend. For example, when tapping out the word *clam*, the standard method is to tap /kl/ /ă/ /m/. The following alternative can be used for students who need additional support: /k/ /l/ (2 taps with the same finger) /ă/ /m/. IMSE gives blends one fingertap to help with coarticulation. **Reminder:** Fingertaps do not always equal the number of sounds.

Sentence Dictation

Red Words are underlined. Students can fingertap the green words. Use the Flip Chart to follow the steps for sentence dictation.

1. I am glad Sam fled with Ben.
2. Why was Fred so glum?
3. She will flip the clam.
4. Did Nan slip in the mud?
5. I will slip it under the slot.
6. He was glad when he slid on the mat.
7. A big slug sat on the slab.
8. She did blab to Fran.
9. Blot the pen on the pad.
10. The flap on the shed was wet.
11. Greg sat down in the club.
12. The plan was to plod.
13. The plan was to let Nan win.
14. She did not drop the flag.

- Below is a sample script for sentence dictation.

    1. (T): Listen to the sentence. *The bedbug bit Pam.*
    2. (T): Listen while I pound the syllables. *The bedbug bit Pam.* (Make sure to pound *bedbug* twice because it has two syllables.)
    3. (T): Pound it with me. (T&S): *The bedbug bit Pam.*
    4. (T): You pound the sentence. (S): *The bedbug bit Pam.*

5. (T): Watch me as I point to the lines while stating the sentence. (Tap the line for *bedbug* twice because it has two syllables.) *The bedbug bit Pam.*

6. (T): You point to the lines while stating the sentence.

7. (S): *The bedbug bit Pam.*

8. (T): Now write the sentence. Fingertap if needed.

- Below is a sample script to check CUPS.*

1. (T): C stands for capitalization. Did you remember a capital letter at the beginning of your sentence? Did you remember a capital letter for *Pam*? It is a name. If you forgot, fix it. If you remembered, put a tally mark above each capital letter. Add a mark in the box for C.

2. (T): U stands for understanding. Is your sentence neat? Reread it to yourself. Does it make sense? Could someone else understand it? If not, fix it. Add a mark in the box for U.

3. (T): P stands for punctuation. Did you remember a period at the end? If not, fix it. If you remembered, put a tally mark above the period. Add a mark in the box for P.

4. (T): S stands for spelling. Did you spell your words correctly? Check them. Now, check yours with mine (shows the teacher's copy). Fix any words you spelled incorrectly. Put a tally mark above the words you spelled correctly. Add a mark in the box for S.

5. (T): Rewrite your sentence with all of the corrections.

6. (T): Check for CUPS again. Put another mark in the boxes.

7. (T): Let's read the sentences.

8. (S) Read the sentences for fluency and automaticity.

***Please note:** Once students understand how to use CUPS, transition to letting them check their sentence independently before showing the teacher's copy.

Weekly Red Words

Materials Needed:
screen, red crayon, red word paper

Introduce on Tuesday, and practice daily. Use the Flip Chart for steps.

New:	Review:	New Read-Only:	Review Read-Only:
under, down	were, does, some, good, there, done, her, here		our, help

Steps for Teaching a New Red Word:

1. (T) States the word. (*under*)

2. (T&S) Use tokens to determine how many sounds are in the word.
   (/ŭ/ /n/ /d/ /er/; 4)

3. (T&S) Discuss how we would expect to spell each sound as the teacher writes the grapheme(s) correctly. Identify what is unexpected or irregular about the spelling of the word. It could also be expected, but the concept hasn't been taught yet.

4. (T&S) Discuss the etymology of the word, if appropriate (lexical words). Visit www.etymonline.com for more information on the word.

5. (T) Defines the word, and writes a sentence using the word.

6. (T) Writes the word on Red Word paper with the screen underneath, using red crayon.

7. (S) Write the word on Red Word paper with the screen underneath, using red crayon. (S) Show the word to the teacher.
   (**NOTE:** The teacher should have students chunk the word if it has more than four letters.)

8. (T&S) Stand up, holding the Red Word in the nondominant hand. Armtap word while naming each letter. Then "underline" the word by sweeping left to right while stating the word, 3x. (**NOTE:** Left-handed students will place their left hand on their right wrist. They tap to their right shoulder. Underline from wrist to shoulder. Right-handed students place their right hand on their left shoulder. They tap to their left wrist. Underline shoulder to wrist.)

9. (T&S) Trace crayon bumps with the pointer finger while naming the letters, 3x.

10. (T&S) Place the screen over the paper and trace the word with the pointer finger while naming the letters, 3x.

11. (S) Turn paper over. With red crayon, write the word without the screen one time, and hold up the word for the teacher to check. (S) Write the word two more times.

12. (S) Write an original sentence in pencil and underline the Red Word with a red crayon. (**NOTE:** The sentence can also be dictated by the teacher while the student writes or dictated by the student while the teacher writes it.)

13. Repeat the steps for *down*. (/d/ /ou/ /n/; 3)

Review Ideas for Red Words:

- Sculpt the word using red Play-Doh or clay. Have students spell the word as they smash each letter.
- Print flashcards from IOG, and practice reading.
- Armtap the word to review.
- Cross-clap the word to review.
- Stomp the letters to review.
- Use a voice jar with popsicle sticks that have a different voice (e.g., robot, baby, cheerleader, monster) listed on each stick. Have a student draw a stick from the jar. The class armtaps the word using the voice selected. (Another option is to have an electronic spinning wheel with the voices listed on the wheel.)

Syllabication (Decoding)

Materials Needed:
IMSE Syllable Division Word Book, Pencil, Highlighter, Syllable Division Posters

Introduce on Wednesday with the new concept. Practice regularly.

- Choose 6 or more words with the new concept in the *IMSE Syllable Division Word Book* for syllabication.

- Use the steps on the Flip Chart and the Syllable Division Posters.

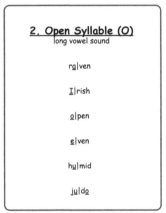

Syllable Division Patterns	1. Closed Syllable (Cl) short vowel sound	2. Open Syllable (O) long vowel sound
1. vc|cv	mag|net	ra|ven
2. v|cv	ten|nis	I|rish
3. vc|v	tip|top	o|pen
4. v|v	tom|tom	e|ven
	up|set	hu|mid
		ju|do

- Below is a sample script for syllabication.

> 1. Find the first two vowels or vowel units. Underline and label with a "v."
> 2. Draw the bridge. Underline the consonants or consonant units and label with a "c."
> 3. Find the pattern and divide the word.
> 4. Is there another vowel (other than an "e" at the end)? If so, repeat steps 1-3. If not, go to step 5.
> 5. Label each syllable.
> 6. Read the word.
>
> **NOTE:** If there are two consonants in the middle of a word, split the word between the two consonants. (Exception: If the two consonants are a digraph [sh, ch, th] they cannot be split.) If there are three or more consonants, some letters go together as one consonant unit (look for known digraphs or blends).

Fluency, Vocabulary, and Comprehension

- Incorporate fluency into your literacy lessons daily/weekly (minimum 30 min/week) by using Rapid Word Charts, IMSE Decodable Readers, words and sentences, Acadience Reading K-6 or DIBELS 8th Edition, repeated reading, and other activities.

- Incorporate vocabulary into your literacy lessons daily/weekly (minimum 50 min/week) by choosing 3-5 appropriate tier two words (can pull from rich literature or decodable readers). Teach the words through explicit, direct instruction using student-friendly definitions, word webs, vocabulary charts, illustrations, and other activities.

© IMSE 2022

- Incorporate oral language comprehension into your literacy lessons daily/weekly (approximately 100 min/week). Comprehension instruction should be explicit, direct instruction that includes teacher modeling, guided practice, and independent practice. Plan ahead to build on students' background knowledge, language structures, verbal reasoning, and literacy knowledge.

Extension Activity Ideas

- Set up a center with a recording of words with blends. Have students use tokens and sound boxes to indicate how many sounds are in each word.
- Have an image of a blender. Have students brainstorm words that have blends.
- Visit IMSE's Orton-Gillingham's Pinterest page for more ideas.

Weekly Lesson Reminders

- Daily practice with writing the weekly Red Word(s)
- Kilpatrick's "One-Minute Activities" for daily phonological awareness practice
- Zgonc's phonological awareness activities
- Listen to rich literature to work on oral language comprehension.
- Target concept practice sheets from IMSE's practice books
- Practice test on Thursday and test on Friday

Notes:

_____

_____

_____

_____

_____

_____

_____

_____

_____

_____

_____

_____

_____

_____

_____

_____

_____

_____

_____

_____

_____

Two-Consonant Beginning S Blends (snail)

Card Pack #34 Decodable Reader #31	
Object Ideas:	**Literature Ideas:**
smoothie, storm, stone, skin, spider, skate, scooter	▪ Flat Stanley series by Jeff Brown ▪ *Stellaluna* by Janell Cannon ▪ *The Real Story of Stone Soup* by Ying Chang Compestine ▪ *Our Tree Named Steve* by Alan Zweibel ▪ *The Skin You Live In* by Michael Tyler ▪ *Anansi the Spider: A Tale From the Ashanti* by Gerald McDermott ▪ *Our Skin: A First Conversation About Race* by Megan Madison and Jessica Ralli ▪ *A Sled for Gabo* Emma Otheguy

Notes

- Use the Comprehensive Flip Chart for the steps on how to teach each part of IMSE's Lesson Plan.
- Use www.etymonline.com to help establish why a word might not follow the expected rules or patterns.
- A blend consists of 2 or more consonants that blend together when speaking and reading.
- Each sound is heard in a blend. However, with coarticulation, sounds may change slightly (e.g., dr- may sound like /jr/ as in *drip*, tr- may sound like /chr/ as in *truck*).
- Use mini sound lines as an extra visual cue for word dictation. This reminds students that we still hear two sounds, but we give the blend one fingertap (to allow for coarticulation).

s　n

- If students struggle with these combinations, use tokens to first represent each sound. Then, use one finger to tap each sound in the blend. Build up to giving the blend one fingertap.
- Both sc- and sk- are included in this week's lesson. These blends include the same sounds (/sk/). Students should use the cat/kite rule to determine how to spell the /sk/ blend within the context of a word.

Phonological Awareness:

Materials Needed:
tokens, sound boxes, one-minute activities, or Zgonc PA book

Use the PAST assessment to determine a starting point for instruction. Incorporate daily phonological awareness activities by using Zgonc's tiered activities and/or Kilpatrick's One-Minute Activities in *Equipped for Reading Success.*

Phonemic awareness warm-up: Use tokens (or letter tiles once concepts have been taught) and sound boxes to do a quick phonemic awareness activity that ties in with the new concept, if appropriate.

Three-Part Drill

Materials Needed:
review cards, sand, blending board, vowel tents or sticks

Do this at least 3x per week. Use the Flip Chart for steps. Include the new concept after Day 1.

- Vowel Intensive: Use the Flip Chart for steps.
  - Do the Vowel Intensive with all 5 vowels.

V	VC	CVC
a	ag, ap, ab	lat, cad, zan
e	et, en, eb	zeg, ren, med
i	ig, ib, im	lin, hib, fid
o	ob, ot, oz	rom, hob, cog
u	un, ud, ub	sup, pum, dut

  - **NOTE:** If students are doing well with the Vowel Intensive, (T) give an assessment with 20 CVC syllables (not real words). If students pass with 80% accuracy or better, discontinue the Vowel Intensive.
- Below is a sample script. Remember to use review concepts only.

  1. **Visual:**
     (T) Tell me the sounds you know for these letters.
     (S) /m/, /l/, etc.
  2. **Auditory/Kinesthetic:**
     (T) You know two ways to spell this. (S) split trays. (T) Eyes on me.
     Spell /k/. Repeat.
     (S) /k/ c says /k/; k says /k/

3. **Blending:**
(T) Tell me the sound for each letter as I point. Then blend the sounds together to read the word or syllable. Give me a thumbs up if it is a real word.
(S) /mmm/ /ŏŏŏ/ /mmm/ *mom* (thumbs up)
Alternative:
(T) Watch me first. /mmm/ /ŏŏŏ/ /mmm/ *mom*
(T) Do it with me. (T&S) /mmm/ /ŏŏŏ/ /mmm/ *mom*
(T) Your turn. (S) /mmm/ /ŏŏŏ/ /mmm/ *mom* (thumbs up)

*Vowel Intensive: Model the visual cue while calling out the sound. Students will do the visual cue as they repeat the sound. Students will then hold up the vowel tent while stating the letter name and sound.

- (T): Eyes on me. The sound is /ă/. Repeat.
- (S): /ă/ a says /ă/

Teaching a New Concept

Materials Needed:
concept card, screen, green crayon, object, sand, decodable readers, literature, P/G chart

Introduce on Monday, and practice daily.

1. (T) Shows the new concept card(s).
   a. (T) Tells students that we will learn a new concept today: beginning S Blends.
   b. (T) Tells students that they already know the sounds for these letters. When the letters live next to each other, sometimes the sounds become blended together. That's why we call them blends.
   c. (T) States "sc-" says /sk/. (S) Repeat. Continue with the other blends: sk-, sm-, sn-, sp-, st-. Reminds students that the blends still make two sounds.
2. (T) Shows an object.
   a. (T) Allows students to manipulate the object and discuss prior knowledge. Reminds (S) that the object has the target sound(s) spelled with the target letter(s).
3. (S) Brainstorm to help establish a spelling rule, if applicable.
   a. Brainstorm words that have the target sound(s) or rule. The brainstorming can be a teacher-directed activity if students need extra support.
4. (T) Teaches Letter Formation, if needed. Can teach cursive writing.
   a. Use the steps for teaching letter formation on the Flip Chart.
   b. Use house paper to teach lowercase letters.
   c. Teach capital letters throughout the week. Capital letters go outside the house.
5. (T) Dictates target sound(s). (S) Practice all known spellings in the sand or other medium.
6. (T) Connects with literature.
   a. Read for language comprehension.
   b. Continue to work on language comprehension with rich literature throughout the week.

7. (S) Use decodable readers to practice the concepts learned.

    a. (S) Highlight words with the new concept. Read those words.

    b. (S) Highlight Red Words. Read those words.

    c. (S) Start reading the decodable reader.

    d. (S) Continue reading throughout the week.

    e. (S) Read a clean copy on Friday.

8. (T&S) Mark the Phoneme/Grapheme (P/G) chart by highlighting the target sound(s).

 ## Word Dictation

Materials Needed:
fingertapping hand, dictation paper, pencil

Practice daily. Use the Flip Chart to follow the steps for word dictation.

Day 1:	1. smell	2. Stan	3. snap	4. pigskin	5. misspell
Day 2:	1. scab	2. snapshot	3. skillet	4. spun	5. stop
Day 3:	1. scuff	2. skeptic	3. skin	4. spin	5. smitten
Days 4-5:	Review prior words. Optional additional words: instill, scan, skim, skip, skit, skittish, smog, smug, sniff, snip, snug, span, spat, spectrum, spell, spit, stash, stem, step, stiff, stub, stucco, stud, stuff				

▪ Below is a sample script for one-syllable word dictation.

1. (T) States word: *boss*. Uses it in a sentence: My *boss* is kind and fair. (Pounds) *boss*. (T) Models fingertapping if needed: /b/ /ŏ/ /s/. (Pounds) *boss*.

2. (S) State while pounding: *boss*. (Fingertap) /b/ /ŏ/ /s/. (Pound) *boss*. Write the letters known for the sounds.

3. (T) When yours looks like mine, rewrite the word.

4. (S) Rewrite.

5. Repeat the process for each word.

6. (S) Read the list of words multiple times to build automaticity.

▪ Below is a sample script for multisyllabic word dictation.

1. (T) States word: *bathtub*. Uses it in a sentence: Clean out the *bathtub*. (Pounds each syllable) *bath/tub*.

2. (S) State while pounding each syllable: *bath/tub*.

3. (T) Models fingertapping, if needed. First syllable: (Pounds) *bath*. (Fingertaps) /b/ /ă/ /th/. (Pounds) *bath*.

4. (S) State first syllable while pounding: *bath*. (Fingertap) /b/ /ă/ /th/. (Pound) *bath*. Write the letters known for the sounds.

5. (T) Second syllable: (Pounds) *tub*. (Fingertaps) /t/ /ŭ/ /b/. (Pounds) *tub*.

6. (S) State second syllable while pounding: *tub*. (Fingertap) /t/ /ŭ/ /b/. (Pound) *tub*. Write the letters known for the sounds.

7. (T) When yours looks like mine, rewrite the word.

8. (S) Rewrite.

9. Repeat the process for each word.

10. (S) Read the list of words multiple times to build automaticity.

Note: For blends, if students need to tap out each sound, use one finger to tap each sound of the blend. For example, when tapping out the word *smell*, the standard method is to tap /sm/ /ĕ/ /l/. The following alternative can be used for students who need additional support: /s/ /m/ (2 taps with the same finger) /ĕ/ /l/. IMSE gives blends one fingertap to help with coarticulation. **Reminder:** Fingertaps do not always equal the number of sounds.

Sentence Dictation

Red Words are underlined. Students can fingertap the green words. Use the Flip Chart to follow the steps for sentence dictation.

1. Kim spun on the log.
2. She hit her shin, and then there was a scab.
3. She will skip to the shed.
4. Bob did snip the stem and put it in the trash.
5. Stan put the sled onto his van.
6. Stan got on the bus with the people at the stop.
7. The snug hat had a big snap.
8. The glass will smash if I drop it.
9. Bill will put the gum on the step.
10. Did she spin the top?
11. She had a snapshot of the sunset.
12. Put the stuff in the trash.

- Below is a sample script for sentence dictation.

1. (T): Listen to the sentence. *The bedbug bit Pam.*
2. (T): Listen while I pound the syllables. *The bedbug bit Pam.* (Make sure to pound *bedbug* twice because it has two syllables.)
3. (T): Pound it with me. (T&S): *The bedbug bit Pam.*
4. (T): You pound the sentence. (S): *The bedbug bit Pam.*
5. (T): Watch me as I point to the lines while stating the sentence. (Tap the line for *bedbug* twice because it has two syllables.) *The bedbug bit Pam.*
6. (T): You point to the lines while stating the sentence.
7. (S): *The bedbug bit Pam.*
8. (T): Now write the sentence. Fingertap if needed.

- Below is a sample script to check CUPS.*

---

1. (T): C stands for capitalization. Did you remember a capital letter at the beginning of your sentence? Did you remember a capital letter for *Pam*? It is a name. If you forgot, fix it. If you remembered, put a tally mark above each capital letter. Add a mark in the box for C.

2. (T): U stands for understanding. Is your sentence neat? Reread it to yourself. Does it make sense? Could someone else understand it? If not, fix it. Add a mark in the box for U.

3. (T): P stands for punctuation. Did you remember a period at the end? If not, fix it. If you remembered, put a tally mark above the period. Add a mark in the box for P.

4. (T): S stands for spelling. Did you spell your words correctly? Check them. Now, check yours with mine (shows the teacher's copy). Fix any words you spelled incorrectly. Put a tally mark above the words you spelled correctly. Add a mark in the box for S.

5. (T): Rewrite your sentence with all of the corrections.

6. (T): Check for CUPS again. Put another mark in the boxes.

7. (T): Let's read the sentences.

8. (S) Read the sentences for fluency and automaticity.

*__Please note:__ Once students understand how to use CUPS, transition to letting them check their sentence independently before showing the teacher's copy.

Weekly Red Words

Materials Needed:
screen, red crayon, red word paper

Introduce on Tuesday, and practice daily. Use the Flip Chart for steps.

New:	Review:	New Read-Only:	Review Read-Only:
onto, people	were, does, some, good, there, done, her, here, under, down	oven	our, help

Steps for Teaching a New Red Word:

1. (T) States the word. (*onto*)

2. (T&S) Use tokens to determine how many sounds are in the word. (/ŏ/ /n/ /t/ /o͞o/; 4)

3. (T&S) Discuss how we would expect to spell each sound as the teacher writes the grapheme(s) correctly. Identify what is unexpected or irregular about the spelling of the word. It could also be expected, but the concept hasn't been taught yet.

© IMSE 2022

4. (T&S) Discuss the etymology of the word, if appropriate (lexical words). Visit www.etymonline.com for more information on the word.

5. (T) Defines the word, and writes a sentence using the word.

6. (T) Writes the word on Red Word paper with the screen underneath, using red crayon.

7. (S) Write the word on Red Word paper with the screen underneath, using red crayon. (S) Show the word to the teacher.
   (**NOTE:** The teacher should have students chunk the word if it has more than four letters.)

8. (T&S) Stand up, holding the Red Word in the nondominant hand. Armtap word while naming each letter. Then "underline" the word by sweeping left to right while stating the word, 3x. (**NOTE:** Left-handed students will place their left hand on their right wrist. They tap to their right shoulder. Underline from wrist to shoulder. Right-handed students place their right hand on their left shoulder. They tap to their left wrist. Underline shoulder to wrist.)

9. (T&S) Trace crayon bumps with the pointer finger while naming the letters, 3x.

10. (T&S) Place the screen over the paper and trace the word with the pointer finger while naming the letters, 3x.

11. (S) Turn paper over. With red crayon, write the word without the screen one time, and hold up the word for the teacher to check. (S) Write the word two more times.

12. (S) Write an original sentence in pencil and underline the Red Word with a red crayon. (**NOTE:** The sentence can also be dictated by the teacher while the student writes or dictated by the student while the teacher writes it.)

13. Repeat the steps for *people*. (/p/ /ē/ /p/ /ə/ /l/; 5)

Review Ideas for Red Words:

- Sculpt the word using red Play-Doh or clay. Have students spell the word as they smash each letter.
- Print flashcards from IOG, and practice reading.
- Armtap the word to review.
- Cross-clap the word to review.
- Stomp the letters to review.
- Use a voice jar with popsicle sticks that have a different voice (e.g., robot, baby, cheerleader, monster) listed on each stick. Have a student draw a stick from the jar. The class armtaps the word using the voice selected. (Another option is to have an electronic spinning wheel with the voices listed on the wheel.)

Syllabication (Decoding)

Materials Needed:
IMSE Syllable Division Word Book, Pencil, Highlighter, Syllable Division Posters

Introduce on Wednesday with the new concept. Practice regularly.

© IMSE 2022

- Choose 6 or more words with the new concept in the *IMSE Syllable Division Word Book* for syllabication.
- Use the steps on the Flip Chart and the Syllable Division Posters.

Syllable Division Patterns	1. Closed Syllable (Cl) short vowel sound	2. Open Syllable (O) long vowel sound
1. vc|cv		ra|ven
	mag|net	I|rish
2. v|cv	ten|nis	o|pen
	tip|top	e|ven
3. vc|v	tom|tom	hu|mid
4. v|v	up|set	ju|do

- Below is a sample script for syllabication.

1. Find the first two vowels or vowel units. Underline and label with a "v."
2. Draw the bridge. Underline the consonants or consonant units and label with a "c."
3. Find the pattern and divide the word.
4. Is there another vowel (other than an "e" at the end)? If so, repeat steps 1-3. If not, go to step 5.
5. Label each syllable.
6. Read the word.

NOTE: If there are two consonants in the middle of a word, split the word between the two consonants. (Exception: If the two consonants are a digraph [sh, ch, th] they cannot be split.) If there are three or more consonants, some letters go together as one consonant unit (look for known digraphs or blends).

Fluency, Vocabulary, and Comprehension

- Incorporate fluency into your literacy lessons daily/weekly (minimum 30 min/week) by using Rapid Word Charts, IMSE Decodable Readers, words and sentences, Acadience Reading K-6 or DIBELS 8th Edition, repeated reading, and other activities.
- Incorporate vocabulary into your literacy lessons daily/weekly (minimum 50 min/week) by choosing 3-5 appropriate tier two words (can pull from rich literature or decodable readers). Teach the words through explicit, direct instruction using student-friendly definitions, word webs, vocabulary charts, illustrations, and other activities.
- Incorporate oral language comprehension into your literacy lessons daily/weekly (approximately 100 min/week). Comprehension instruction should be explicit, direct instruction that includes teacher modeling, guided practice, and independent practice. Plan ahead to build on students' background knowledge, language structures, verbal reasoning, and literacy knowledge.

Extension Activity Ideas

- Set up a center with a recording of words with blends. Have students use tokens and sound boxes to indicate how many sounds are in each word.
- Have an image of a blender. Have students brainstorm words that have blends.
- Visit IMSE's Orton-Gillingham's Pinterest page for more ideas.

Weekly Lesson Reminders

- Daily practice with writing the weekly Red Word(s)
- Kilpatrick's "One-Minute Activities" for daily phonological awareness practice
- Zgonc's phonological awareness activities
- Listen to rich literature to work on oral language comprehension.
- Target concept practice sheets from IMSE's practice books
- Practice test on Thursday and test on Friday

Notes:

Two-Consonant Beginning W Blends (swing)

Card Pack #35 Decodable Reader #32	
Object Ideas:	**Literature Ideas:**
swing, swirl, twirl, twin, twine, swine, sweets	▪ *Phonics Through Poetry* by Babs Bell Hajdusiewicz ▪ *Sweet Clara and the Freedom Quilt* by Deborah Hopkinson ▪ There Was an Old Lady Who Swallowed... series by Lucille Colandro ▪ *A Picture Book of Dwight David Eisenhower* by David Adler ▪ *Swashby and the Sea* by Beth Ferry

 ## Notes

- Use the Comprehensive Flip Chart for the steps on how to teach each part of IMSE's Lesson Plan.
- Use www.etymonline.com to help establish why a word might not follow the expected rules or patterns.
- A blend consists of 2 or more consonants that blend together when speaking and reading.
- Each sound is heard in a blend. However, with coarticulation, sounds may change slightly (e.g., dr- may sound like /jr/ as in *drip*, tr- may sound like /chr/ as in *truck*).
- Use mini sound lines as an extra visual cue for word dictation. This reminds students that we still hear two sounds, but we give the blend one fingertap (to allow for coarticulation).

- If students struggle with these combinations, use tokens to first represent each sound. Then, use one finger to tap each sound in the blend. Build up to giving the blend one fingertap.

 ## Phonological Awareness:

Materials Needed:
tokens, sound boxes, one-minute activities, or Zgonc PA book

Use the PAST assessment to determine a starting point for instruction. Incorporate daily phonological awareness activities by using Zgonc's tiered activities and/or Kilpatrick's One-Minute Activities in *Equipped for Reading Success*.

Phonemic awareness warm-up: Use tokens (or letter tiles once concepts have been taught) and sound boxes to do a quick phonemic awareness activity that ties in with the new concept, if appropriate.

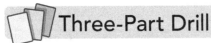

Three-Part Drill

Materials Needed:
review cards, sand, blending board, vowel tents or sticks

Do this at least 3x per week. Use the Flip Chart for steps. Include the new concept after Day 1.

- Vowel Intensive: Use the Flip Chart for steps.
  - Do the Vowel Intensive with all 5 vowels.

V	VC	CVC
a	ag, ap, ab	lat, cad, zan
e	et, en, eb	zeg, ren, med
i	ig, ib, im	lin, hib, fid
o	ob, ot, oz	rom, hob, cog
u	un, ud, ub	sup, pum, dut

  - **NOTE:** If students are doing well with the Vowel Intensive, (T) give an assessment with 20 CVC syllables (not real words). If students pass with 80% accuracy or better, discontinue the Vowel Intensive.
- Below is a sample script. Remember to use review concepts only.

1. **Visual:**
   (T) Tell me the sounds you know for these letters.
   (S) /m/, /l/, etc.

2. **Auditory/Kinesthetic:**
   (T) You know two ways to spell this. (S) split trays. (T) Eyes on me.
   Spell /k/. Repeat.
   (S) /k/ c says /k/; k says /k/

3. **Blending:**
   (T) Tell me the sound for each letter as I point. Then blend the sounds together to read the word or syllable. Give me a thumbs up if it is a real word.
   (S) /mmm/ /ŏŏŏ/ /mmm/ *mom* (thumbs up)
   Alternative:
   (T) Watch me first. /mmm/ /ŏŏŏ/ /mmm/ *mom*
   (T) Do it with me. (T&S) /mmm/ /ŏŏŏ/ /mmm/ *mom*
   (T) Your turn. (S) /mmm/ /ŏŏŏ/ /mmm/ *mom* (thumbs up)

*Vowel Intensive:** Model the visual cue while calling out the sound. Students will do the visual cue as they repeat the sound. Students will then hold up the vowel tent while stating the letter name and sound.

- (T): Eyes on me. The sound is /ă/. Repeat.
- (S): /ă/ a says /ă/

Teaching a New Concept

Materials Needed:
concept card, screen, green crayon, object, sand, decodable readers, literature, P/G chart

Introduce on Monday, and practice daily.

1. (T) Shows the new concept card(s).
   a. (T) Tells students that we will learn a new concept today: beginning W Blends.
   b. (T) Tells students that they already know the sounds for these letters. When the letters live next to each other, sometimes the sounds become blended together. That's why we call them blends.
   c. (T) States "dw-" says /dw/. (S) Repeat. Continue with the other blends: sw-, tw-. Reminds students that the blends still make two sounds.
2. (T) Shows an object.
   a. (T) Allows students to manipulate the object and discuss prior knowledge. Reminds (S) that the object has the target sound(s) spelled with the target letter(s).
3. (S) Brainstorm to help establish a spelling rule, if applicable.
   a. Brainstorm words that have the target sound(s) or rule. The brainstorming can be a teacher-directed activity if students need extra support.
4. (T) Teaches Letter Formation, if needed. Can teach cursive writing.
   a. Use the steps for teaching letter formation on the Flip Chart.
   b. Use house paper to teach lowercase letters.
   c. Teach capital letters throughout the week. Capital letters go outside the house.
5. (T) Dictates target sound(s). (S) Practice all known spellings in the sand or other medium.
6. (T) Connects with literature.
   a. Read for language comprehension.
   b. Continue to work on language comprehension with rich literature throughout the week.
7. (S) Use decodable readers to practice the concepts learned.
   a. (S) Highlight words with the new concept. Read those words.
   b. (S) Highlight Red Words. Read those words.
   c. (S) Start reading the decodable reader.
   d. (S) Continue reading throughout the week.
   e. (S) Read a clean copy on Friday.
8. (T&S) Mark the Phoneme/Grapheme (P/G) chart by highlighting the target sound(s).

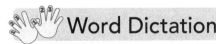 Word Dictation

Materials Needed:
fingertapping hand, dictation paper, pencil

Practice daily. Use the Flip Chart to follow the steps for word dictation.

Day 1:	1. twin	2. swam	3. dwell	4. swig	5. snapshot
Day 2:	1. dwell	2. swim	3. pigskin	4. twig	5. swum
Day 3:	1. swim	2. skeptic	3. twill	4. twin	5. swum
Days 4-5:	Review prior words.				

- Below is a sample script for one-syllable word dictation.

  1. (T) States word: *boss*. Uses it in a sentence: My *boss* is kind and fair. (Pounds) *boss*. (T) Models fingertapping if needed: /b/ /ŏ/ /s/. (Pounds) *boss*.
  2. (S) State while pounding: *boss*. (Fingertap) /b/ /ŏ/ /s/. (Pound) *boss*. Write the letters known for the sounds.
  3. (T) When yours looks like mine, rewrite the word.
  4. (S) Rewrite.
  5. Repeat the process for each word.
  6. (S) Read the list of words multiple times to build automaticity.

- Below is a sample script for multisyllabic word dictation.

  1. (T) States word: *bathtub*. Uses it in a sentence: Clean out the *bathtub*. (Pounds each syllable) *bath/tub*.
  2. (S) State while pounding each syllable: *bath/tub*.
  3. (T) Models fingertapping, if needed. First syllable: (Pounds) *bath*. (Fingertaps) /b/ /ă/ /th/. (Pounds) *bath*.
  4. (S) State first syllable while pounding: *bath*. (Fingertap) /b/ /ă/ /th/. (Pound) *bath*. Write the letters known for the sounds.
  5. (T) Second syllable: (Pounds) *tub*. (Fingertaps) /t/ /ŭ/ /b/. (Pounds) *tub*.
  6. (S) State second syllable while pounding: *tub*. (Fingertap) /t/ /ŭ/ /b/. (Pound) *tub*. Write the letters known for the sounds.
  7. (T) When yours looks like mine, rewrite the word.
  8. (S) Rewrite.
  9. Repeat the process for each word.
  10. (S) Read the list of words multiple times to build automaticity.

Note: For blends, if students need to tap out each sound, use one finger to tap each sound of the blend. For example, when tapping out the word *twig*, the standard method is to tap /tw/ /ĭ/ /g/. The following alternative can be used for students who need additional support: /t/ /w/ (2 taps with the same finger) /ĭ/ /g/. IMSE gives blends one fingertap to help with coarticulation.
Reminder: Fingertaps do not always equal the number of sounds.

Sentence Dictation

Red Words are underlined. Students can fingertap the green words. Use the Flip Chart to follow the steps for sentence dictation.

1. The bed is a twin.
2. The twig on the log was cut by Stan.
3. Bob can swim!
4. Do you like the twill fabric?
5. The rabbit did dwell in the hut.
6. Nan and Jan had a big swig.
7. We swam with both Sal and Sam.
8. She saw a twin.
9. The pup can swim in the bathtub.
10. The rat will swim in the tub.

- Below is a sample script for sentence dictation.

> 1. (T): Listen to the sentence. *The bedbug bit Pam.*
> 2. (T): Listen while I pound the syllables. *The bedbug bit Pam.* (Make sure to pound *bedbug* twice because it has two syllables.)
> 3. (T): Pound it with me. (T&S): *The bedbug bit Pam.*
> 4. (T): You pound the sentence. (S): *The bedbug bit Pam.*
> 5. (T): Watch me as I point to the lines while stating the sentence. (Tap the line for *bedbug* twice because it has two syllables.) *The bedbug bit Pam.*
> 6. (T): You point to the lines while stating the sentence.
> 7. (S): *The bedbug bit Pam.*
> 8. (T): Now write the sentence. Fingertap if needed.

- Below is a sample script to check CUPS.*

> 1. (T): C stands for capitalization. Did you remember a capital letter at the beginning of your sentence? Did you remember a capital letter for *Pam*? It is a name. If you forgot, fix it. If you remembered, put a tally mark above each capital letter. Add a mark in the box for C.
> 2. (T): U stands for understanding. Is your sentence neat? Reread it to yourself. Does it make sense? Could someone else understand it? If not, fix it. Add a mark in the box for U.
> 3. (T): P stands for punctuation. Did you remember a period at the end? If not, fix it. If you remembered, put a tally mark above the period. Add a mark in the box for P.

4. (T): S stands for spelling. Did you spell your words correctly? Check them. Now, check yours with mine (shows the teacher's copy). Fix any words you spelled incorrectly. Put a tally mark above the words you spelled correctly. Add a mark in the box for S.

5. (T): Rewrite your sentence with all of the corrections.

6. (T): Check for CUPS again. Put another mark in the boxes.

7. (T): Let's read the sentences.

8. (S) Read the sentences for fluency and automaticity.

***Please note:** Once students understand how to use CUPS, transition to letting them check their sentence independently before showing the teacher's copy.

Weekly Red Words

Materials Needed:
screen, red crayon, red word paper

Introduce on Tuesday, and practice daily. Use the Flip Chart for steps.

New:	Review:	New Read-Only:	Review Read-Only:
saw, both	were, does, some, good, there, done, her, here, under, down, onto, people	park	our, help, oven

Steps for Teaching a New Red Word:

1. (T) States the word. (*saw*)

2. (T&S) Use tokens to determine how many sounds are in the word. (/s/ /aw/; 2)

3. (T&S) Discuss how we would expect to spell each sound as the teacher writes the grapheme(s) correctly. Identify what is unexpected or irregular about the spelling of the word. It could also be expected, but the concept hasn't been taught yet.

4. (T&S) Discuss the etymology of the word, if appropriate (lexical words). Visit www.etymonline.com for more information on the word.

5. (T) Defines the word, and writes a sentence using the word.

6. (T) Writes the word on Red Word paper with the screen underneath, using red crayon.

7. (S) Write the word on Red Word paper with the screen underneath, using red crayon. (S) Show the word to the teacher.
   (**NOTE:** The teacher should have students chunk the word if it has more than four letters.)

8. (T&S) Stand up, holding the Red Word in the nondominant hand. Armtap word while naming each letter. Then "underline" the word by sweeping left to right while stating the word, 3x. (**NOTE:** Left-handed students will place their left hand on their

right wrist. They tap to their right shoulder. Underline from wrist to shoulder. Right-handed students place their right hand on their left shoulder. They tap to their left wrist. Underline shoulder to wrist.)

9. (T&S) Trace crayon bumps with the pointer finger while naming the letters, 3x.

10. (T&S) Place the screen over the paper and trace the word with the pointer finger while naming the letters, 3x.

11. (S) Turn paper over. With red crayon, write the word without the screen one time, and hold up the word for the teacher to check. (S) Write the word two more times.

12. (S) Write an original sentence in pencil and underline the Red Word with a red crayon. (**NOTE:** The sentence can also be dictated by the teacher while the student writes or dictated by the student while the teacher writes it.)

13. Repeat the steps for both. (/b/ /ō/ /th/; 3)

Review Ideas for Red Words:

- Sculpt the word using red Play-Doh or clay. Have students spell the word as they smash each letter.
- Print flashcards from IOG, and practice reading.
- Armtap the word to review.
- Cross-clap the word to review.
- Stomp the letters to review.
- Use a voice jar with popsicle sticks that have a different voice (e.g., robot, baby, cheerleader, monster) listed on each stick. Have a student draw a stick from the jar. The class armtaps the word using the voice selected. (Another option is to have an electronic spinning wheel with the voices listed on the wheel.)

Syllabication (Decoding)

Materials Needed:
IMSE Syllable Division Word Book, Pencil, Highlighter, Syllable Division Posters

Introduce on Wednesday with the new concept. Practice regularly.

- Choose 6 or more words with the new concept in the *IMSE Syllable Division Word Book* for syllabication.
- Use the steps on the Flip Chart and the Syllable Division Posters.

Syllable Division Patterns	1. Closed Syllable (Cl) short vowel sound	2. Open Syllable (O) long vowel sound
1. vc|cv	mag|net	ra|ven
2. v|cv	ten|nis	I|rish
3. vc|v	tip|top	o|pen
4. v|v	tom|tom	e|ven
	up|set	hu|mid
		ju|do

- Below is a sample script for syllabication.

> 1. Find the first two vowels or vowel units. Underline and label with a "v."
> 2. Draw the bridge. Underline the consonants or consonant units and label with a "c."
> 3. Find the pattern and divide the word.
> 4. Is there another vowel (other than an "e" at the end)? If so, repeat steps 1-3. If not, go to step 5.
> 5. Label each syllable.
> 6. Read the word.
>
> **NOTE:** If there are two consonants in the middle of a word, split the word between the two consonants. (Exception: If the two consonants are a digraph [sh, ch, th] they cannot be split.) If there are three or more consonants, some letters go together as one consonant unit (look for known digraphs or blends).

Fluency, Vocabulary, and Comprehension

- Incorporate fluency into your literacy lessons daily/weekly (minimum 30 min/week) by using Rapid Word Charts, IMSE Decodable Readers, words and sentences, Acadience Reading K-6 or DIBELS 8th Edition, repeated reading, and other activities.

- Incorporate vocabulary into your literacy lessons daily/weekly (minimum 50 min/week) by choosing 3-5 appropriate tier two words (can pull from rich literature or decodable readers). Teach the words through explicit, direct instruction using student-friendly definitions, word webs, vocabulary charts, illustrations, and other activities.

- Incorporate oral language comprehension into your literacy lessons daily/weekly (approximately 100 min/week). Comprehension instruction should be explicit, direct instruction that includes teacher modeling, guided practice, and independent practice. Plan ahead to build on students' background knowledge, language structures, verbal reasoning, and literacy knowledge.

Extension Activity Ideas

- Set up a center with a recording of words with blends. Have students use tokens and sound boxes to indicate how many sounds are in each word.
- Have an image of a blender. Have students brainstorm words that have blends.
- Visit IMSE's Orton-Gillingham's Pinterest page for more ideas.

Weekly Lesson Reminders

- Daily practice with writing the weekly Red Word(s)
- Kilpatrick's "One-Minute Activities" for daily phonological awareness practice
- Zgonc's phonological awareness activities
- Listen to rich literature to work on oral language comprehension.
- Target concept practice sheets from IMSE's practice books
- Practice test on Thursday and test on Friday

Notes:

_____

_____

_____

_____

_____

_____

_____

_____

_____

_____

_____

_____

_____

_____

_____

_____

_____

_____

_____

_____

_____

Ending T Blends (left)

Card Pack #36 Decodable Reader #33	
Object Ideas:	**Literature Ideas:**
craft, belt, melt, felt, Crest®, twist, vest, west, swept, subtract, text	▪ *Grace for President* by Kelly DiPucchio ▪ *Salt in His Shoes: Michael Jordan in Pursuit of a Dream* by Deloris and Roslyn Jordan ▪ *The Sand Castle Contest* by Robert Munsch ▪ *Be a Perfect Person in Just Three Days!* by Stephen Manes ▪ *Hugh Manatee for President* by Carla Siravo ▪ *More! Phonics Through Poetry* by Babs Bell Hajdusiewicz

Notes

▪ Use the Comprehensive Flip Chart for the steps on how to teach each part of IMSE's Lesson Plan.

▪ Use www.etymonline.com to help establish why a word might not follow the expected rules or patterns.

▪ A blend consists of 2 or more consonants that blend together when speaking and reading.

▪ Each sound is heard in a blend. However, with coarticulation, sounds may change slightly (e.g., dr- may sound like /jr/ as in *drip*, tr- may sound like /chr/ as in *truck*).

▪ Use mini sound lines as an extra visual cue for word dictation. This reminds students that we still hear two sounds, but we give the blend one fingertap (to allow for coarticulation).

▪ If students struggle with these combinations, use tokens to first represent each sound. Then, use one finger to tap each sound in the blend. Build up to giving the blend one fingertap.

▪ Avoid "olt" and "ost" on the blending board for now because the "o" is often long in words like *bolt* and *post*.

Phonological Awareness:

Materials Needed:
tokens, sound boxes, one-minute activities, or Zgonc PA book

Use the PAST assessment to determine a starting point for instruction. Incorporate daily phonological awareness activities by using Zgonc's tiered activities and/or Kilpatrick's One-Minute Activities in *Equipped for Reading Success.*

Phonemic awareness warm-up: Use tokens (or letter tiles once concepts have been taught) and sound boxes to do a quick phonemic awareness activity that ties in with the new concept, if appropriate.

Three-Part Drill

Materials Needed:
review cards, sand, blending board, vowel tents or sticks

Do this at least 3x per week. Use the Flip Chart for steps. Include the new concept after Day 1.

- Vowel Intensive: Use the Flip Chart for steps.
  - Do the Vowel Intensive with all 5 vowels.

V	VC	CVC
a	ag, ap, ab	lat, cad, zan
e	et, en, eb	zeg, ren, med
i	ig, ib, im	lin, hib, fid
o	ob, ot, oz	rom, hob, cog
u	un, ud, ub	sup, pum, dut

  - **NOTE:** If students are doing well with the Vowel Intensive, (T) give an assessment with 20 CVC syllables (not real words). If students pass with 80% accuracy or better, discontinue the Vowel Intensive.
- Below is a sample script. Remember to use review concepts only.

---

1. **Visual:**
   (T) Tell me the sounds you know for these letters.
   (S) /m/, /l/, etc.
2. **Auditory/Kinesthetic:**
   (T) You know two ways to spell this. (S) split trays. (T) Eyes on me.
   Spell /k/. Repeat.
   (S) /k/ c says /k/; k says /k/

---

3. **Blending:**
   (T) Tell me the sound for each letter as I point. Then blend the sounds together to read the word or syllable. Give me a thumbs up if it is a real word.
   (S) /mmm/ /ŏŏŏ/ /mmm/ *mom* (thumbs up)
   Alternative:
   (T) Watch me first. /mmm/ /ŏŏŏ/ /mmm/ *mom*
   (T) Do it with me. (T&S) /mmm/ /ŏŏŏ/ /mmm/ *mom*
   (T) Your turn. (S) /mmm/ /ŏŏŏ/ /mmm/ *mom* (thumbs up)

Vowel Intensive: Model the visual cue while calling out the sound. Students will do the visual cue as they repeat the sound. Students will then hold up the vowel tent while stating the letter name and sound.

- (T): Eyes on me. The sound is /ă/. Repeat.
- (S): /ă/ a says /ă/

Teaching a New Concept

Materials Needed:
concept card, screen, green crayon, object, sand, decodable readers, literature, P/G chart

Introduce on Monday, and practice daily.

1. (T) Shows the new concept card(s).
   a. (T) Tells students that we will learn a new concept today: ending T Blends.
   b. (T) Tells students that they already know the sounds for these letters. When the letters live next to each other, sometimes the sounds become blended together. That's why we call them blends.
   c. (T) States "-ct" says /kt/. (S) Repeat. Continue with the other blends: -ft, -lt, -nt, -pt, -st, -xt. Reminds students that the blends still make two sounds. (Note that -xt actually has three sounds [/kst/] because "x" has two phonemes [/k/ and /s/].)
2. (T) Shows an object.
   a. (T) Allows students to manipulate the object and discuss prior knowledge. Reminds (S) that the object has the target sound(s) spelled with the target letter(s).
3. (S) Brainstorm to help establish a spelling rule, if applicable.
   a. Brainstorm words that have the target sound(s) or rule. The brainstorming can be a teacher-directed activity if students need extra support.
4. (T) Teaches Letter Formation, if needed. Can teach cursive writing.
   a. Use the steps for teaching letter formation on the Flip Chart.
   b. Use house paper to teach lowercase letters.
   c. Teach capital letters throughout the week. Capital letters go outside the house.
5. (T) Dictates target sound(s). (S) Practice all known spellings in the sand or other medium.
6. (T) Connects with literature.
   a. Read for language comprehension.
   b. Continue to work on language comprehension with rich literature throughout the week.

7. (S) Use decodable readers to practice the concepts learned.

   a. (S) Highlight words with the new concept. Read those words.

   b. (S) Highlight Red Words. Read those words.

   c. (S) Start reading the decodable reader.

   d. (S) Continue reading throughout the week.

   e. (S) Read a clean copy on Friday.

8. (T&S) Mark the Phoneme/Grapheme (P/G) chart by highlighting the target sound(s).

 ## Word Dictation

Materials Needed:
fingertapping hand, dictation paper, pencil

Practice daily. Use the Flip Chart to follow the steps for word dictation.

Day 1:	1. craft	2. chant	3. trust	4. silent	5. district
Day 2:	1. act	2. comment	3. disrupt	4. text	5. felt
Day 3:	1. grunt	2. dentist	3. slept	4. melt	5. subtract
Days 4-5:	Review prior words. Optional additional words: ant, belt, bent, best, blunt, bust, cast, contact, cost, crept, crest, crust, draft, dust, event, fact, fist, frost, grant, hilt, hunt, Kent, kept, last, left, lent, lint, list, loft, mint, mist, must, nest, next, object, pact, pant, pelt, pest, plant, print, rant, rent, runt, rust, sent, silt, slant, spent, student, swept, swift, tent, test, tilt, tint, tract, twist, vest, went, west, wilt				

- Below is a sample script for one-syllable word dictation.

  1. (T) States word: *boss.* Uses it in a sentence: My *boss* is kind and fair. (Pounds) *boss.* (T) Models fingertapping if needed: /b/ /ŏ/ /s/. (Pounds) *boss.*

  2. (S) State while pounding: *boss.* (Fingertap) /b/ /ŏ/ /s/. (Pound) *boss.* Write the letters known for the sounds.

  3. (T) When yours looks like mine, rewrite the word.

  4. (S) Rewrite.

  5. Repeat the process for each word.

  6. (S) Read the list of words multiple times to build automaticity.

- Below is a sample script for multisyllabic word dictation.

  1. (T) States word: *bathtub.* Uses it in a sentence: Clean out the *bathtub.* (Pounds each syllable) *bath/tub.*

  2. (S) State while pounding each syllable: *bath/tub.*

  3. (T) Models fingertapping, if needed. First syllable: (Pounds) *bath.* (Fingertaps) /b/ /ă/ /th/. (Pounds) *bath.*

© IMSE 2022

4. (S) State first syllable while pounding: *bath*. (Fingertap) /b/ /ă/ /th/. (Pound) *bath*. Write the letters known for the sounds.

5. (T) Second syllable: (Pounds) *tub*. (Fingertaps) /t/ /ŭ/ /b/. (Pounds) *tub*.

6. (S) State second syllable while pounding: *tub*. (Fingertap) /t/ /ŭ/ /b/. (Pound) *tub*. Write the letters known for the sounds.

7. (T) When yours looks like mine, rewrite the word.

8. (S) Rewrite.

9. Repeat the process for each word.

10. (S) Read the list of words multiple times to build automaticity.

Note: For blends, if students need to tap out each sound, use one finger to tap each sound of the blend. For example, when tapping out the word *bent*, the standard method is to tap /b/ /ĕ/ /nt/. The following alternative can be used for students who need additional support: /b/ /ĕ/ /n/ /t/ (tapping the last two sounds [/n/ and /t/] with the same finger). IMSE gives blends one fingertap to help with coarticulation. **Reminder:** Fingertaps do not always equal the number of sounds.

Sentence Dictation

Red Words are underlined. Students can fingertap the green words. Use the Flip Chart to follow the steps for sentence dictation.

1. Sam had a red vest.
2. The rust was on the tin shed.
3. Did you see the plant next to the grass?
4. Did you contact the student?
5. She was silent when the cup fell over.
6. Ben could swim fast, but I could swim best.
7. The bug was a big pest.
8. Should Kent go on a rant?
9. She did comment to the dentist.
10. He will subtract the cost of the tent from the bill.
11. Fran can act in the skit.
12. Kent kept the cast from his left leg.
13. Do not disrupt the test!
14. We must trust him with the fact.
15. Would you subtract the cash in the cashbox?
16. I saw the people from the district.

- Below is a sample script for sentence dictation.

> 1. (T): Listen to the sentence. *The bedbug bit Pam.*
> 2. (T): Listen while I pound the syllables. *The bedbug bit Pam.* (Make sure to pound *bedbug* twice because it has two syllables.)
> 3. (T): Pound it with me. (T&S): *The bedbug bit Pam.*
> 4. (T): You pound the sentence. (S): *The bedbug bit Pam.*
> 5. (T): Watch me as I point to the lines while stating the sentence. (Tap the line for *bedbug* twice because it has two syllables.) *The bedbug bit Pam.*
> 6. (T): You point to the lines while stating the sentence.
> 7. (S): *The bedbug bit Pam.*
> 8. (T): Now write the sentence. Fingertap if needed.

- Below is a sample script to check CUPS.*

> 1. (T): C stands for capitalization. Did you remember a capital letter at the beginning of your sentence? Did you remember a capital letter for *Pam*? It is a name. If you forgot, fix it. If you remembered, put a tally mark above each capital letter. Add a mark in the box for C.
> 2. (T): U stands for understanding. Is your sentence neat? Reread it to yourself. Does it make sense? Could someone else understand it? If not, fix it. Add a mark in the box for U.
> 3. (T): P stands for punctuation. Did you remember a period at the end? If not, fix it. If you remembered, put a tally mark above the period. Add a mark in the box for P.
> 4. (T): S stands for spelling. Did you spell your words correctly? Check them. Now, check yours with mine (shows the teacher's copy). Fix any words you spelled incorrectly. Put a tally mark above the words you spelled correctly. Add a mark in the box for S.
> 5. (T): Rewrite your sentence with all of the corrections.
> 6. (T): Check for CUPS again. Put another mark in the boxes.
> 7. (T): Let's read the sentences.
> 8. (S) Read the sentences for fluency and automaticity.
>
> *Please note: Once students understand how to use CUPS, transition to letting them check their sentence independently before showing the teacher's copy.

Weekly Red Words

Materials Needed:
screen, red crayon, red word paper

Introduce on Tuesday, and practice daily. Use the Flip Chart for steps.

New:	Review:	New Read-Only:	Review Read-Only:
should, could, would, over	were, does, some, good, there, done, her, here, under, down, onto, people, saw, both		our, help, oven, park

Steps for Teaching a New Red Word:

1. (T) States the word. (*should*)
2. (T&S) Use tokens to determine how many sounds are in the word. (/sh/ /o͞o/ /d/; 3)
3. (T&S) Discuss how we would expect to spell each sound as the teacher writes the grapheme(s) correctly. Identify what is unexpected or irregular about the spelling of the word. It could also be expected, but the concept hasn't been taught yet.
4. (T&S) Discuss the etymology of the word, if appropriate (lexical words). Visit www.etymonline.com for more information on the word.
5. (T) Defines the word, and writes a sentence using the word.
6. (T) Writes the word on Red Word paper with the screen underneath, using red crayon.
7. (S) Write the word on Red Word paper with the screen underneath, using red crayon. (S) Show the word to the teacher.
(**NOTE:** The teacher should have students chunk the word if it has more than four letters.)
8. (T&S) Stand up, holding the Red Word in the nondominant hand. Armtap word while naming each letter. Then "underline" the word by sweeping left to right while stating the word, 3x. (**NOTE:** Left-handed students will place their left hand on their right wrist. They tap to their right shoulder. Underline from wrist to shoulder. Right-handed students place their right hand on their left shoulder. They tap to their left wrist. Underline shoulder to wrist.)
9. (T&S) Trace crayon bumps with the pointer finger while naming the letters, 3x.
10. (T&S) Place the screen over the paper and trace the word with the pointer finger while naming the letters, 3x.
11. (S) Turn paper over. With red crayon, write the word without the screen one time, and hold up the word for the teacher to check. (S) Write the word two more times.
12. (S) Write an original sentence in pencil and underline the Red Word with a red crayon. (**NOTE:** The sentence can also be dictated by the teacher while the student writes or dictated by the student while the teacher writes it.)
13. Repeat the steps for *could* (/k/ /o͞o/ /d/; 3), *would* (/w/ /o͞o/ /d/; 3), *over* (/ō/ /v/ /er/; 3).

Review Ideas for Red Words:

- Sculpt the word using red Play-Doh or clay. Have students spell the word as they smash each letter.
- Print flashcards from IOG, and practice reading.
- Armtap the word to review.
- Cross-clap the word to review.
- Stomp the letters to review.
- Use a voice jar with popsicle sticks that have a different voice (e.g., robot, baby, cheerleader, monster) listed on each stick. Have a student draw a stick from the jar. The class armtaps the word using the voice selected. (Another option is to have an electronic spinning wheel with the voices listed on the wheel.)

Syllabication (Decoding)

Materials Needed:
IMSE Syllable Division Word Book, Pencil, Highlighter, Syllable Division Posters

Introduce on Wednesday with the new concept. Practice regularly.

- Choose 6 or more words with the new concept in the *IMSE Syllable Division Word Book* for syllabication.
- Use the steps on the Flip Chart and the Syllable Division Posters.

Syllable Division Patterns	1. Closed Syllable (Cl) short vowel sound	2. Open Syllable (O) long vowel sound
1. vc|cv	mag|net	ra|ven
2. v|cv	ten|nis	I|rish
3. vc|v	tip|top	o|pen
4. v|v	tom|tom	e|ven
	up|set	hu|mid
		ju|do

- Below is a sample script for syllabication.

1. Find the first two vowels or vowel units. Underline and label with a "v."
2. Draw the bridge. Underline the consonants or consonant units and label with a "c."
3. Find the pattern and divide the word.
4. Is there another vowel (other than an "e" at the end)? If so, repeat steps 1-3. If not, go to step 5.
5. Label each syllable.
6. Read the word.

> **NOTE:** If there are two consonants in the middle of a word, split the word between the two consonants. (Exception: If the two consonants are a digraph [sh, ch, th] they cannot be split.) If there are three or more consonants, some letters go together as one consonant unit (look for known digraphs or blends).

Fluency, Vocabulary, and Comprehension

- Incorporate fluency into your literacy lessons daily/weekly (minimum 30 min/week) by using Rapid Word Charts, IMSE Decodable Readers, words and sentences, Acadience Reading K-6 or DIBELS 8th Edition, repeated reading, and other activities.
- Incorporate vocabulary into your literacy lessons daily/weekly (minimum 50 min/week) by choosing 3-5 appropriate tier two words (can pull from rich literature or decodable readers). Teach the words through explicit, direct instruction using student-friendly definitions, word webs, vocabulary charts, illustrations, and other activities.
- Incorporate oral language comprehension into your literacy lessons daily/weekly (approximately 100 min/week). Comprehension instruction should be explicit, direct instruction that includes teacher modeling, guided practice, and independent practice. Plan ahead to build on students' background knowledge, language structures, verbal reasoning, and literacy knowledge.

Extension Activity Ideas

- Set up a center with a recording of words with blends. Have students use tokens and sound boxes to indicate how many sounds are in each word.
- Have an image of a blender. Have students brainstorm words that have blends.
- Visit IMSE's Orton-Gillingham's Pinterest page for more ideas.

Weekly Lesson Reminders

- Daily practice with writing the weekly Red Word(s)
- Kilpatrick's "One-Minute Activities" for daily phonological awareness practice
- Zgonc's phonological awareness activities
- Listen to rich literature to work on oral language comprehension.
- Target concept practice sheets from IMSE's practice books
- Practice test on Thursday and test on Friday

Notes:

_____

_____

_____

_____

_____

_____

_____

_____

_____

_____

_____

_____

_____

_____

_____

_____

_____

_____

_____

_____

Ending L Blends (milk)

Object Ideas:	Literature Ideas:
elf, golf, shelf, self, milk, Hulk®, silk, elk	• *The Milk Makers* by Gail Gibbons • *No Moon, No Milk!* by Chris Babcock • *The Elf on the Shelf: A Christmas Tradition* by Carol V. Aebersold and Chanda A. Bell • *Help!: A Story of Friendship* by Holly Keller

Notes

- Use the Comprehensive Flip Chart for the steps on how to teach each part of IMSE's Lesson Plan.
- Use www.etymonline.com to help establish why a word might not follow the expected rules or patterns.
- A blend consists of 2 or more consonants that blend together when speaking and reading.
- Each sound is heard in a blend. However, with coarticulation, sounds may change slightly (e.g., dr- may sound like /jr/ as in *drip*, tr- may sound like /chr/ as in *truck*).
- Use mini sound lines as an extra visual cue for word dictation. This reminds students that we still hear two sounds, but we give the blend one fingertap (to allow for coarticulation)

- If students struggle with these combinations, use tokens to first represent each sound. Then, use one finger to tap each sound in the blend. Build up to giving the blend one fingertap.
- Avoid "ild" and "old" on the blending board for now because the "o" and "i" are often long in words like *wild* and *scold*.

Phonological Awareness:

Materials Needed:
tokens, sound boxes, one-minute activities, or Zgonc PA book

Use the PAST assessment to determine a starting point for instruction. Incorporate daily phonological awareness activities by using Zgonc's tiered activities and/or Kilpatrick's One-Minute Activities in *Equipped for Reading Success*.

Phonemic awareness warm-up: Use tokens (or letter tiles once concepts have been taught) and sound boxes to do a quick phonemic awareness activity that ties in with the new concept, if appropriate.

 ## Three-Part Drill

Materials Needed:
review cards, sand, blending board, vowel tents or sticks

Do this at least 3x per week. Use the Flip Chart for steps. Include the new concept after Day 1.

- Vowel Intensive: Use the Flip Chart for steps.
  - Do the Vowel Intensive with all 5 vowels.

V	VC	CVC
a	ag, ap, ab	lat, cad, zan
e	et, en, eb	zeg, ren, med
i	ig, ib, im	lin, hib, fid
o	ob, ot, oz	rom, hob, cog
u	un, ud, ub	sup, pum, dut

  - **NOTE:** If students are doing well with the Vowel Intensive, (T) give an assessment with 20 CVC syllables (not real words). If students pass with 80% accuracy or better, discontinue the Vowel Intensive.
- Below is a sample script. Remember to use review concepts only.

1. **Visual:**
   (T) Tell me the sounds you know for these letters.
   (S) /m/, /l/, etc.
2. **Auditory/Kinesthetic:**
   (T) You know two ways to spell this. (S) split trays. (T) Eyes on me.
   Spell /k/. Repeat.
   (S) /k/ c says /k/; k says /k/
3. **Blending:**
   (T) Tell me the sound for each letter as I point. Then blend the sounds together to read the word or syllable. Give me a thumbs up if it is a real word.
   (S) /mmm/ /ŏŏŏ/ /mmm/ *mom* (thumbs up)
   Alternative:
   (T) Watch me first. /mmm/ /ŏŏŏ/ /mmm/ *mom*
   (T) Do it with me. (T&S) /mmm/ /ŏŏŏ/ /mmm/ *mom*
   (T) Your turn. (S) /mmm/ /ŏŏŏ/ /mmm/ *mom* (thumbs up)

> ***Vowel Intensive:** Model the visual cue while calling out the sound. Students will do the visual cue as they repeat the sound. Students will then hold up the vowel tent while stating the letter name and sound.
> - (T): Eyes on me. The sound is /ă/. Repeat.
> - (S): /ă/ a says /ă/

 ## Teaching a New Concept

Materials Needed:
concept card, screen, green crayon, object, sand, decodable readers, literature, P/G chart

Introduce on Monday, and practice daily.

1. (T) Shows the new concept card(s).
   a. (T) Tells students that we will learn a new concept today: ending L Blends.
   b. (T) Tells students that they already know the sounds for these letters. When the letters live next to each other, sometimes the sounds become blended together. That's why we call them blends.
   c. (T) States "-ld" says /ld/. (S) Repeat. Continue with the other blends: -lf, -lk, -lp. Reminds students that the blends still make two sounds.
2. (T) Shows an object.
   a. (T) Allows students to manipulate the object and discuss prior knowledge. Reminds (S) that the object has the target sound(s) spelled with the target letter(s).
3. (S) Brainstorm to help establish a spelling rule, if applicable.
   a. Brainstorm words that have the target sound(s) or rule. The brainstorming can be a teacher-directed activity if students need extra support.
4. (T) Teaches Letter Formation, if needed. Can teach cursive writing.
   a. Use the steps for teaching letter formation on the Flip Chart.
   b. Use house paper to teach lowercase letters.
   c. Teach capital letters throughout the week. Capital letters go outside the house.
5. (T) Dictates target sound(s). (S) Practice all known spellings in the sand or other medium.
6. (T) Connects with literature.
   a. Read for language comprehension.
   b. Continue to work on language comprehension with rich literature throughout the week.
7. (S) Use decodable readers to practice the concepts learned.
   a. (S) Highlight words with the new concept. Read those words.
   b. (S) Highlight Red Words. Read those words.
   c. (S) Start reading the decodable reader.
   d. (S) Continue reading throughout the week.
   e. (S) Read a clean copy on Friday.
8. (T&S) Mark the Phoneme/Grapheme (P/G) chart by highlighting the target sound(s).

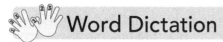 Word Dictation

Materials Needed:
fingertapping hand, dictation paper, pencil

Practice daily. Use the Flip Chart to follow the steps for word dictation.

Day 1:	1. silk	2. gulf	3. weld	4. help	5. himself
Day 2:	1. shelf	2. held	3. engulf	4. milkman	5. sulk
Day 3:	1. withheld	2. milk	3. bulk	4. itself	5. yelp
Days 4-5:	Review prior words. Optional additional words: elf, elk, golf, hulk, ilk, kelp, meld, self, selfless, upheld				

- Below is a sample script for one-syllable word dictation.

> 1. (T) States word: *boss*. Uses it in a sentence: My *boss* is kind and fair. (Pounds) *boss*. (T) Models fingertapping if needed: /b/ /ŏ/ /s/. (Pounds) *boss*.
> 2. (S) State while pounding: *boss*. (Fingertap) /b/ /ŏ/ /s/. (Pound) *boss*. Write the letters known for the sounds.
> 3. (T) When yours looks like mine, rewrite the word.
> 4. (S) Rewrite.
> 5. Repeat the process for each word.
> 6. (S) Read the list of words multiple times to build automaticity.

- Below is a sample script for multisyllabic word dictation.

> 1. (T) States word: *bathtub*. Uses it in a sentence: Clean out the *bathtub*. (Pounds each syllable) *bath/tub*.
> 2. (S) State while pounding each syllable: *bath/tub*.
> 3. (T) Models fingertapping, if needed. First syllable: (Pounds) *bath*. (Fingertaps) /b/ /ă/ /th/. (Pounds) *bath*.
> 4. (S) State first syllable while pounding: *bath*. (Fingertap) /b/ /ă/ /th/. (Pound) *bath*. Write the letters known for the sounds.
> 5. (T) Second syllable: (Pounds) *tub*. (Fingertaps) /t/ /ŭ/ /b/. (Pounds) *tub*.
> 6. (S) State second syllable while pounding: *tub*. (Fingertap) /t/ /ŭ/ /b/. (Pound) *tub*. Write the letters known for the sounds.
> 7. (T) When yours looks like mine, rewrite the word.
> 8. (S) Rewrite.
> 9. Repeat the process for each word.
> 10. (S) Read the list of words multiple times to build automaticity.

Note: For blends, if students need to tap out each sound, use one finger to tap each sound of the blend. For example, when tapping out the word *sulk*, the standard method is to tap /s/ /ŭ/ /lk/. The following alternative can be used for students who need additional support: /s/ /ŭ/ /l/ /k/ (tapping the last two sounds [/l/ and /k/] with the same finger). IMSE gives blends one fingertap to help with coarticulation. **Reminder:** Fingertaps do not always equal the number of sounds.

Sentence Dictation

Red Words are underlined. Students can fingertap the green words. Use the Flip Chart to follow the steps for sentence dictation.

1. The elf sat on the shelf.
2. She held the can of milk.
3. Does the pup yelp?
4. Jan will run to get help.
5. The elk will live out on the path.
6. I love the silk hat on top of the shelf!
7. Can you help me weld the tin?
8. Stan is good at golf.
9. Did he sulk for milk?
10. We get the milk in bulk.
11. He held the kelp.

- Below is a sample script for sentence dictation.

> 1. (T): Listen to the sentence. *The bedbug bit Pam.*
> 2. (T): Listen while I pound the syllables. *The bedbug bit Pam.* (Make sure to pound *bedbug* twice because it has two syllables.)
> 3. (T): Pound it with me. (T&S): *The bedbug bit Pam.*
> 4. (T): You pound the sentence. (S): *The bedbug bit Pam.*
> 5. (T): Watch me as I point to the lines while stating the sentence. (Tap the line for *bedbug* twice because it has two syllables.) *The bedbug bit Pam.*
> 6. (T): You point to the lines while stating the sentence.
> 7. (S): *The bedbug bit Pam.*
> 8. (T): Now write the sentence. Fingertap if needed.

- Below is a sample script to check CUPS.*

> 1. (T): C stands for capitalization. Did you remember a capital letter at the beginning of your sentence? Did you remember a capital letter for *Pam*? It is a name. If you forgot, fix it. If you remembered, put a tally mark above each capital letter. Add a mark in the box for C.
> 2. (T): U stands for understanding. Is your sentence neat? Reread it to yourself. Does it make sense? Could someone else understand it? If not, fix it. Add a mark in the box for U.
> 3. (T): P stands for punctuation. Did you remember a period at the end? If not, fix it. If you remembered, put a tally mark above the period. Add a mark in the box for P.

4. (T): S stands for spelling. Did you spell your words correctly? Check them. Now, check yours with mine (shows the teacher's copy). Fix any words you spelled incorrectly. Put a tally mark above the words you spelled correctly. Add a mark in the box for S.

5. (T): Rewrite your sentence with all of the corrections.

6. (T): Check for CUPS again. Put another mark in the boxes.

7. (T): Let's read the sentences.

8. (S) Read the sentences for fluency and automaticity.

*__Please note:__ Once students understand how to use CUPS, transition to letting them check their sentence independently before showing the teacher's copy.

Weekly Red Words

Materials Needed:
screen, red crayon, red word paper

Introduce on Tuesday, and practice daily. Use the Flip Chart for steps.

New:	Review:	New Read-Only:	Review Read-Only:
love, live, out	were, does, some, good, there, done, her, here, under, down, onto, people, saw, both, should, could, would, over		our, oven, park

Steps for Teaching a New Red Word:

1. (T) States the word. (*love*)

2. (T&S) Use tokens to determine how many sounds are in the word. (/l/ /ŭ/ /v/; 3)

3. (T&S) Discuss how we would expect to spell each sound as the teacher writes the grapheme(s) correctly. Identify what is unexpected or irregular about the spelling of the word. It could also be expected, but the concept hasn't been taught yet.

4. (T&S) Discuss the etymology of the word, if appropriate (lexical words). Visit www.etymonline.com for more information on the word.

5. (T) Defines the word, and writes a sentence using the word.

6. (T) Writes the word on Red Word paper with the screen underneath, using red crayon.

7. (S) Write the word on Red Word paper with the screen underneath, using red crayon. (S) Show the word to the teacher.
(**NOTE:** The teacher should have students chunk the word if it has more than four letters.)

8. (T&S) Stand up, holding the Red Word in the nondominant hand. Armtap word while naming each letter. Then "underline" the word by sweeping left to right while stating the word, 3x. (**NOTE:** Left-handed students will place their left hand on their right wrist. They tap to their right shoulder. Underline from wrist to shoulder. Right-handed students place their right hand on their left shoulder. They tap to their left wrist. Underline shoulder to wrist.)

9. (T&S) Trace crayon bumps with the pointer finger while naming the letters, 3x.

10. (T&S) Place the screen over the paper and trace the word with the pointer finger while naming the letters, 3x.

11. (S) Turn paper over. With red crayon, write the word without the screen one time, and hold up the word for the teacher to check. (S) Write the word two more times.

12. (S) Write an original sentence in pencil and underline the Red Word with a red crayon. (**NOTE:** The sentence can also be dictated by the teacher while the student writes or dictated by the student while the teacher writes it.)

13. Repeat the steps for *live* (/l/ /ĭ/ /v/; 3), *out* (/ou/ /t/; 2).

Review Ideas for Red Words:

- Sculpt the word using red Play-Doh or clay. Have students spell the word as they smash each letter.
- Print flashcards from IOG, and practice reading.
- Armtap the word to review.
- Cross-clap the word to review.
- Stomp the letters to review.
- Use a voice jar with popsicle sticks that have a different voice (e.g., robot, baby, cheerleader, monster) listed on each stick. Have a student draw a stick from the jar. The class armtaps the word using the voice selected. (Another option is to have an electronic spinning wheel with the voices listed on the wheel.)

Syllabication (Decoding)

Materials Needed:
IMSE Syllable Division Word Book, Pencil, Highlighter, Syllable Division Posters

Introduce on Wednesday with the new concept. Practice regularly.

- Choose 6 or more words with the new concept in the *IMSE Syllable Division Word Book* for syllabication.
- Use the steps on the Flip Chart and the Syllable Division Posters.

Syllable Division Patterns	1. Closed Syllable (Cl) short vowel sound	2. Open Syllable (O) long vowel sound
1. vc|cv	mag|net	ra|ven
2. v|cv	ten|nis	I|rish
3. vc|v	tip|top	o|pen
4. v|v	tom|tom	e|ven
	up|set	hu|mid
		ju|do

- Below is a sample script for syllabication.

1. Find the first two vowels or vowel units. Underline and label with a "v."
2. Draw the bridge. Underline the consonants or consonant units and label with a "c."
3. Find the pattern and divide the word.
4. Is there another vowel (other than an "e" at the end)? If so, repeat steps 1-3. If not, go to step 5.
5. Label each syllable.
6. Read the word.

NOTE: If there are two consonants in the middle of a word, split the word between the two consonants. (Exception: If the two consonants are a digraph [sh, ch, th] they cannot be split.) If there are three or more consonants, some letters go together as one consonant unit (look for known digraphs or blends).

Fluency, Vocabulary, and Comprehension

- Incorporate fluency into your literacy lessons daily/weekly (minimum 30 min/week) by using Rapid Word Charts, IMSE Decodable Readers, words and sentences, Acadience Reading K-6 or DIBELS 8th Edition, repeated reading, and other activities.
- Incorporate vocabulary into your literacy lessons daily/weekly (minimum 50 min/week) by choosing 3-5 appropriate tier two words (can pull from rich literature or decodable readers). Teach the words through explicit, direct instruction using student-friendly definitions, word webs, vocabulary charts, illustrations, and other activities.
- Incorporate oral language comprehension into your literacy lessons daily/weekly (approximately 100 min/week). Comprehension instruction should be explicit, direct instruction that includes teacher modeling, guided practice, and independent practice. Plan ahead to build on students' background knowledge, language structures, verbal reasoning, and literacy knowledge.

Extension Activity Ideas

- Set up a center with a recording of words with blends. Have students use tokens and sound boxes to indicate how many sounds are in each word.
- Have an image of a blender. Have students brainstorm words that have blends.
- Visit IMSE's Orton-Gillingham's Pinterest page for more ideas.

Weekly Lesson Reminders

- Daily practice with writing the weekly Red Word(s)
- Kilpatrick's "One-Minute Activities" for daily phonological awareness practice
- Zgonc's phonological awareness activities
- Listen to rich literature to work on oral language comprehension.
- Target concept practice sheets from IMSE's practice books
- Practice test on Thursday and test on Friday

Review for Concepts m-ending l blends

After teaching the first 41 concepts, the following words and sentences may be utilized for review. Teachers can dictate a different list (A, B, C, or D) and three sentences each day of the review. Teachers can spend up to a week on review *if needed*. If a review is not needed, this page can be skipped or partially utilized. Students can use IMSE workbooks or age-appropriate paper for recording their answers.

List A	List B	List C	List D
1. fizz	1. bobcat	1. express	1. grill
2. plan	2. even	2. stop	2. district
3. zero	3. spell	3. hill	3. dishpan
4. twin	4. trumpet	4. dwell	4. yelp
5. cashbox	5. help	5. banjo	5. flip
6. shelf	6. pass	6. held	6. combo
7. frog	7. subtract	7. dentist	7. twig
8. open	8. dogsled	8. bathtub	8. off
9. craft	9. swim	9. silk	9. skeptic
10. misspell	10. himself	10. clam	10. hundred

Sentences:
1. The rabbit sat on the hippo.
2. She did not drop the flag.
3. Does that cat hiss at you?
4. Fran can act in the skit.
5. The velvet dress was for Fran.
6. Did you see the sunfish at sunset?
7. She had a snapshot of the sunset.
8. Stan is good at golf.
9. Mom is upset with the mess!
10. The pup can swim in the bathtub.
11. The gull will sit by a shell.
12. Do not disrupt the test!

Remaining Ending Blends (jump)

and syllabication of 3 or more syllables (hob/gob/lin)

Card Pack #38 Decodable Reader #35	
Object Ideas:	**Literature Ideas:**
jump rope, pumpkin, stamp, ranch, bench, Band-Aid®, hand	▪ *The Kissing Hand* by Audrey Penn ▪ *The Vanishing Pumpkin* by Tony Johnston ▪ *The Runaway Pumpkin* by Kevin Lewis ▪ *The Biggest Pumpkin Ever* by Steven Kroll ▪ *It's Pumpkin Day, Mouse!* by Laura Numeroff ▪ *These Hands* by Margaret H. Mason ▪ *Jabari Jumps* by Gaia Cornwall ▪ *More! Phonics Through Poetry* by Babs Bell Hajdusiewicz

Notes

- Use the Comprehensive Flip Chart for the steps on how to teach each part of IMSE's Lesson Plan.
- Use www.etymonline.com to help establish why a word might not follow the expected rules or patterns.
- A blend consists of 2 or more consonants that blend together when speaking and reading.
- Each sound is heard in a blend. However, with coarticulation, sounds may change slightly (e.g., dr- may sound like /jr/ as in *drip*, tr- may sound like /chr/ as in *truck*).
- Use mini sound lines as an extra visual cue for word dictation. This reminds students that we still hear two sounds, but we give the blend one fingertap (to allow for coarticulation).

- If students struggle with these combinations, use tokens to first represent each sound. Then, use one finger to tap each sound in the blend. Build up to giving the blend one fingertap.
- After all blends are taught, teachers can also teach students how to decode 3-syllable words (e.g., hobgoblin, Atlantic). See the Syllabication section of this lesson.
- Avoid "ind" on the blending board for now because the "i" is often long in words like *find*.

Reviewing Blends

- **Visual:** Do not flash every card; randomly flip through card pack to keep review to ten minutes. Remember to include long vowel sounds.
- **Auditory/Kinesthetic:** Do not state every highlighted sound; randomly state sounds, focusing on problem areas.
- **Blending:** When blending, be mindful of beginning and ending blends on the blending board at the same time because students may have difficulty with pronunciation. Be sure to practice open syllables on the blending board.
- **Vowel Intensive:** Continue to practice short vowel drill with students if needed.

Phonological Awareness:

Materials Needed:
tokens, sound boxes, one-minute activities, or Zgonc PA book

Use the PAST assessment to determine a starting point for instruction. Incorporate daily phonological awareness activities by using Zgonc's tiered activities and/or Kilpatrick's One-Minute Activities in *Equipped for Reading Success*.

Phonemic awareness warm-up: Use tokens (or letter tiles once concepts have been taught) and sound boxes to do a quick phonemic awareness activity that ties in with the new concept, if appropriate.

Three-Part Drill

Materials Needed:
review cards, sand, blending board, vowel tents or sticks

Do this at least 3x per week. Use the Flip Chart for steps. Include the new concept after Day 1.

- Vowel Intensive: Use the Flip Chart for steps.
  - Do the Vowel Intensive with all 5 vowels.

V	VC	CVC
a	ag, ap, ab	lat, cad, zan
e	et, en, eb	zeg, ren, med
i	ig, ib, im	lin, hib, fid
o	ob, ot, oz	rom, hob, cog
u	un, ud, ub	sup, pum, dut

  - **NOTE:** If students are doing well with the Vowel Intensive, (T) give an assessment with 20 CVC syllables (not real words). If students pass with 80% accuracy or better, discontinue the Vowel Intensive.
- Below is a sample script. Remember to use review concepts only.

1. **Visual:**
   (T) Tell me the sounds you know for these letters.
   (S) /m/, /l/, etc.

2. **Auditory/Kinesthetic:**
   (T) You know two ways to spell this. (S) split trays. (T) Eyes on me.
   Spell /k/. Repeat.
   (S) /k/ c says /k/; k says /k/

3. **Blending:**
   (T) Tell me the sound for each letter as I point. Then blend the sounds together
   to read the word or syllable. Give me a thumbs up if it is a real word.
   (S) /mmm/ /ŏŏŏ/ /mmm/ *mom* (thumbs up)
   Alternative:
   (T) Watch me first. /mmm/ /ŏŏŏ/ /mmm/ *mom*
   (T) Do it with me. (T&S) /mmm/ /ŏŏŏ/ /mmm/ *mom*
   (T) Your turn. (S) /mmm/ /ŏŏŏ/ /mmm/ *mom* (thumbs up)

Vowel Intensive: Model the visual cue while calling out the sound. Students will
do the visual cue as they repeat the sound. Students will then hold up the vowel
tent while stating the letter name and sound.

- (T): Eyes on me. The sound is /ă/. Repeat.
- (S): /ă/ a says /ă/

Teaching a New Concept

Materials Needed:
concept card, screen, green crayon, object, sand, decodable readers, literature, P/G chart

Introduce on Monday, and practice daily.

1. (T) Shows the new concept card(s).
   a. (T) Tells students that we will learn a new concept today: remaining ending
      blends.
   b. (T) Tells students that they already know the sounds for these letters. When the
      letters live next to each other, sometimes the sounds become blended together.
      That's why we call them blends.
   c. (T) States "-mp" says /mp/. (S) Repeat. Continue with the other blends: -nch, -nd,
      -sk, -sp. Reminds students that the blends still make two sounds.

2. (T) Shows an object.
   a. (T) Allows students to manipulate the object and discuss prior knowledge.
      Reminds (S) that the object has the target sound(s) spelled with the target letter(s).

3. (S) Brainstorm to help establish a spelling rule, if applicable.
   a. Brainstorm words that have the target sound(s) or rule. The brainstorming can be
      a teacher-directed activity if students need extra support.

4. (T) Teaches Letter Formation, if needed. Can teach cursive writing.
   a. Use the steps for teaching letter formation on the Flip Chart.
   b. Use house paper to teach lowercase letters.
   c. Teach capital letters throughout the week. Capital letters go outside the house.

5. (T) Dictates target sound(s). (S) Practice all known spellings in the sand or other medium.

6. (T) Connects with literature.

   a. Read for language comprehension.

   b. Continue to work on language comprehension with rich literature throughout the week.

7. (S) Use decodable readers to practice the concepts learned.

   a. (S) Highlight words with the new concept. Read those words.

   b. (S) Highlight Red Words. Read those words.

   c. (S) Start reading the decodable reader.

   d. (S) Continue reading throughout the week.

   e. (S) Read a clean copy on Friday.

8. (T&S) Mark the Phoneme/Grapheme (P/G) chart by highlighting the target sound(s).

 ## Word Dictation

Materials Needed:
fingertapping hand, dictation paper, pencil

Practice daily. Use the Flip Chart to follow the steps for word dictation.

Day 1:	1. bump	2. dusk	3. branch	4. pretend	5. windmill
Day 2:	1. stomp	2. brunch	3. standstill	4. crisp	5. context
Day 3:	1. pumpkin	2. clasp	3. brisk	4. intend	5. lunch
Days 4-5:	Review prior words. Optional additional words: amp, and, ask, band, bask, bench, bend, blend, bond, brand, bunch, camp, champ, clench, clump, cramp, desk, disk, drench, dump, end, expand, fend, finch, flask, fond, fund, gasp, grand, grasp, hand, handstand, hump, hunch, husk, inch, jump, lamp, land, lend, limp, lisp, lump, mask, mend, muskrat, pinch, plump, pond, pump, ramp, ranch, romp, rump, sand, send, skimp, spend, stamp, stump, suspend, task, tend, trend, winch, wind (pronounced /wĭnd/), wisp				

- Below is a sample script for one-syllable word dictation.

1. (T) States word: *boss.* Uses it in a sentence: My *boss* is kind and fair. (Pounds) *boss.* (T) Models fingertapping if needed: /b/ /ŏ/ /s/. (Pounds) *boss.*

2. (S) State while pounding: *boss.* (Fingertap) /b/ /ŏ/ /s/. (Pound) *boss.* Write the letters known for the sounds.

3. (T) When yours looks like mine, rewrite the word.

4. (S) Rewrite.

5. Repeat the process for each word.

6. (S) Read the list of words multiple times to build automaticity.

- Below is a sample script for multisyllabic word dictation.

---

1. (T) States word: *bathtub*. Uses it in a sentence: Clean out the *bathtub*. (Pounds each syllable) *bath/tub*.
2. (S) State while pounding each syllable: *bath/tub*.
3. (T) Models fingertapping, if needed. First syllable: (Pounds) *bath*. (Fingertaps) /b/ /ă/ /th/. (Pounds) *bath*.
4. (S) State first syllable while pounding: *bath*. (Fingertap) /b/ /ă/ /th/. (Pound) *bath*. Write the letters known for the sounds.
5. (T) Second syllable: (Pounds) *tub*. (Fingertaps) /t/ /ŭ/ /b/. (Pounds) *tub*.
6. (S) State second syllable while pounding: *tub*. (Fingertap) /t/ /ŭ/ /b/. (Pound) *tub*. Write the letters known for the sounds.
7. (T) When yours looks like mine, rewrite the word.
8. (S) Rewrite.
9. Repeat the process for each word.
10. (S) Read the list of words multiple times to build automaticity.

Sentence Dictation

Red Words are underlined. Students can fingertap the green words. Use the Flip Chart to follow the steps for sentence dictation.

1. A frog can hop and land in the sand.
2. Tad was fond of his pet cat.
3. The stem can bend and snap.
4. Lend me the mask to put on the cub.
5. Ask Ben, and he will send it to Tim too.
6. Kim will end the task for the day.
7. Did he gasp when he swam?
8. The wind cost him the win.
9. The branch hit me in the eye.
10. The flat desk was in the class.
11. The camp had a blue tent.
12. Ben was a champ to stomp on the bug.
13. Mend the red band, and send it to Dad.
14. Will you suspend the student?
15. Grasp the pumpkin by the stem.
16. The finch had cod for lunch.

- Below is a sample script for sentence dictation.

> 1. (T): Listen to the sentence. *The bedbug bit Pam.*
> 2. (T): Listen while I pound the syllables. *The bedbug bit Pam.* (Make sure to pound *bedbug* twice because it has two syllables.)
> 3. (T): Pound it with me. (T&S): *The bedbug bit Pam.*
> 4. (T): You pound the sentence. (S): *The bedbug bit Pam.*
> 5. (T): Watch me as I point to the lines while stating the sentence. (Tap the line for *bedbug* twice because it has two syllables.) *The bedbug bit Pam.*
> 6. (T): You point to the lines while stating the sentence.
> 7. (S): *The bedbug bit Pam.*
> 8. (T): Now write the sentence. Fingertap if needed.

- Below is a sample script to check CUPS.*

> 1. (T): C stands for capitalization. Did you remember a capital letter at the beginning of your sentence? Did you remember a capital letter for *Pam*? It is a name. If you forgot, fix it. If you remembered, put a tally mark above each capital letter. Add a mark in the box for C.
> 2. (T): U stands for understanding. Is your sentence neat? Reread it to yourself. Does it make sense? Could someone else understand it? If not, fix it. Add a mark in the box for U.
> 3. (T): P stands for punctuation. Did you remember a period at the end? If not, fix it. If you remembered, put a tally mark above the period. Add a mark in the box for P.
> 4. (T): S stands for spelling. Did you spell your words correctly? Check them. Now, check yours with mine (shows the teacher's copy). Fix any words you spelled incorrectly. Put a tally mark above the words you spelled correctly. Add a mark in the box for S.
> 5. (T): Rewrite your sentence with all of the corrections.
> 6. (T): Check for CUPS again. Put another mark in the boxes.
> 7. (T): Let's read the sentences.
> 8. (S) Read the sentences for fluency and automaticity.
>
> ***Please note:** Once students understand how to use CUPS, transition to letting them check their sentence independently before showing the teacher's copy.

 ## Weekly Red Words

Materials Needed:
screen, red crayon, red word paper

Introduce on Tuesday, and practice daily. Use the Flip Chart for steps.

New:	Review:	New Read-Only:	Review Read-Only:
day, too, eye	were, does, some, good, there, done, her, here, under, down, onto, people, saw, both, should, could, would, over, love, live, out		our, oven, park

Steps for Teaching a New Red Word:

1. (T) States the word. (*day*)
2. (T&S) Use tokens to determine how many sounds are in the word. (/d/ /ā/; 2)
3. (T&S) Discuss how we would expect to spell each sound as the teacher writes the grapheme(s) correctly. Identify what is unexpected or irregular about the spelling of the word. It could also be expected, but the concept hasn't been taught yet.
4. (T&S) Discuss the etymology of the word, if appropriate (lexical words). Visit www.etymonline.com for more information on the word.
5. (T) Defines the word, and writes a sentence using the word.
6. (T) Writes the word on Red Word paper with the screen underneath, using red crayon.
7. (S) Write the word on Red Word paper with the screen underneath, using red crayon. (S) Show the word to the teacher.
   (**NOTE:** The teacher should have students chunk the word if it has more than four letters.)
8. (T&S) Stand up, holding the Red Word in the nondominant hand. Armtap word while naming each letter. Then "underline" the word by sweeping left to right while stating the word, 3x. (**NOTE:** Left-handed students will place their left hand on their right wrist. They tap to their right shoulder. Underline from wrist to shoulder. Right-handed students place their right hand on their left shoulder. They tap to their left wrist. Underline shoulder to wrist.)
9. (T&S) Trace crayon bumps with the pointer finger while naming the letters, 3x.
10. (T&S) Place the screen over the paper and trace the word with the pointer finger while naming the letters, 3x.
11. (S) Turn paper over. With red crayon, write the word without the screen one time, and hold up the word for the teacher to check. (S) Write the word two more times.

12. (S) Write an original sentence in pencil and underline the Red Word with a red crayon. (**NOTE:** The sentence can also be dictated by the teacher while the student writes or dictated by the student while the teacher writes it.)

13. Repeat the steps for *too* (/t/ /o͞o/; 2), *eye* (/ī/; 1).

Review Ideas for Red Words:

- Sculpt the word using red Play-Doh or clay. Have students spell the word as they smash each letter.
- Print flashcards from IOG, and practice reading.
- Armtap the word to review.
- Cross-clap the word to review.
- Stomp the letters to review.
- Use a voice jar with popsicle sticks that have a different voice (e.g., robot, baby, cheerleader, monster) listed on each stick. Have a student draw a stick from the jar. The class armtaps the word using the voice selected. (Another option is to have an electronic spinning wheel with the voices listed on the wheel.)

Syllabication (Decoding)

Materials Needed:
IMSE Syllable Division Word Book, Pencil, Highlighter, Syllable Division Posters

Introduce on Wednesday with the new concept. Practice regularly.

1. Choose 6 or more words with the new concept in the *IMSE Syllable Division Word Book* for syllabication.

2. Use the steps on the Flip Chart and the Syllable Division Posters.

Syllable Division Patterns	1. Closed Syllable (Cl) short vowel sound	2. Open Syllable (O) long vowel sound
1. vc|cv	mag|net	ra|ven
2. v|cv	ten|nis	I|rish
3. vc|v	tip|top	o|pen
4. v|v	tom|tom	e|ven
	up|set	hu|mid
		ju|do

- Below is a sample script for syllabication.

> 1. Find the first two vowels or vowel units. Underline and label with a "v."
> 2. Draw the bridge. Underline the consonants or consonant units and label with a "c."
> 3. Find the pattern and divide the word.

4. Is there another vowel (other than an "e" at the end)? If so, repeat steps 1-3. If not, go to step 5.

5. Label each syllable.

6. Read the word.

NOTE: If there are two consonants in the middle of a word, split the word between the two consonants. (Exception: If the two consonants are a digraph [sh, ch, th] they cannot be split.) If there are three or more consonants, some letters go together as one consonant unit (look for known digraphs or blends).

Fluency, Vocabulary, and Comprehension

- Incorporate fluency into your literacy lessons daily/weekly (minimum 30 min/week) by using Rapid Word Charts, IMSE Decodable Readers, words and sentences, Acadience Reading K-6 or DIBELS 8th Edition, repeated reading, and other activities.

- Incorporate vocabulary into your literacy lessons daily/weekly (minimum 50 min/week) by choosing 3-5 appropriate tier two words (can pull from rich literature or decodable readers). Teach the words through explicit, direct instruction using student-friendly definitions, word webs, vocabulary charts, illustrations, and other activities.

- Incorporate oral language comprehension into your literacy lessons daily/weekly (approximately 100 min/week). Comprehension instruction should be explicit, direct instruction that includes teacher modeling, guided practice, and independent practice. Plan ahead to build on students' background knowledge, language structures, verbal reasoning, and literacy knowledge.

Extension Activity Ideas

- Set up a center with a recording of words with blends. Have students use tokens and sound boxes to indicate how many sounds are in each word.

- Have an image of a blender. Have students brainstorm words that have blends.

- Visit IMSE's Orton-Gillingham's Pinterest page for more ideas.

Weekly Lesson Reminders

- Daily practice with writing the weekly Red Word(s)
- Kilpatrick's "One-Minute Activities" for daily phonological awareness practice
- Zgonc's phonological awareness activities
- Listen to rich literature to work on oral language comprehension.
- Target concept practice sheets from IMSE's practice books
- Practice test on Thursday and test on Friday

Notes:

_____

_____

_____

_____

_____

_____

_____

_____

_____

_____

_____

_____

_____

_____

_____

_____

_____

_____

y as a vowel /ī/ (cry)

Card Pack #39 Decodable Reader #36	
Object Ideas:	**Literature Ideas:**
fly, sky, July, fry, spy, butterfly	▪ *Y the Sometimes Vowel: A Story About the Letter Y* by Linda DeFeudis ▪ *My Little Yellow Taxi* by Stephen T. Johnson ▪ *My Little Red Toolbox* by Stephen T. Johnson ▪ *Don't Cry, Baby Sam* by Harriet Ziefert ▪ *The Shy Little Kitten* by Cathleen Schurr ▪ *Dealing With Feeling...Shy* by Isabel Thomas ▪ *More! Phonics Through Poetry* by Babs Bell Hajdusiewicz ▪ *Fry Bread: A Native American Family Story* by Kevin Noble Maillard

Notes

- Use the Comprehensive Flip Chart for the steps on how to teach each part of IMSE's Lesson Plan.
- Use www.etymonline.com to help establish why a word might not follow the expected rules or patterns.
- Y says /ī/ at the end of an open, stressed syllable (e.g., cry, July).
  - For younger students, you can start by telling them that when y comes at the end of a one-syllable word, it usually says /ī/.
  - Refer to the *Spelling Teacher's Guide (3rd Grade Plus)* for older students.
- When practicing this concept on the blending board, remove the final pile to create an open syllable (e.g., fry, sly).
- Y also says /ī/ when used with Magic E (e.g., type, Skype). Revisit this concept after Magic E has been taught.
- When the white consonant y card is shown in the Visual Drill, students say /y/. When the yellow vowel y card is shown, students say /ī/.
- In the Auditory/Kinesthetic Drill, students know two ways to spell the /ī/ sound: i, y.

Phonological Awareness:

Materials Needed:
tokens, sound boxes, one-minute activities, or Zgonc PA book

Use the PAST assessment to determine a starting point for instruction. Incorporate daily phonological awareness activities by using Zgonc's tiered activities and/or Kilpatrick's One-Minute Activities in *Equipped for Reading Success*.

Phonemic awareness warm-up: Use tokens (or letter tiles once concepts have been taught) and sound boxes to do a quick phonemic awareness activity that ties in with the new concept, if appropriate.

 ## Three-Part Drill

Materials Needed:
review cards, sand, blending board, vowel tents or sticks

Do this at least 3x per week. Use the Flip Chart for steps. Include the new concept after Day 1.

- Vowel Intensive: Use the Flip Chart for steps.
  - Do the Vowel Intensive with all 5 vowels.

V	VC	CVC
a	ag, ap, ab	lat, cad, zan
e	et, en, eb	zeg, ren, med
i	ig, ib, im	lin, hib, fid
o	ob, ot, oz	rom, hob, cog
u	un, ud, ub	sup, pum, dut

  - **NOTE:** If students are doing well with the Vowel Intensive, (T) give an assessment with 20 CVC syllables (not real words). If students pass with 80% accuracy or better, discontinue the Vowel Intensive.

- Below is a sample script. Remember to use review concepts only.

1. **Visual:**
   (T) Tell me the sounds you know for these letters.
   (S) /m/, /l/, etc.

2. **Auditory/Kinesthetic:**
   (T) You know two ways to spell this. (S) split trays. (T) Eyes on me.
   Spell /k/. Repeat.
   (S) /k/ c says /k/; k says /k/

3. **Blending:**
   (T) Tell me the sound for each letter as I point. Then blend the sounds together to read the word or syllable. Give me a thumbs up if it is a real word.
   (S) /mmm/ /ŏŏŏ/ /mmm/ *mom* (thumbs up)
   Alternative:
   (T) Watch me first. /mmm/ /ŏŏŏ/ /mmm/ *mom*
   (T) Do it with me. (T&S) /mmm/ /ŏŏŏ/ /mmm/ *mom*
   (T) Your turn. (S) /mmm/ /ŏŏŏ/ /mmm/ *mom* (thumbs up)

> ***Vowel Intensive:** Model the visual cue while calling out the sound. Students will do the visual cue as they repeat the sound. Students will then hold up the vowel tent while stating the letter name and sound.
> - (T): Eyes on me. The sound is /ǎ/. Repeat.
> - (S): /ǎ/ a says /ǎ/

 ## Teaching a New Concept

Materials Needed:
concept card, screen, green crayon, object, sand, decodable readers, literature, P/G chart

Introduce on Monday, and practice daily.

1. (T) Shows the new concept card(s).
   a. (T) Tells students that we will learn a new concept today.
   b. (T) Tells students that they know y is a consonant that says /y/. Today they will learn that sometimes y is a vowel that says /ī/.
   c. (T) States "y" says /ī/. (S) Repeat.
2. (T) Shows an object.
   a. (T) Allows students to manipulate the object and discuss prior knowledge. Reminds (S) that the object has the target sound(s) spelled with the target letter(s).
3. (S) Brainstorm to help establish a spelling rule, if applicable.
   a. Brainstorm words that have the target sound(s) or rule. The brainstorming can be a teacher-directed activity if students need extra support.
4. (T) Teaches Letter Formation, if needed. Can teach cursive writing.
   a. Use the steps for teaching letter formation on the Flip Chart.
   b. Use house paper to teach lowercase letters.
   c. Teach capital letters throughout the week. Capital letters go outside the house.
5. (T) Dictates target sound(s). (S) Practice all known spellings in the sand or other medium.
6. (T) Connects with literature.
   a. Read for language comprehension.
   b. Continue to work on language comprehension with rich literature throughout the week.
7. (S) Use decodable readers to practice the concepts learned.
   a. (S) Highlight words with the new concept. Read those words.
   b. (S) Highlight Red Words. Read those words.
   c. (S) Start reading the decodable reader.
   d. (S) Continue reading throughout the week.
   e. (S) Read a clean copy on Friday.
8. (T&S) Mark the Phoneme/Grapheme (P/G) chart by highlighting the target sound(s).

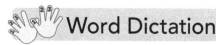 **Word Dictation**

Materials Needed:
fingertapping hand, dictation paper, pencil

Practice daily. Use the Flip Chart to follow the steps for word dictation.

Day 1:	1. fly	2. shy	3. cry	4. sty	5. fry
Day 2:	1. dry	2. my	3. sky	4. why	5. ply
Day 3:	1. by	2. try	3. sly	4. pry	5. fly
Days 4-5:	Review prior words. Optional additional words: deny*, imply*, July*, rely*, reply*, supply* *Please note: In these words, "y" says /ī/ because the second syllable is an open, stressed (i.e., accented) syllable. Teachers should consider students' age and experience level when selecting words for this concept.				

- Below is a sample script for one-syllable word dictation.

1. (T) States word: *boss*. Uses it in a sentence: My *boss* is kind and fair. (Pounds) *boss*. (T) Models fingertapping if needed: /b/ /ŏ/ /s/. (Pounds) *boss*.
2. (S) State while pounding: *boss*. (Fingertap) /b/ /ŏ/ /s/. (Pound) *boss*. Write the letters known for the sounds.
3. (T) When yours looks like mine, rewrite the word.
4. (S) Rewrite.
5. Repeat the process for each word.
6. (S) Read the list of words multiple times to build automaticity.

- Below is a sample script for multisyllabic word dictation.

1. (T) States word: *bathtub*. Uses it in a sentence: Clean out the *bathtub*. (Pounds each syllable) *bath/tub*.
2. (S) State while pounding each syllable: *bath/tub*.
3. (T) Models fingertapping, if needed. First syllable: (Pounds) *bath*. (Fingertaps) /b/ /ă/ /th/. (Pounds) *bath*.
4. (S) State first syllable while pounding: *bath*. (Fingertap) /b/ /ă/ /th/. (Pound) *bath*. Write the letters known for the sounds.
5. (T) Second syllable: (Pounds) *tub*. (Fingertaps) /t/ /ŭ/ /b/. (Pounds) *tub*.
6. (S) State second syllable while pounding: *tub*. (Fingertap) /t/ /ŭ/ /b/. (Pound) *tub*. Write the letters known for the sounds.
7. (T) When yours looks like mine, rewrite the word.
8. (S) Rewrite.
9. Repeat the process for each word.
10. (S) Read the list of words multiple times to build automaticity.

Sentence Dictation

Red Words are underlined. Students can fingertap the green words. Use the Flip Chart to follow the steps for sentence dictation.

1. The big bug will try to hiss.
2. I have a sty in my eye.
3. Beth will try to swim.
4. The fox was sly.
5. The fly was on my hand again.
6. Sam was shy and did not try at all.
7. Why did she not reply?
8. I do not wish to fly.
9. Can I rely on you to help me?
10. July is so hot.

- Below is a sample script for sentence dictation.

> 1. (T): Listen to the sentence. *The bedbug bit Pam.*
> 2. (T): Listen while I pound the syllables. *The bedbug bit Pam.* (Make sure to pound *bedbug* twice because it has two syllables.)
> 3. (T): Pound it with me. (T&S): *The bedbug bit Pam.*
> 4. (T): You pound the sentence. (S): *The bedbug bit Pam.*
> 5. (T): Watch me as I point to the lines while stating the sentence. (Tap the line for *bedbug* twice because it has two syllables.) *The bedbug bit Pam.*
> 6. (T): You point to the lines while stating the sentence.
> 7. (S): *The bedbug bit Pam.*
> 8. (T): Now write the sentence. Fingertap if needed.

- Below is a sample script to check CUPS.*

> 1. (T): C stands for capitalization. Did you remember a capital letter at the beginning of your sentence? Did you remember a capital letter for *Pam*? It is a name. If you forgot, fix it. If you remembered, put a tally mark above each capital letter. Add a mark in the box for C.
> 2. (T): U stands for understanding. Is your sentence neat? Reread it to yourself. Does it make sense? Could someone else understand it? If not, fix it. Add a mark in the box for U.
> 3. (T): P stands for punctuation. Did you remember a period at the end? If not, fix it. If you remembered, put a tally mark above the period. Add a mark in the box for P.
> 4. (T): S stands for spelling. Did you spell your words correctly? Check them. Now, check yours with mine (shows the teacher's copy). Fix any words you spelled incorrectly. Put a tally mark above the words you spelled correctly. Add a mark in the box for S.

5. (T): Rewrite your sentence with all of the corrections.

6. (T): Check for CUPS again. Put another mark in the boxes.

7. (T): Let's read the sentences.

8. (S) Read the sentences for fluency and automaticity.

*Please note: Once students understand how to use CUPS, transition to letting them check their sentence independently before showing the teacher's copy.

Weekly Red Words

Materials Needed:
screen, red crayon, red word paper

Introduce on Tuesday, and practice daily. Use the Flip Chart for steps.

New:	Review:	New Read-Only:	Review Read-Only:
all*, again	were, does, some, good, there, done, her, here, under, down, onto, people, saw, both, should, could, would, over, love, live, out, day, too, eye		our, oven, park

NOTE: If the -all word family was taught with Concept 33 in the Grade 1 sequence, students will not need to go through the Red Word process with *all*.

Steps for Teaching a New Red Word:

1. (T) States the word. (*all*)

2. (T&S) Use tokens to determine how many sounds are in the word. (/aw/ /l/; 2)

3. (T&S) Discuss how we would expect to spell each sound as the teacher writes the grapheme(s) correctly. Identify what is unexpected or irregular about the spelling of the word. It could also be expected, but the concept hasn't been taught yet.

4. (T&S) Discuss the etymology of the word, if appropriate (lexical words). Visit www.etymonline.com for more information on the word.

5. (T) Defines the word, and writes a sentence using the word.

6. (T) Writes the word on Red Word paper with the screen underneath, using red crayon.

7. (S) Write the word on Red Word paper with the screen underneath, using red crayon. (S) Show the word to the teacher.
   (**NOTE:** The teacher should have students chunk the word if it has more than four letters.)

8. (T&S) Stand up, holding the Red Word in the nondominant hand. Armtap word while naming each letter. Then "underline" the word by sweeping left to right while

stating the word, 3x. (**NOTE:** Left-handed students will place their left hand on their right wrist. They tap to their right shoulder. Underline from wrist to shoulder. Right-handed students place their right hand on their left shoulder. They tap to their left wrist. Underline shoulder to wrist.)

9. (T&S) Trace crayon bumps with the pointer finger while naming the letters, 3x.

10. (T&S) Place the screen over the paper and trace the word with the pointer finger while naming the letters, 3x.

11. (S) Turn paper over. With red crayon, write the word without the screen one time, and hold up the word for the teacher to check. (S) Write the word two more times.

12. (S) Write an original sentence in pencil and underline the Red Word with a red crayon. (**NOTE:** The sentence can also be dictated by the teacher while the student writes or dictated by the student while the teacher writes it.)

13. Repeat the steps for *again*. (/ə/ /g/ /ĕ/ /n/; 4).

Review Ideas for Red Words:

- Sculpt the word using red Play-Doh or clay. Have students spell the word as they smash each letter.
- Print flashcards from IOG, and practice reading.
- Armtap the word to review.
- Cross-clap the word to review.
- Stomp the letters to review.
- Use a voice jar with popsicle sticks that have a different voice (e.g., robot, baby, cheerleader, monster) listed on each stick. Have a student draw a stick from the jar. The class armtaps the word using the voice selected. (Another option is to have an electronic spinning wheel with the voices listed on the wheel.)

Syllabication (Decoding)

Materials Needed:
IMSE Syllable Division Word Book, Pencil, Highlighter, Syllable Division Posters

Introduce on Wednesday with the new concept. Practice regularly.

1. Choose 6 or more words with the new concept in the *IMSE Syllable Division Word Book* for syllabication.

2. Use the steps on the Flip Chart and the Syllable Division Posters.

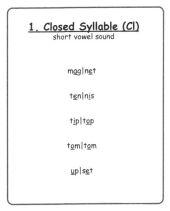

- Below is a sample script for syllabication.

> 1. Find the first two vowels or vowel units. Underline and label with a "v."
> 2. Draw the bridge. Underline the consonants or consonant units and label with a "c."
> 3. Find the pattern and divide the word.
> 4. Is there another vowel (other than an "e" at the end)? If so, repeat steps 1-3. If not, go to step 5.
> 5. Label each syllable.
> 6. Read the word.
>
> **NOTE:** If there are two consonants in the middle of a word, split the word between the two consonants. (Exception: If the two consonants are a digraph [sh, ch, th] they cannot be split.) If there are three or more consonants, some letters go together as one consonant unit (look for known digraphs or blends).

Fluency, Vocabulary, and Comprehension

- Incorporate fluency into your literacy lessons daily/weekly (minimum 30 min/week) by using Rapid Word Charts, IMSE Decodable Readers, words and sentences, Acadience Reading K-6 or DIBELS 8th Edition, repeated reading, and other activities.
- Incorporate vocabulary into your literacy lessons daily/weekly (minimum 50 min/week) by choosing 3-5 appropriate tier two words (can pull from rich literature or decodable readers). Teach the words through explicit, direct instruction using student-friendly definitions, word webs, vocabulary charts, illustrations, and other activities.
- Incorporate oral language comprehension into your literacy lessons daily/weekly (approximately 100 min/week). Comprehension instruction should be explicit, direct instruction that includes teacher modeling, guided practice, and independent practice. Plan ahead to build on students' background knowledge, language structures, verbal reasoning, and literacy knowledge.

Extension Activity Ideas

- Start a bulletin board with the sounds of "y." (Include only the sounds that have been taught thus far [/y/, /ī/].)
- Visit IMSE's Orton-Gillingham's Pinterest page for more ideas.

Weekly Lesson Reminders

- Daily practice with writing the weekly Red Word(s)
- Kilpatrick's "One-Minute Activities" for daily phonological awareness practice
- Zgonc's phonological awareness activities
- Listen to rich literature to work on oral language comprehension.
- Target concept practice sheets from IMSE's practice books
- Practice test on Thursday and test on Friday

Velar Nasal: -ng/-nk Units

(sang, sink)

Card Pack #40 Decodable Reader #37	
Object Ideas:	**Literature Ideas:**
bang, clang, mustang, ring, sing, bling, spring, trunk, swing, drink, king, skunk	▪ *Noisy Poems* by Jill Bennett ▪ *Mae Among the Stars* by Roda Ahmed ▪ *The Ring Bearer* by Floyd Cooper ▪ *The King of Kindergarten* by Derrick Barnes ▪ *Louis I, King of the Sheep* by Olivier Tallec ▪ *More! Phonics Through Poetry* by Babs Bell Hajdusiewicz

Notes

- Use the Comprehensive Flip Chart for the steps on how to teach each part of IMSE's Lesson Plan.

- Use www.etymonline.com to help establish why a word might not follow the expected rules or patterns.

- The velar nasal /ŋ/ is one nasal sound. It is formed with the lips parted and the back of the tongue against the back roof of the mouth.

- The /ŋ/ sound is represented with the grapheme "ng." However, when the /ŋ/ sound is followed by the /k/, it is spelled with just the *n* (e.g., bank). In addition, when the /ŋ/ sound is followed by a hard /g/, it is spelled with just the *n* (e.g., mango).
  - How many sounds are in the word *sang*? (3)
  - How many sounds are in the word *bank*? (4)
  - How many sounds are in the word *mango*? (5)

- The ng/nk units are on a yellow card because the vowel is difficult to isolate from the velar nasal. Therefore, they go in the middle pile on the blending board. Simply remove the final consonant pile when these units appear on the board.

- For word dictation, the ng/nk unit receives one fingertap and is written on one line. Again, this is because coarticulation causes the vowel to be nasalized, thus making it difficult to isolate from the velar nasal. No extra visual cue is used for the ng/nk units.

- For syllabication, students can just circle the ng/nk unit because these units typically end a syllable. Just be careful with words like *mango* and *finger* where the /ŋ/ is spelled with an *n* and the *g* is a hard /g/. This often happens when a vowel comes after the "g." In that case, *mango* would be split *man/go*.

- If students struggle with this concept, you can teach *-ng* one week and *-nk* the next.

Phonological Awareness:

Materials Needed:
tokens, sound boxes, one-minute activities, or Zgonc PA book

Use the PAST assessment to determine a starting point for instruction. Incorporate daily phonological awareness activities by using Zgonc's tiered activities and/or Kilpatrick's One-Minute Activities in *Equipped for Reading Success.*

Phonemic awareness warm-up: Use tokens (or letter tiles once concepts have been taught) and sound boxes to do a quick phonemic awareness activity that ties in with the new concept, if appropriate.

Three-Part Drill

Materials Needed:
review cards, sand, blending board, vowel tents or sticks

Do this at least 3x per week. Use the Flip Chart for steps. Include the new concept after Day 1.

- Vowel Intensive: Use the Flip Chart for steps.
  - Do the Vowel Intensive with all 5 vowels.

V	VC	CVC
a	ag, ap, ab	lat, cad, zan
e	et, en, eb	zeg, ren, med
i	ig, ib, im	lin, hib, fid
o	ob, ot, oz	rom, hob, cog
u	un, ud, ub	sup, pum, dut

  - **NOTE:** If students are doing well with the Vowel Intensive, (T) give an assessment with 20 CVC syllables (not real words). If students pass with 80% accuracy or better, discontinue the Vowel Intensive.

- Below is a sample script. Remember to use review concepts only.

---

1. **Visual:**
   (T) Tell me the sounds you know for these letters.
   (S) /m/, /l/, etc.
2. **Auditory/Kinesthetic:**
   (T) You know two ways to spell this. (S) split trays. (T) Eyes on me.
   Spell /k/. Repeat.
   (S) /k/ c says /k/; k says /k/

---

3. **Blending:**
(T) Tell me the sound for each letter as I point. Then blend the sounds together to read the word or syllable. Give me a thumbs up if it is a real word.
(S) /mmm/ /ŏŏŏ/ /mmm/ *mom* (thumbs up)
Alternative:
(T) Watch me first. /mmm/ /ŏŏŏ/ /mmm/ *mom*
(T) Do it with me. (T&S) /mmm/ /ŏŏŏ/ /mmm/ *mom*
(T) Your turn. (S) /mmm/ /ŏŏŏ/ /mmm/ *mom* (thumbs up)

Vowel Intensive: Model the visual cue while calling out the sound. Students will do the visual cue as they repeat the sound. Students will then hold up the vowel tent while stating the letter name and sound.

- (T): Eyes on me. The sound is /ă/. Repeat.
- (S): /ă/ a says /ă/

Teaching a New Concept

Materials Needed:
concept card, screen, green crayon, object, sand, decodable readers, literature, P/G chart

Introduce on Monday, and practice daily.

1. (T) Shows the new concept card(s).
   a. (T) Tells students that we will learn a new concept today.
   b. (T) Tells students the new sound, /ŋ/, and discusses articulators.
   c. (S) Use mirrors as they practice forming the /ŋ/ sound.
   d. (T) Tells students that the /ŋ/ sound is spelled with *ng* or just *n* when a *k* follows.
   e. (T) Tells students that it's difficult to separate the vowel sound, so we will say the sounds together.
   f. (T) States "ang" says /ang/. (S) Repeat. Continue with the other cards: -ing, -ong, -ung, -ank, -ink, -onk, -unk.
2. (T) Shows an object.
   a. (T) Allows students to manipulate the object and discuss prior knowledge. Reminds (S) that the object has the target sound(s) spelled with the target letter(s).
3. (S) Brainstorm to help establish a spelling rule, if applicable.
   a. Brainstorm words that have the target sound(s) or rule. The brainstorming can be a teacher-directed activity if students need extra support.
4. (T) Teaches Letter Formation, if needed. Can teach cursive writing.
   a. Use the steps for teaching letter formation on the Flip Chart.
   b. Use house paper to teach lowercase letters.
   c. Teach capital letters throughout the week. Capital letters go outside the house.
5. (T) Dictates target sound(s). (S) Practice all known spellings in the sand or other medium.

6. (T) Connects with literature.
   a. Read for language comprehension.
   b. Continue to work on language comprehension with rich literature throughout the week.
7. (S) Use decodable readers to practice the concepts learned.
   a. (S) Highlight words with the new concept. Read those words.
   b. (S) Highlight Red Words. Read those words.
   c. (S) Start reading the decodable reader.
   d. (S) Continue reading throughout the week.
   e. (S) Read a clean copy on Friday.
8. (T&S) Mark the Phoneme/Grapheme (P/G) chart by highlighting the target sound(s).

 ## Word Dictation

Materials Needed:
fingertapping hand, dictation paper, pencil

Practice daily. Use the Flip Chart to follow the steps for word dictation.

Day 1:	1. drink	2. stung	3. honk	4. mustang	5. chipmunk
Day 2:	1. blank	2. sing	3. sibling	4. trunk	5. belong
Day 3:	1. stink	2. prolong	3. rang	4. bring	5. bankrupt
Days 4-5:	Review prior words. Optional additional words: bang, bank, blink, bonk, brink, bunk, chunk, clang, clank, cling, clonk, clung, clunk, conk, drank, drunk, dunk, fang, flank, fling, flung, flunk, Frank, funk, gang, gong, Hank, hung, hunk, ink, inkwell, junk, king, kingfish, link, long, mink, ping, pink, plank, prank, prong, rank, ring, ringlet, rink, rung, sang, sank, singsong, sink, slink, song, spank, sting, stunk, sung, swing, swung, tank, thank, thing, think, tong, trinket, unsung, upswing, wing, wink, yank, zonk				

- Below is a sample script for one-syllable word dictation.

> 1. (T) States word: *boss*. Uses it in a sentence: My *boss* is kind and fair. (Pounds) *boss*. (T) Models fingertapping if needed: /b/ /ŏ/ /s/. (Pounds) *boss*.
> 2. (S) State while pounding: *boss*. (Fingertap) /b/ /ŏ/ /s/. (Pound) *boss*. Write the letters known for the sounds.
> 3. (T) When yours looks like mine, rewrite the word.
> 4. (S) Rewrite.
> 5. Repeat the process for each word.
> 6. (S) Read the list of words multiple times to build automaticity.

- Below is a sample script for multisyllabic word dictation.

1. (T) States word: *bathtub*. Uses it in a sentence: Clean out the *bathtub*. (Pounds each syllable) *bath/tub*.
2. (S) State while pounding each syllable: *bath/tub*.
3. (T) Models fingertapping, if needed. First syllable: (Pounds) *bath*. (Fingertaps) */b/ /ă/ /th/*. (Pounds) *bath*.
4. (S) State first syllable while pounding: *bath*. (Fingertap) */b/ /ă/ /th/*. (Pound) *bath*. Write the letters known for the sounds.
5. (T) Second syllable: (Pounds) *tub*. (Fingertaps) */t/ /ŭ/ /b/*. (Pounds) *tub*.
6. (S) State second syllable while pounding: *tub*. (Fingertap) */t/ /ŭ/ /b/*. (Pound) *tub*. Write the letters known for the sounds.
7. (T) When yours looks like mine, rewrite the word.
8. (S) Rewrite.
9. Repeat the process for each word.
10. (S) Read the list of words multiple times to build automaticity.

Sentence Dictation

Red Words are underlined. Students can fingertap the green words. Use the Flip Chart to follow the steps for sentence dictation.

1. Beth and Greg will sing for the king.
2. Bring it with you.
3. The dog had a long fang.
4. She clung to the rung.
5. The boy will swing on the hill.
6. The girl will sing a song.
7. She drank a glass of milk.
8. Frank was stung by the bug.
9. An ink spot was on the hat.
10. Frank drank a hot glass of milk.
11. She said thank you to Kim.
12. My best vest did stink!
13. Mom had to go to the bank to sign it.
14. He put the skunk in the trunk.
15. Honk if you open the trunk.
16. I did not flunk in math!

- Below is a sample script for sentence dictation.

  1. (T): Listen to the sentence. *The bedbug bit Pam.*
  2. (T): Listen while I pound the syllables. *The bedbug bit Pam.* (Make sure to pound *bedbug* twice because it has two syllables.)
  3. (T): Pound it with me. (T&S): *The bedbug bit Pam.*
  4. (T): You pound the sentence. (S): *The bedbug bit Pam.*
  5. (T): Watch me as I point to the lines while stating the sentence. (Tap the line for *bedbug* twice because it has two syllables.) *The bedbug bit Pam.*
  6. (T): You point to the lines while stating the sentence.
  7. (S): *The bedbug bit Pam.*
  8. (T): Now write the sentence. Fingertap if needed.

- Below is a sample script to check CUPS.*

  1. (T): C stands for capitalization. Did you remember a capital letter at the beginning of your sentence? Did you remember a capital letter for *Pam*? It is a name. If you forgot, fix it. If you remembered, put a tally mark above each capital letter. Add a mark in the box for C.
  2. (T): U stands for understanding. Is your sentence neat? Reread it to yourself. Does it make sense? Could someone else understand it? If not, fix it. Add a mark in the box for U.
  3. (T): P stands for punctuation. Did you remember a period at the end? If not, fix it. If you remembered, put a tally mark above the period. Add a mark in the box for P.
  4. (T): S stands for spelling. Did you spell your words correctly? Check them. Now, check yours with mine (shows the teacher's copy). Fix any words you spelled incorrectly. Put a tally mark above the words you spelled correctly. Add a mark in the box for S.
  5. (T): Rewrite your sentence with all of the corrections.
  6. (T): Check for CUPS again. Put another mark in the boxes.
  7. (T): Let's read the sentences.
  8. (S) Read the sentences for fluency and automaticity.

  ***Please note:** Once students understand how to use CUPS, transition to letting them check their sentence independently before showing the teacher's copy.

Weekly Red Words

Materials Needed:
screen, red crayon, red word paper

Introduce on Tuesday, and practice daily. Use the Flip Chart for steps.

New:	Review:	New Read-Only:	Review Read-Only:
boy, girl, sign	were, does, some, good, there, done, her, here, under, down, onto, people, saw, both, should, could, would, over, love, live, out, day, too, eye, all, again	play	our, oven, park

Steps for Teaching a New Red Word:

1. (T) States the word. (*boy*)

2. (T&S) Use tokens to determine how many sounds are in the word. (/b/ /oi/; 2)

3. (T&S) Discuss how we would expect to spell each sound as the teacher writes the grapheme(s) correctly. Identify what is unexpected or irregular about the spelling of the word. It could also be expected, but the concept hasn't been taught yet.

4. (T&S) Discuss the etymology of the word, if appropriate (lexical words). Visit www.etymonline.com for more information on the word.

5. (T) Defines the word, and writes a sentence using the word.

6. (T) Writes the word on Red Word paper with the screen underneath, using red crayon.

7. (S) Write the word on Red Word paper with the screen underneath, using red crayon. (S) Show the word to the teacher.
   (**NOTE:** The teacher should have students chunk the word if it has more than four letters.)

8. (T&S) Stand up, holding the Red Word in the nondominant hand. Armtap word while naming each letter. Then "underline" the word by sweeping left to right while stating the word, 3x. (**NOTE:** Left-handed students will place their left hand on their right wrist. They tap to their right shoulder. Underline from wrist to shoulder. Right-handed students place their right hand on their left shoulder. They tap to their left wrist. Underline shoulder to wrist.)

9. (T&S) Trace crayon bumps with the pointer finger while naming the letters, 3x.

10. (T&S) Place the screen over the paper and trace the word with the pointer finger while naming the letters, 3x.

11. (S) Turn paper over. With red crayon, write the word without the screen one time, and hold up the word for the teacher to check. (S) Write the word two more times.

12. (S) Write an original sentence in pencil and underline the Red Word with a red crayon. (**NOTE:** The sentence can also be dictated by the teacher while the student writes or dictated by the student while the teacher writes it.)

13. Repeat the steps for *girl* (/g/ /er/ /l/; 3), *sign* (/s/ /ī/ /n/; 3).

Review Ideas for Red Words:

- Sculpt the word using red Play-Doh or clay. Have students spell the word as they smash each letter.
- Print flashcards from IOG, and practice reading.
- Armtap the word to review.
- Cross-clap the word to review.
- Stomp the letters to review.
- Use a voice jar with popsicle sticks that have a different voice (e.g., robot, baby, cheerleader, monster) listed on each stick. Have a student draw a stick from the jar. The class armtaps the word using the voice selected. (Another option is to have an electronic spinning wheel with the voices listed on the wheel.)

VC/CV
V/CV
VC/V
V/V

Syllabication (Decoding)

Materials Needed:
IMSE Syllable Division Word Book, Pencil, Highlighter, Syllable Division Posters

Introduce on Wednesday with the new concept. Practice regularly.

1. Choose 6 or more words with the new concept in the *IMSE Syllable Division Word Book* for syllabication.

2. Use the steps on the Flip Chart and the Syllable Division Posters.

Syllable Division Patterns	1. Closed Syllable (Cl) short vowel sound	2. Open Syllable (O) long vowel sound
1. vc|cv	mag|net	ra|ven
2. v|cv	ten|nis	I|rish
3. vc|v	tip|top	o|pen
4. v|v	tom|tom	e|ven
	up|set	hu|mid
		ju|do

- Below is a sample script for syllabication.

1. Find the first two vowels or vowel units. Underline and label with a "v."

2. Draw the bridge. Underline the consonants or consonant units and label with a "c."

© IMSE 2022

3. Find the pattern and divide the word.

4. Is there another vowel (other than an "e" at the end)? If so, repeat steps 1-3. If not, go to step 5.

5. Label each syllable.

6. Read the word.

NOTE: If there are two consonants in the middle of a word, split the word between the two consonants. (Exception: If the two consonants are a digraph [sh, ch, th] they cannot be split.) If there are three or more consonants, some letters go together as one consonant unit (look for known digraphs or blends).

 ## Fluency, Vocabulary, and Comprehension

- Incorporate fluency into your literacy lessons daily/weekly (minimum 30 min/week) by using Rapid Word Charts, IMSE Decodable Readers, words and sentences, Acadience Reading K-6 or DIBELS 8th Edition, repeated reading, and other activities.

- Incorporate vocabulary into your literacy lessons daily/weekly (minimum 50 min/week) by choosing 3-5 appropriate tier two words (can pull from rich literature or decodable readers). Teach the words through explicit, direct instruction using student-friendly definitions, word webs, vocabulary charts, illustrations, and other activities.

- Incorporate oral language comprehension into your literacy lessons daily/weekly (approximately 100 min/week). Comprehension instruction should be explicit, direct instruction that includes teacher modeling, guided practice, and independent practice. Plan ahead to build on students' background knowledge, language structures, verbal reasoning, and literacy knowledge.

 ## Extension Activity Ideas

- Have students create limericks using ng/nk words. A limerick is a poem that has 5 lines. The first two lines have 7 syllables, the third and fourth lines have 5 syllables, and the fifth line has 7 syllables. The first, second, and fifth lines end with rhyming words. The third and fourth lines end with rhyming words. Example:
  - There once was a boy named **Hank**.   (7 syllables)
  - Some children said that he **stank**.   (7 syllables)
  - He was sprayed by *Skunk*,   (5 syllables)
  - Oh, who would have *thunk*?   (5 syllables)
  - Still to this day, he smells **rank**.   (7 syllables)

- Use sound boxes to have students write words and also indicate how many sounds are in each word.

- Visit IMSE's Orton-Gillingham's Pinterest page for more ideas.

Weekly Lesson Reminders

- Daily practice with writing the weekly Red Word(s)
- Kilpatrick's "One-Minute Activities" for daily phonological awareness practice
- Zgonc's phonological awareness activities
- Listen to rich literature to work on oral language comprehension.
- Target concept practice sheets from IMSE's practice books
- Practice test on Thursday and test on Friday

-ck /k/ (rock)

(1-1-1 Rule)

Card Pack #41 Decodable Reader #38	
Object Ideas:	**Literature Ideas:**
backpack, rock, shack, jacks, snack, chick, brick, stick, clock, duck, truck	<ul><li>*Black Is a Rainbow Color* by Angela Joy</li><li>*Click, Clack, Moo: Cows That Type* by Doreen Cronin</li><li>*The Stuck Truck* by Michelle Reinshuttle</li><li>*Clocks and More Clocks* by Pat Hutchins</li><li>*Clocks and How They Go* by Gail Gibbons</li><li>*My Grandmother's Clock* by Geraldine McCaughrean</li><li>*Tick-Tock* by Eileen Browne</li><li>*The Clock* by Trent Duffy</li><li>*Stick Man* by Julia Donaldson</li></ul>

 ## Notes

- Use the Comprehensive Flip Chart for the steps on how to teach each part of IMSE's Lesson Plan.
- Use www.etymonline.com to help establish why a word might not follow the expected rules or patterns.
- The /k/ sound is spelled -ck when it immediately follows a short vowel in a stressed syllable.
- An easier way to teach young children this rule would be to call this another 1-1-1 rule: If you have a word that has *one* syllable, *one* short vowel, and ends with *one* consonant sound that says /k/, spell /k/ with -ck.
- The /k/ sound must *immediately* follow the short vowel. For example, *task* and *frisk* aren't spelled with -ck because the /k/ sound doesn't immediately follow the short vowel.
- In the Auditory/Kinesthetic Drill, students will know 3 ways to spell the /k/ sound: c, k, -ck.
- There is no extra visual cue for word dictation. Because this is a spelling rule, students should know the rule.

 ## Phonological Awareness:

Materials Needed:
tokens, sound boxes, one-minute activities, or Zgonc PA book

Use the PAST assessment to determine a starting point for instruction. Incorporate daily phonological awareness activities by using Zgonc's tiered activities and/or Kilpatrick's One-Minute Activities in *Equipped for Reading Success*.

Phonemic awareness warm-up: Use tokens (or letter tiles once concepts have been taught) and sound boxes to do a quick phonemic awareness activity that ties in with the new concept, if appropriate.

 ## Three-Part Drill

Materials Needed:
review cards, sand, blending board, vowel tents or sticks

Do this at least 3x per week. Use the Flip Chart for steps. Include the new concept after Day 1.

- Vowel Intensive: Use the Flip Chart for steps.
  - Do the Vowel Intensive with all 5 vowels.

V	VC	CVC
a	ag, ap, ab	lat, cad, zan
e	et, en, eb	zeg, ren, med
i	ig, ib, im	lin, hib, fid
o	ob, ot, oz	rom, hob, cog
u	un, ud, ub	sup, pum, dut

  - **NOTE:** If students are doing well with the Vowel Intensive, (T) give an assessment with 20 CVC syllables (not real words). If students pass with 80% accuracy or better, discontinue the Vowel Intensive.
- Below is a sample script. Remember to use review concepts only.

---

1. **Visual:**
   (T) Tell me the sounds you know for these letters.
   (S) /m/, /l/, etc.

2. **Auditory/Kinesthetic:**
   (T) You know two ways to spell this. (S) split trays. (T) Eyes on me.
   Spell /k/. Repeat.
   (S) /k/ c says /k/; k says /k/
   NOTE: Once the Day 1 lesson has been taught, children will then know three ways to spell /k/ (c, k, ck).

3. **Blending:**
   (T) Tell me the sound for each letter as I point. Then blend the sounds together to read the word or syllable. Give me a thumbs up if it is a real word.
   (S) /mmm/ /ŏŏŏ/ /mmm/ *mom* (thumbs up)
   Alternative:
   (T) Watch me first. /mmm/ /ŏŏŏ/ /mmm/ *mom*
   (T) Do it with me. (T&S) /mmm/ /ŏŏŏ/ /mmm/ *mom*
   (T) Your turn. (S) /mmm/ /ŏŏŏ/ /mmm/ *mom* (thumbs up)

> *Vowel Intensive:** Model the visual cue while calling out the sound. Students will do the visual cue as they repeat the sound. Students will then hold up the vowel tent while stating the letter name and sound.
>
> - (T): Eyes on me. The sound is /ă/. Repeat.
> - (S): /ă/ a says /ă/

 ## Teaching a New Concept

Materials Needed:
concept card, screen, green crayon, object, sand, decodable readers, literature, P/G chart

Introduce on Monday, and practice daily.

1. (T) Shows the new concept card(s).
    a. (T) Tells students that they will learn another way to spell the /k/ sound.
    b. (T) Tells students that "-ck" says /k/. (S) Repeat.
    c. (T) Tells students that they will need to learn when to use the -ck spelling.
    d. (T) Tells students that when they hear the /k/ sound directly after a short vowel sound in a one-syllable word, it is spelled with "-ck."
2. (T) Shows an object.
    a. (T) Allows students to manipulate the object and discuss prior knowledge. Reminds (S) that the object has the target sound(s) spelled with the target letter(s).
3. (S) Brainstorm to help establish a spelling rule, if applicable.
    a. Brainstorm words that have the target sound(s) or rule. The brainstorming can be a teacher-directed activity if students need extra support.
4. (T) Teaches Letter Formation, if needed. Can teach cursive writing.
    a. Use the steps for teaching letter formation on the Flip Chart.
    b. Use house paper to teach lowercase letters.
    c. Teach capital letters throughout the week. Capital letters go outside the house.
5. (T) Dictates target sound(s). (S) Practice all known spellings in the sand or other medium.
6. (T) Connects with literature.
    a. Read for language comprehension.
    b. Continue to work on language comprehension with rich literature throughout the week.
7. (S) Use decodable readers to practice the concepts learned.
    a. (S) Highlight words with the new concept. Read those words.
    b. (S) Highlight Red Words. Read those words.
    c. (S) Start reading the decodable reader.
    d. (S) Continue reading throughout the week.
    e. (S) Read a clean copy on Friday.
8. (T&S) Mark the Phoneme/Grapheme (P/G) chart by highlighting the target sound(s).

Word Dictation

Materials Needed:
fingertapping hand, dictation paper, pencil

Practice daily. Use the Flip Chart to follow the steps for word dictation.

Day 1:	1. brick	2. snack	3. neck	4. flock	5. stuck
Day 2:	1. lick	2. thick	3. clock	4. shack	5. truck
Day 3:	1. stick	2. deck	3. block	4. track	5. cluck
Days 4-5:	Review prior words. Optional additional words: back, buck, bucket, check, chick, chock, click, crack, crock, dock, duck, fleck, hack, jack (Jack), kick, lack, lock, mock, muck, Nick, pack, peck, pick, pluck, pocket, rack, sack, shock, smock, sock, socket, stack, stock, tick, trick, tuck				

- Below is a sample script for one-syllable word dictation.

1. (T) States word: *boss*. Uses it in a sentence: My *boss* is kind and fair. (Pounds) *boss*. (T) Models fingertapping if needed: /b/ /ŏ/ /s/. (Pounds) *boss*.
2. (S) State while pounding: *boss*. (Fingertap) /b/ /ŏ/ /s/. (Pound) *boss*. Write the letters known for the sounds.
3. (T) When yours looks like mine, rewrite the word.
4. (S) Rewrite.
5. Repeat the process for each word.
6. (S) Read the list of words multiple times to build automaticity.

- Below is a sample script for multisyllabic word dictation.

1. (T) States word: *bathtub*. Uses it in a sentence: Clean out the *bathtub*. (Pounds each syllable) *bath/tub*.
2. (S) State while pounding each syllable: *bath/tub*.
3. (T) Models fingertapping, if needed. First syllable: (Pounds) *bath*. (Fingertaps) /b/ /ă/ /th/. (Pounds) *bath*.
4. (S) State first syllable while pounding: *bath*. (Fingertap) /b/ /ă/ /th/. (Pound) *bath*. Write the letters known for the sounds.
5. (T) Second syllable: (Pounds) *tub*. (Fingertaps) /t/ /ŭ/ /b/. (Pounds) *tub*.
6. (S) State second syllable while pounding: *tub*. (Fingertap) /t/ /ŭ/ /b/. (Pound) *tub*. Write the letters known for the sounds.
7. (T) When yours looks like mine, rewrite the word.
8. (S) Rewrite.
9. Repeat the process for each word.
10. (S) Read the list of words multiple times to build automaticity.

Sentence Dictation

Red Words are underlined. Students can fingertap the green words. Use the Flip Chart to follow the steps for sentence dictation.

1. Put the stick on the dock.
2. The black block was on the deck.
3. The ship got to the dock at sunset.
4. She put the hot dog on the stick.
5. Your clock on the shelf rang at six.
6. I can fix the crack in the dock.
7. A tick bit Jack on the neck.
8. Do not lick the sock!
9. Beth and Bill had a snack in the shack.
10. A duck was stuck in the pond.
11. Which chick can peck at the flock?
12. Look at the tick on the back of Jack.
13. Pluck the thick tick from the chick!
14. I had to pack a sock in a sack.
15. Nick had to lock the duck in the truck.
16. The trick to get the buck is luck.

- Below is a sample script for sentence dictation.

> 1. (T): Listen to the sentence. *The bedbug bit Pam.*
> 2. (T): Listen while I pound the syllables. *The bedbug bit Pam.* (Make sure to pound *bedbug* twice because it has two syllables.)
> 3. (T): Pound it with me. (T&S): *The bedbug bit Pam.*
> 4. (T): You pound the sentence. (S): *The bedbug bit Pam.*
> 5. (T): Watch me as I point to the lines while stating the sentence. (Tap the line for *bedbug* twice because it has two syllables.) *The bedbug bit Pam.*
> 6. (T): You point to the lines while stating the sentence.
> 7. (S): *The bedbug bit Pam.*
> 8. (T): Now write the sentence. Fingertap if needed.

- Below is a sample script to check CUPS.*

> 1. (T): C stands for capitalization. Did you remember a capital letter at the beginning of your sentence? Did you remember a capital letter for *Pam*? It is a name. If you forgot, fix it. If you remembered, put a tally mark above each capital letter. Add a mark in the box for C.

2. (T): U stands for understanding. Is your sentence neat? Reread it to yourself. Does it make sense? Could someone else understand it? If not, fix it. Add a mark in the box for U.

3. (T): P stands for punctuation. Did you remember a period at the end? If not, fix it. If you remembered, put a tally mark above the period. Add a mark in the box for P.

4. (T): S stands for spelling. Did you spell your words correctly? Check them. Now, check yours with mine (shows the teacher's copy). Fix any words you spelled incorrectly. Put a tally mark above the words you spelled correctly. Add a mark in the box for S.

5. (T): Rewrite your sentence with all of the corrections.

6. (T): Check for CUPS again. Put another mark in the boxes.

7. (T): Let's read the sentences.

8. (S) Read the sentences for fluency and automaticity.

*Please note: Once students understand how to use CUPS, transition to letting them check their sentence independently before showing the teacher's copy.

 ## Weekly Red Words

Materials Needed:
screen, red crayon, red word paper

Introduce on Tuesday, and practice daily. Use the Flip Chart for steps.

New:	Review:	New Read-Only:	Review Read-Only:
your, which, look	were, does, some, good, there, done, her, here, under, down, onto, people, saw, both, should, could, would, over, love, live, out, day, too, eye, all, again, boy, girl, sign	way	our, oven, park, play

Steps for Teaching a New Red Word:

1. (T) States the word. (*your*)

2. (T&S) Use tokens to determine how many sounds are in the word. (/y/ /or/; 2)

3. (T&S) Discuss how we would expect to spell each sound as the teacher writes the grapheme(s) correctly. Identify what is unexpected or irregular about the spelling of the word. It could also be expected, but the concept hasn't been taught yet.

4. (T&S) Discuss the etymology of the word, if appropriate (lexical words). Visit www.etymonline.com for more information on the word.

5. (T) Defines the word, and writes a sentence using the word.

6. (T) Writes the word on Red Word paper with the screen underneath, using red crayon.

7. (S) Write the word on Red Word paper with the screen underneath, using red crayon. (S) Show the word to the teacher. (**NOTE:** The teacher should have students chunk the word if it has more than four letters.)

8. (T&S) Stand up, holding the Red Word in the nondominant hand. Armtap word while naming each letter. Then "underline" the word by sweeping left to right while stating the word, 3x. (**NOTE:** Left-handed students will place their left hand on their right wrist. They tap to their right shoulder. Underline from wrist to shoulder. Right-handed students place their right hand on their left shoulder. They tap to their left wrist. Underline shoulder to wrist.)

9. (T&S) Trace crayon bumps with the pointer finger while naming the letters, 3x.

10. (T&S) Place the screen over the paper and trace the word with the pointer finger while naming the letters, 3x.

11. (S) Turn paper over. With red crayon, write the word without the screen one time, and hold up the word for the teacher to check. (S) Write the word two more times.

12. (S) Write an original sentence in pencil and underline the Red Word with a red crayon. (**NOTE:** The sentence can also be dictated by the teacher while the student writes or dictated by the student while the teacher writes it.)

13. Repeat the steps for *which* (/w/ /ĭ/ /ch/; 3), *look* (/l/ /o͞o/ /k/; 3). (Note: Students may associate the sounds in *which* with the correct spelling. However, *which* does not follow the -tch rule that comes next in the sequence.)

Review Ideas for Red Words:

▪ Sculpt the word using red Play-Doh or clay. Have students spell the word as they smash each letter.

▪ Print flashcards from IOG, and practice reading.

▪ Armtap the word to review.

▪ Cross-clap the word to review.

▪ Stomp the letters to review.

▪ Use a voice jar with popsicle sticks that have a different voice (e.g., robot, baby, cheerleader, monster) listed on each stick. Have a student draw a stick from the jar. The class armtaps the word using the voice selected. (Another option is to have an electronic spinning wheel with the voices listed on the wheel.)

Syllabication (Decoding)

Materials Needed:
IMSE Syllable Division Word Book, Pencil, Highlighter, Syllable Division Posters

Introduce on Wednesday with the new concept. Practice regularly.

1. Choose 6 or more words with the new concept in the *IMSE Syllable Division Word Book* for syllabication.

2. Use the steps on the Flip Chart and the Syllable Division Posters.

Syllable Division Patterns	1. Closed Syllable (Cl) short vowel sound	2. Open Syllable (O) long vowel sound
1. vc|cv	mag|net	ra|ven
2. v|cv	ten|nis	I|rish
3. vc|v	tip|top	o|pen
4. v|v	tom|tom	e|ven
	up|set	hu|mid
		ju|do

- Below is a sample script for syllabication.

1. Find the first two vowels or vowel units. Underline and label with a "v."
2. Draw the bridge. Underline the consonants or consonant units and label with a "c."
3. Find the pattern and divide the word.
4. Is there another vowel (other than an "e" at the end)? If so, repeat steps 1-3. If not, go to step 5.
5. Label each syllable.
6. Read the word.

NOTE: If there are two consonants in the middle of a word, split the word between the two consonants. (Exception: If the two consonants are a digraph [sh, ch, th] they cannot be split.) If there are three or more consonants, some letters go together as one consonant unit (look for known digraphs or blends).

Fluency, Vocabulary, and Comprehension

- Incorporate fluency into your literacy lessons daily/weekly (minimum 30 min/week) by using Rapid Word Charts, IMSE Decodable Readers, words and sentences, Acadience Reading K-6 or DIBELS 8th Edition, repeated reading, and other activities.

- Incorporate vocabulary into your literacy lessons daily/weekly (minimum 50 min/week) by choosing 3-5 appropriate tier two words (can pull from rich literature or decodable readers). Teach the words through explicit, direct instruction using student-friendly definitions, word webs, vocabulary charts, illustrations, and other activities.

- Incorporate oral language comprehension into your literacy lessons daily/weekly (approximately 100 min/week). Comprehension instruction should be explicit, direct instruction that includes teacher modeling, guided practice, and independent practice. Plan ahead to build on students' background knowledge, language structures, verbal reasoning, and literacy knowledge.

Extension Activity Ideas

- Have words with the /k/ sound at the end that are missing either a "k" or "-ck." Have students fill in the blank with the correct grapheme (k or -ck).
- Visit IMSE's Orton-Gillingham's Pinterest page for more ideas.

Weekly Lesson Reminders

- Daily practice with writing the weekly Red Word(s)
- Kilpatrick's "One-Minute Activities" for daily phonological awareness practice
- Zgonc's phonological awareness activities
- Listen to rich literature to work on oral language comprehension.
- Target concept practice sheets from IMSE's practice books
- Practice test on Thursday and test on Friday

Notes:

_____

_____

_____

_____

_____

_____

_____

_____

_____

_____

_____

_____

_____

_____

_____

_____

_____

_____

_____

_____

-tch /ch/ (match)

(1-1-1 Rule)

Card Pack #42 Decodable Reader #39	
Object Ideas:	**Literature Ideas:**
match, witch, batch, latch, sketch, Stitch® (*Lilo and Stitch*)	■ *The Patchwork Path: A Quilt Map to Freedom* by Bettye Stroud ■ *The Patchwork Quilt* by Valerie Flournoy ■ *How to Catch a Turkey* or other books in the How to Catch series by Adam Wallace ■ Lilo and Stitch books ■ *The Patchwork Bike* by Maxine Beneba Clarke

Notes

- Use the Comprehensive Flip Chart for the steps on how to teach each part of IMSE's Lesson Plan.
- Use www.etymonline.com to help establish why a word might not follow the expected rules or patterns.
- The /ch/ sound is spelled -tch when it immediately follows a short vowel in a stressed syllable.
- An easier way to teach young children this rule would be to call this another 1-1-1 rule: If you have a word that has *one* syllable, *one* short vowel, and ends with *one* consonant sound that says /ch/, spell /ch/ with -tch.
- The /ch/ sound must *immediately* follow the short vowel. For example, *lunch* and *cinch* aren't spelled with -tch because the /ch/ sound doesn't immediately follow the short vowel.
- Some exceptions include *such, rich, much,* and *which*.
- In the Auditory/Kinesthetic Drill, students will know 2 ways to spell the /ch/ sound: ch, -tch.
- There is no extra visual cue for word dictation. Because this is a spelling rule, students should know the rule.

Phonological Awareness:

Materials Needed:
tokens, sound boxes, one-minute activities, or Zgonc PA book

Use the PAST assessment to determine a starting point for instruction. Incorporate daily phonological awareness activities by using Zgonc's tiered activities and/or Kilpatrick's One-Minute Activities in *Equipped for Reading Success*.

Phonemic awareness warm-up: Use tokens (or letter tiles once concepts have been taught) and sound boxes to do a quick phonemic awareness activity that ties in with the new concept, if appropriate.

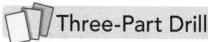

Three-Part Drill

Materials Needed:
review cards, sand, blending board, vowel tents or sticks

Do this at least 3x per week. Use the Flip Chart for steps. Include the new concept after Day 1.

- Vowel Intensive: Use the Flip Chart for steps.
  - Do the Vowel Intensive with all 5 vowels.

V	VC	CVC
a	ag, ap, ab	lat, cad, zan
e	et, en, eb	zeg, ren, med
i	ig, ib, im	lin, hib, fid
o	ob, ot, oz	rom, hob, cog
u	un, ud, ub	sup, pum, dut

  - **NOTE:** If students are doing well with the Vowel Intensive, (T) give an assessment with 20 CVC syllables (not real words). If students pass with 80% accuracy or better, discontinue the Vowel Intensive.
- Below is a sample script. Remember to use review concepts only.

---

1. **Visual:**
   (T) Tell me the sounds you know for these letters.
   (S) /m/, /l/, etc.

2. **Auditory/Kinesthetic:**
   (T) You know three ways to spell this. (S) split trays. (T) Eyes on me.
   Spell /k/. Repeat.
   (S) /k/ c says /k/; k says /k/; ck says /k/

3. **Blending:**
   (T) Tell me the sound for each letter as I point. Then blend the sounds together to read the word or syllable. Give me a thumbs up if it is a real word.
   (S) /mmm/ /ŏŏŏ/ /mmm/ *mom* (thumbs up)
   Alternative:
   (T) Watch me first. /mmm/ /ŏŏŏ/ /mmm/ *mom*
   (T) Do it with me. (T&S) /mmm/ /ŏŏŏ/ /mmm/ *mom*
   (T) Your turn. (S) /mmm/ /ŏŏŏ/ /mmm/ *mom* (thumbs up)

   ***Vowel Intensive:** Model the visual cue while calling out the sound. Students will do the visual cue as they repeat the sound. Students will then hold up the vowel tent while stating the letter name and sound.
   - (T): Eyes on me. The sound is /ă/. Repeat.
   - (S): /ă/ a says /ă/

Teaching a New Concept

Materials Needed:
concept card, screen, green crayon, object, sand, decodable readers, literature, P/G chart

Introduce on Monday, and practice daily.

1. (T) Shows the new concept card(s).
   a. (T) Tells students that they will learn another way to spell the /ch/ sound.
   b. (T) Tells students that "-tch" says /ch/. (S) Repeat.
   c. (T) Tells students that they will need to learn when to use the -tch spelling.
   d. (T) Tells students that when they hear the /ch/ sound directly after a short vowel sound in a one-syllable word, it is spelled with "-tch."
2. (T) Shows an object.
   a. (T) Allows students to manipulate the object and discuss prior knowledge. Reminds (S) that the object has the target sound(s) spelled with the target letter(s).
3. (S) Brainstorm to help establish a spelling rule, if applicable.
   a. Brainstorm words that have the target sound(s) or rule. The brainstorming can be a teacher-directed activity if students need extra support.
4. (T) Teaches Letter Formation, if needed. Can teach cursive writing.
   a. Use the steps for teaching letter formation on the Flip Chart.
   b. Use house paper to teach lowercase letters.
   c. Teach capital letters throughout the week. Capital letters go outside the house.
5. (T) Dictates target sound(s). (S) Practice all known spellings in the sand or other medium.
6. (T) Connects with literature.
   a. Read for language comprehension.
   b. Continue to work on language comprehension with rich literature throughout the week.
7. (S) Use decodable readers to practice the concepts learned.
   a. (S) Highlight words with the new concept. Read those words.
   b. (S) Highlight Red Words. Read those words.
   c. (S) Start reading the decodable reader.
   d. (S) Continue reading throughout the week.
   e. (S) Read a clean copy on Friday.
8. (T&S) Mark the Phoneme/Grapheme (P/G) chart by highlighting the target sound(s).

 Word Dictation

Materials Needed:
fingertapping hand, dictation paper, pencil

Practice daily. Use the Flip Chart to follow the steps for word dictation.

Day 1:	1. fetch	2. patch	3. notch	4. hitch	5. stitch
Day 2:	1. ditch	2. snatch	3. hutch	4. sketch	5. etch
Day 3:	1. switch	2. catch	3. pitch	4. crutch	5. botch
Days 4-5:	Review prior words. Optional additional words: batch, Dutch, hatch, itch, latch, match, witch				

- Below is a sample script for one-syllable word dictation.

> 1. (T) States word: *boss*. Uses it in a sentence: My *boss* is kind and fair. (Pounds) *boss*. (T) Models fingertapping if needed: /b/ /ŏ/ /s/. (Pounds) *boss*.
> 2. (S) State while pounding: *boss*. (Fingertap) /b/ /ŏ/ /s/. (Pound) *boss*. Write the letters known for the sounds.
> 3. (T) When yours looks like mine, rewrite the word.
> 4. (S) Rewrite.
> 5. Repeat the process for each word.
> 6. (S) Read the list of words multiple times to build automaticity.

- Below is a sample script for multisyllabic word dictation.

> 1. (T) States word: *bathtub*. Uses it in a sentence: Clean out the *bathtub*. (Pounds each syllable) *bath/tub*.
> 2. (S) State while pounding each syllable: *bath/tub*.
> 3. (T) Models fingertapping, if needed. First syllable: (Pounds) *bath*. (Fingertaps) /b/ /ă/ /th/. (Pounds) *bath*.
> 4. (S) State first syllable while pounding: *bath*. (Fingertap) /b/ /ă/ /th/. (Pound) *bath*. Write the letters known for the sounds.
> 5. (T) Second syllable: (Pounds) *tub*. (Fingertaps) /t/ /ŭ/ /b/. (Pounds) *tub*.
> 6. (S) State second syllable while pounding: *tub*. (Fingertap) /t/ /ŭ/ /b/. (Pound) *tub*. Write the letters known for the sounds.
> 7. (T) When yours looks like mine, rewrite the word.
> 8. (S) Rewrite.
> 9. Repeat the process for each word.
> 10. (S) Read the list of words multiple times to build automaticity.

C U P S Sentence Dictation

Red Words are underlined. Students can fingertap the green words. Use the Flip Chart to follow the steps for sentence dictation.

1. Bob will catch the fast pitch.
2. Did the dog catch the cat?
3. We dug a ditch in the patch of grass.
4. The red rash did itch!
5. I will have to stitch the patch.
6. Ken can also pitch fast!
7. My pup will fetch the big stick.
8. He will use a hitch on the truck.
9. The chick will hatch in the shed.
10. Do not botch the sketch!

- Below is a sample script for sentence dictation.

> 1. (T): Listen to the sentence. *The bedbug bit Pam.*
> 2. (T): Listen while I pound the syllables. *The bedbug bit Pam.* (Make sure to pound *bedbug* twice because it has two syllables.)
> 3. (T): Pound it with me. (T&S): *The bedbug bit Pam.*
> 4. (T): You pound the sentence. (S): *The bedbug bit Pam.*
> 5. (T): Watch me as I point to the lines while stating the sentence. (Tap the line for *bedbug* twice because it has two syllables.) *The bedbug bit Pam.*
> 6. (T): You point to the lines while stating the sentence.
> 7. (S): *The bedbug bit Pam.*
> 8. (T): Now write the sentence. Fingertap if needed.

- Below is a sample script to check CUPS.*

> 1. (T): C stands for capitalization. Did you remember a capital letter at the beginning of your sentence? Did you remember a capital letter for *Pam*? It is a name. If you forgot, fix it. If you remembered, put a tally mark above each capital letter. Add a mark in the box for C.
> 2. (T): U stands for understanding. Is your sentence neat? Reread it to yourself. Does it make sense? Could someone else understand it? If not, fix it. Add a mark in the box for U.
> 3. (T): P stands for punctuation. Did you remember a period at the end? If not, fix it. If you remembered, put a tally mark above the period. Add a mark in the box for P.
> 4. (T): S stands for spelling. Did you spell your words correctly? Check them. Now, check yours with mine (shows the teacher's copy). Fix any words you spelled incorrectly. Put a tally mark above the words you spelled correctly. Add a mark in the box for S.
> 5. (T): Rewrite your sentence with all of the corrections.
> 6. (T): Check for CUPS again. Put another mark in the boxes.
> 7. (T): Let's read the sentences.
> 8. (S) Read the sentences for fluency and automaticity.
>
> **Please note:** Once students understand how to use CUPS, transition to letting them check their sentence independently before showing the teacher's copy.

Weekly Red Words

Materials Needed:
screen, red crayon, red word paper

Introduce on Tuesday, and practice daily. Use the Flip Chart for steps.

New:	Review:	New Read-Only:	Review Read-Only:
also, use	were, does, some, good, there, done, her, here, under, down, onto, people, saw, both, should, could, would, over, love, live, out, day, too, eye, all, again, boy, girl, sign, your, which, look		our, oven, park, play, way

Steps for Teaching a New Red Word:

1. (T) States the word. (*also*)
2. (T&S) Use tokens to determine how many sounds are in the word. (/aw/ /l/ /s/ /ō/; 4)
3. (T&S) Discuss how we would expect to spell each sound as the teacher writes the grapheme(s) correctly. Identify what is unexpected or irregular about the spelling of the word. It could also be expected, but the concept hasn't been taught yet.
4. (T&S) Discuss the etymology of the word, if appropriate (lexical words). Visit www. etymonline.com for more information on the word.
5. (T) Defines the word, and writes a sentence using the word.
6. (T) Writes the word on Red Word paper with the screen underneath, using red crayon.
7. (S) Write the word on Red Word paper with the screen underneath, using red crayon. (S) Show the word to the teacher.
   (**NOTE:** The teacher should have students chunk the word if it has more than four letters.)
8. (T&S) Stand up, holding the Red Word in the nondominant hand. Armtap word while naming each letter. Then "underline" the word by sweeping left to right while stating the word, 3x. (**NOTE:** Left-handed students will place their left hand on their right wrist. They tap to their right shoulder. Underline from wrist to shoulder. Right-handed students place their right hand on their left shoulder. They tap to their left wrist. Underline shoulder to wrist.)
9. (T&S) Trace crayon bumps with the pointer finger while naming the letters, 3x.
10. (T&S) Place the screen over the paper and trace the word with the pointer finger while naming the letters, 3x.
11. (S) Turn paper over. With red crayon, write the word without the screen one time, and hold up the word for the teacher to check. (S) Write the word two more times.
12. (S) Write an original sentence in pencil and underline the Red Word with a red crayon. (**NOTE:** The sentence can also be dictated by the teacher while the student writes or dictated by the student while the teacher writes it.)
13. Repeat the steps for *use*. (/y/ /oo/ /z/; 3)

Review Ideas for Red Words:

- Sculpt the word using red Play-Doh or clay. Have students spell the word as they smash each letter.
- Print flashcards from IOG, and practice reading.
- Armtap the word to review.
- Cross-clap the word to review.
- Stomp the letters to review.
- Use a voice jar with popsicle sticks that have a different voice (e.g., robot, baby, cheerleader, monster) listed on each stick. Have a student draw a stick from the jar. The class armtaps the word using the voice selected. (Another option is to have an electronic spinning wheel with the voices listed on the wheel.)

Syllabication (Decoding)

Materials Needed:
IMSE Syllable Division Word Book, Pencil, Highlighter, Syllable Division Posters

Introduce on Wednesday with the new concept. Practice regularly.

1. Choose 6 or more words with the new concept in the *IMSE Syllable Division Word Book* for syllabication.
2. Use the steps on the Flip Chart and the Syllable Division Posters.

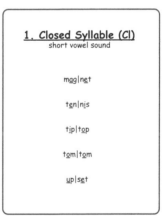

- Below is a sample script for syllabication.

> 1. Find the first two vowels or vowel units. Underline and label with a "v."
> 2. Draw the bridge. Underline the consonants or consonant units and label with a "c."
> 3. Find the pattern and divide the word.
> 4. Is there another vowel (other than an "e" at the end)? If so, repeat steps 1-3. If not, go to step 5.
> 5. Label each syllable.
> 6. Read the word.

> **NOTE:** If there are two consonants in the middle of a word, split the word between the two consonants. (Exception: If the two consonants are a digraph [sh, ch, th] they cannot be split.) If there are three or more consonants, some letters go together as one consonant unit (look for known digraphs or blends).

Fluency, Vocabulary, and Comprehension

- Incorporate fluency into your literacy lessons daily/weekly (minimum 30 min/week) by using Rapid Word Charts, IMSE Decodable Readers, words and sentences, Acadience Reading K-6 or DIBELS 8th Edition, repeated reading, and other activities.
- Incorporate vocabulary into your literacy lessons daily/weekly (minimum 50 min/week) by choosing 3-5 appropriate tier two words (can pull from rich literature or decodable readers). Teach the words through explicit, direct instruction using student-friendly definitions, word webs, vocabulary charts, illustrations, and other activities.
- Incorporate oral language comprehension into your literacy lessons daily/weekly (approximately 100 min/week). Comprehension instruction should be explicit, direct instruction that includes teacher modeling, guided practice, and independent practice. Plan ahead to build on students' background knowledge, language structures, verbal reasoning, and literacy knowledge.

Extension Activity Ideas

- Have words with the /ch/ sound at the end that are missing either a "ch" or "-tch." Have students fill in the blank with the correct grapheme (ch or -tch).
- Visit IMSE's Orton-Gillingham's Pinterest page for more ideas.

Weekly Lesson Reminders

- Daily practice with writing the weekly Red Word(s)
- Kilpatrick's "One-Minute Activities" for daily phonological awareness practice
- Zgonc's phonological awareness activities
- Listen to rich literature to work on oral language comprehension.
- Target concept practice sheets from IMSE's practice books
- Practice test on Thursday and test on Friday

-dge /j/ (fudge)

(1-1-1 Rule)

Card Pack #43 Decodable Reader #40	
Object Ideas:	**Literature Ideas:**
fudge, judge, bridge, badge, hedge	▪ *The Story of Ruby Bridges* by Robert Coles ▪ Fudge series by Judy Blume ▪ *Peeny Butter Fudge* by Toni and Slade Morrison ▪ Henry and Mudge series by Cynthia Rylant

Notes

- Use the Comprehensive Flip Chart for the steps on how to teach each part of IMSE's Lesson Plan.
- Use www.etymonline.com to help establish why a word might not follow the expected rules or patterns.
- The /j/ sound is spelled -dge when it immediately follows a short vowel in a stressed syllable.
- An easier way to teach young children this rule would be to call this another 1-1-1 rule: If you have a word that has *one* syllable, *one* short vowel, and ends with *one* consonant sound that says /j/, spell /j/ with -dge.
- The /j/ sound must *immediately* follow the short vowel. For example, *lunge* and *fringe* aren't spelled with -dge because the /j/ sound doesn't immediately follow the short vowel.
- In the Auditory/Kinesthetic Drill, students will know 2 ways to spell the /j/ sound: j, -dge.
- There is no extra visual cue for word dictation. Because this is a spelling rule, students should know the rule.

Phonological Awareness:

Materials Needed:
tokens, sound boxes, one-minute activities, or Zgonc PA book

Use the PAST assessment to determine a starting point for instruction. Incorporate daily phonological awareness activities by using Zgonc's tiered activities and/or Kilpatrick's One-Minute Activities in *Equipped for Reading Success*.

Phonemic awareness warm-up: Use tokens (or letter tiles once concepts have been taught) and sound boxes to do a quick phonemic awareness activity that ties in with the new concept, if appropriate.

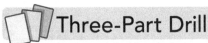 **Three-Part Drill**

Materials Needed:
review cards, sand, blending board, vowel tents or sticks

Do this at least 3x per week. Use the Flip Chart for steps. Include the new concept after Day 1.

- Vowel Intensive: Use the Flip Chart for steps.
  - Do the Vowel Intensive with all 5 vowels.

V	VC	CVC
a	ag, ap, ab	lat, cad, zan
e	et, en, eb	zeg, ren, med
i	ig, ib, im	lin, hib, fid
o	ob, ot, oz	rom, hob, cog
u	un, ud, ub	sup, pum, dut

  - **NOTE:** If students are doing well with the Vowel Intensive, (T) give an assessment with 20 CVC syllables (not real words). If students pass with 80% accuracy or better, discontinue the Vowel Intensive.
- Below is a sample script. Remember to use review concepts only.

1. **Visual:**
   (T) Tell me the sounds you know for these letters.
   (S) /m/, /l/, etc.

2. **Auditory/Kinesthetic:**
   (T) You know three ways to spell this. (S) split trays. (T) Eyes on me. Spell /k/. Repeat.
   (S) /k/ c says /k/; k says /k/; ck says /k/

3. **Blending:**
   (T) Tell me the sound for each letter as I point. Then blend the sounds together to read the word or syllable. Give me a thumbs up if it is a real word.
   (S) /mmm/ /ŏŏŏ/ /mmm/ *mom* (thumbs up)
   Alternative:
   (T) Watch me first. /mmm/ /ŏŏŏ/ /mmm/ *mom*
   (T) Do it with me. (T&S) /mmm/ /ŏŏŏ/ /mmm/ *mom*
   (T) Your turn. (S) /mmm/ /ŏŏŏ/ /mmm/ *mom* (thumbs up)

*Vowel Intensive:** Model the visual cue while calling out the sound. Students will do the visual cue as they repeat the sound. Students will then hold up the vowel tent while stating the letter name and sound.
- (T): Eyes on me. The sound is /ă/. Repeat.
- (S): /ă/ a says /ă/

Teaching a New Concept

Materials Needed:
concept card, screen, green crayon, object, sand, decodable readers, literature, P/G chart

Introduce on Monday, and practice daily.

1. (T) Shows the new concept card(s).
   a. (T) Tells students that they will learn another way to spell the /j/ sound.
   b. (T) Tells students that "-dge" says /j/. (S) Repeat.
   c. (T) Tells students that they will need to learn when to use the -dge spelling.
   d. (T) Tells students that when they hear the /j/ sound directly after a short vowel sound in a one-syllable word, it is spelled with "-dge."
2. (T) Shows an object.
   a. (T) Allows students to manipulate the object and discuss prior knowledge. Reminds (S) that the object has the target sound(s) spelled with the target letter(s).
3. (S) Brainstorm to help establish a spelling rule, if applicable.
   a. Brainstorm words that have the target sound(s) or rule. The brainstorming can be a teacher-directed activity if students need extra support.
4. (T) Teaches Letter Formation, if needed. Can teach cursive writing.
   a. Use the steps for teaching letter formation on the Flip Chart.
   b. Use house paper to teach lowercase letters.
   c. Teach capital letters throughout the week. Capital letters go outside the house.
5. (T) Dictates target sound(s). (S) Practice all known spellings in the sand or other medium.
6. (T) Connects with literature.
   a. Read for language comprehension.
   b. Continue to work on language comprehension with rich literature throughout the week.
7. (S) Use decodable readers to practice the concepts learned.
   a. (S) Highlight words with the new concept. Read those words.
   b. (S) Highlight Red Words. Read those words.
   c. (S) Start reading the decodable reader.
   d. (S) Continue reading throughout the week.
   e. (S) Read a clean copy on Friday.
8. (T&S) Mark the Phoneme/Grapheme (P/G) chart by highlighting the target sound(s).

Word Dictation

Materials Needed:
fingertapping hand, dictation paper, pencil

Practice daily. Use the Flip Chart to follow the steps for word dictation.

Day 1:	1. dodge	2. fudge	3. fridge	4. ledge	5. trudge
Day 2:	1. badge	2. judge	3. hedge	4. lodge	5. wedge
Day 3:	1. bridge	2. smudge	3. edge	4. badge	5. trudge
Days 4-5:	Review prior words.				

- Below is a sample script for one-syllable word dictation.

> 1. (T) States word: *boss*. Uses it in a sentence: My *boss* is kind and fair. (Pounds) *boss*. (T) Models fingertapping if needed: /b/ /ŏ/ /s/. (Pounds) *boss*.
> 2. (S) State while pounding: *boss*. (Fingertap) /b/ /ŏ/ /s/. (Pound) *boss*. Write the letters known for the sounds.
> 3. (T) When yours looks like mine, rewrite the word.
> 4. (S) Rewrite.
> 5. Repeat the process for each word.
> 6. (S) Read the list of words multiple times to build automaticity.

- Below is a sample script for multisyllabic word dictation.

> 1. (T) States word: *bathtub*. Uses it in a sentence: Clean out the *bathtub*. (Pounds each syllable) *bath/tub*.
> 2. (S) State while pounding each syllable: *bath/tub*.
> 3. (T) Models fingertapping, if needed. First syllable: (Pounds) *bath*. (Fingertaps) /b/ /ă/ /th/. (Pounds) *bath*.
> 4. (S) State first syllable while pounding: *bath*. (Fingertap) /b/ /ă/ /th/. (Pound) *bath*. Write the letters known for the sounds.
> 5. (T) Second syllable: (Pounds) *tub*. (Fingertaps) /t/ /ŭ/ /b/. (Pounds) *tub*.
> 6. (S) State second syllable while pounding: *tub*. (Fingertap) /t/ /ŭ/ /b/. (Pound) *tub*. Write the letters known for the sounds.
> 7. (T) When yours looks like mine, rewrite the word.
> 8. (S) Rewrite.
> 9. Repeat the process for each word.
> 10. (S) Read the list of words multiple times to build automaticity.

Sentence Dictation

Red Words are underlined. Students can fingertap the green words. Use the Flip Chart to follow the steps for sentence dictation.

1. The judge put the badge on the ledge.
2. We will cross the bridge to get to the lodge.
3. Bill ran to the ledge and got the cat.
4. Nick sat on the edge and drank the milk.
5. Today Ben will trim the hedge.
6. Yesterday we went to a lodge and swam.
7. We had to dodge the truck.
8. Deb got a snack from the fridge.
9. The cat and dog ran to the hedge and hid.
10. On the edge of the bridge was a nest.

- Below is a sample script for sentence dictation.

> 1. (T): Listen to the sentence. *The bedbug bit Pam.*
> 2. (T): Listen while I pound the syllables. *The bedbug bit Pam.* (Make sure to pound *bedbug* twice because it has two syllables.)
> 3. (T): Pound it with me. (T&S): *The bedbug bit Pam.*
> 4. (T): You pound the sentence. (S): *The bedbug bit Pam.*
> 5. (T): Watch me as I point to the lines while stating the sentence. (Tap the line for *bedbug* twice because it has two syllables.) *The bedbug bit Pam.*
> 6. (T): You point to the lines while stating the sentence.
> 7. (S): *The bedbug bit Pam.*
> 8. (T): Now write the sentence. Fingertap if needed.

- Below is a sample script to check CUPS.*

> 1. (T): C stands for capitalization. Did you remember a capital letter at the beginning of your sentence? Did you remember a capital letter for *Pam*? It is a name. If you forgot, fix it. If you remembered, put a tally mark above each capital letter. Add a mark in the box for C.
> 2. (T): U stands for understanding. Is your sentence neat? Reread it to yourself. Does it make sense? Could someone else understand it? If not, fix it. Add a mark in the box for U.
> 3. (T): P stands for punctuation. Did you remember a period at the end? If not, fix it. If you remembered, put a tally mark above the period. Add a mark in the box for P.
> 4. (T): S stands for spelling. Did you spell your words correctly? Check them. Now, check yours with mine (shows the teacher's copy). Fix any words you spelled incorrectly. Put a tally mark above the words you spelled correctly. Add a mark in the box for S.
> 5. (T): Rewrite your sentence with all of the corrections.
> 6. (T): Check for CUPS again. Put another mark in the boxes.
> 7. (T): Let's read the sentences.
> 8. (S) Read the sentences for fluency and automaticity.
>
> ***Please note:** Once students understand how to use CUPS, transition to letting them check their sentence independently before showing the teacher's copy.

Weekly Red Words

Materials Needed:
screen, red crayon, red word paper

Introduce on Tuesday, and practice daily. Use the Flip Chart for steps.

New:	Review:	New Read-Only:	Review Read-Only:
today, yesterday	were, does, some, good, there, done, her, here, under, down, onto, people, saw, both, should, could, would, over, love, live, out, day, too, eye, all, again, boy, girl, sign, your, which, look, also, use	chair	our, oven, park, play, way

Steps for Teaching a New Red Word:

1. (T) States the word. (*today*)
2. (T&S) Use tokens to determine how many sounds are in the word. (/t/ /o͞o/ /d/ /ā/; 4)
3. (T&S) Discuss how we would expect to spell each sound as the teacher writes the grapheme(s) correctly. Identify what is unexpected or irregular about the spelling of the word. It could also be expected, but the concept hasn't been taught yet.
4. (T&S) Discuss the etymology of the word, if appropriate (lexical words). Visit www.etymonline.com for more information on the word.
5. (T) Defines the word, and writes a sentence using the word.
6. (T) Writes the word on Red Word paper with the screen underneath, using red crayon.
7. (S) Write the word on Red Word paper with the screen underneath, using red crayon. (S) Show the word to the teacher.
   (**NOTE:** The teacher should have students chunk the word if it has more than four letters.)
8. (T&S) Stand up, holding the Red Word in the nondominant hand. Armtap word while naming each letter. Then "underline" the word by sweeping left to right while stating the word, 3x. (**NOTE:** Left-handed students will place their left hand on their right wrist. They tap to their right shoulder. Underline from wrist to shoulder. Right-handed students place their right hand on their left shoulder. They tap to their left wrist. Underline shoulder to wrist.)
9. (T&S) Trace crayon bumps with the pointer finger while naming the letters, 3x.
10. (T&S) Place the screen over the paper and trace the word with the pointer finger while naming the letters, 3x.

© IMSE 2022

11. (S) Turn paper over. With red crayon, write the word without the screen one time, and hold up the word for the teacher to check. (S) Write the word two more times.

12. (S) Write an original sentence in pencil and underline the Red Word with a red crayon. (**NOTE:** The sentence can also be dictated by the teacher while the student writes or dictated by the student while the teacher writes it.)

13. Repeat the steps for *yesterday*. (/y/ /ĕ/ /s/ /t/ /er/ /d/ /ā/; 7)

Review Ideas for Red Words:

- Sculpt the word using red Play-Doh or clay. Have students spell the word as they smash each letter.
- Print flashcards from IOG, and practice reading.
- Armtap the word to review.
- Cross-clap the word to review.
- Stomp the letters to review.
- Use a voice jar with popsicle sticks that have a different voice (e.g., robot, baby, cheerleader, monster) listed on each stick. Have a student draw a stick from the jar. The class armtaps the word using the voice selected. (Another option is to have an electronic spinning wheel with the voices listed on the wheel.)

Syllabication (Decoding)

Materials Needed:
IMSE Syllable Division Word Book, Pencil, Highlighter, Syllable Division Posters

Introduce on Wednesday with the new concept. Practice regularly.

1. Choose 6 or more words with the new concept in the *IMSE Syllable Division Word Book* for syllabication.

2. Use the steps on the Flip Chart and the Syllable Division Posters.

Syllable Division Patterns	1. Closed Syllable (Cl) short vowel sound	2. Open Syllable (O) long vowel sound
1. vc|cv	mag|net	ra|ven
2. v|cv	ten|nis	I|rish
3. vc|v	tip|top	o|pen
4. v|v	tom|tom	e|ven
	up|set	hu|mid
		ju|do

- Below is a sample script for syllabication.

1. Find the first two vowels or vowel units. Underline and label with a "v."

2. Draw the bridge. Underline the consonants or consonant units and label with a "c."

3. Find the pattern and divide the word.

4. Is there another vowel (other than an "e" at the end)? If so, repeat steps 1-3. If not, go to step 5.

5. Label each syllable.

6. Read the word.

NOTE: If there are two consonants in the middle of a word, split the word between the two consonants. (Exception: If the two consonants are a digraph [sh, ch, th] they cannot be split.) If there are three or more consonants, some letters go together as one consonant unit (look for known digraphs or blends).

Fluency, Vocabulary, and Comprehension

- Incorporate fluency into your literacy lessons daily/weekly (minimum 30 min/ week) by using Rapid Word Charts, IMSE Decodable Readers, words and sentences, Acadience Reading K-6 or DIBELS 8th Edition, repeated reading, and other activities.

- Incorporate vocabulary into your literacy lessons daily/weekly (minimum 50 min/ week) by choosing 3-5 appropriate tier two words (can pull from rich literature or decodable readers). Teach the words through explicit, direct instruction using student-friendly definitions, word webs, vocabulary charts, illustrations, and other activities.

- Incorporate oral language comprehension into your literacy lessons daily/weekly (approximately 100 min/week). Comprehension instruction should be explicit, direct instruction that includes teacher modeling, guided practice, and independent practice. Plan ahead to build on students' background knowledge, language structures, verbal reasoning, and literacy knowledge

Extension Activity Ideas

- Visit IMSE's Orton-Gillingham's Pinterest page for ideas.

Weekly Lesson Reminders

- Daily practice with writing the weekly Red Word(s)
- Kilpatrick's "One-Minute Activities" for daily phonological awareness practice
- Zgonc's phonological awareness activities
- Listen to rich literature to work on oral language comprehension.
- Target concept practice sheets from IMSE's practice books
- Practice test on Thursday and test on Friday

Magic E (bike)

Syllable Type 3 (ME)
VC/V Syllable Pattern 3 (fixate)

Card Pack #44 Decodable Reader #41	
Object Ideas:	**Literature Ideas:**
mule, bone, rope, bike, tape, cake, athlete, dime, slime, stone, cube	<ul><li>*Stone Soup* by Ann McGovern</li><li>*A Bad Case of Stripes* by David Shannon</li><li>*Bones* by Stephen Krensky</li><li>*Here We Are: Notes for Living on Planet Earth* by Oliver Jeffers</li><li>*I Like Myself!* by Karen Beaumont</li><li>*The Real Story of Stone Soup* by Ying Chang Compestine</li><li>*Same, Same but Different* by Jenny Sue Kostecki-Shaw</li><li>*Pete the Cat: I Love My White Shoes* by Eric Litwin</li><li>*The Other Side* by Jacqueline Woodson</li></ul>

Notes

- Use the Comprehensive Flip Chart for the steps on how to teach each part of IMSE's Lesson Plan.
- Use www.etymonline.com to help establish why a word might not follow the expected rules or patterns.
- A Magic E is when the "e" jumps over one consonant to make the vowel "say its name." This is also known as VCe.
- Decorate the Magic E card to distinguish it from the regular "e" card.
- Use the a-e, e-e, i-e, o-e, u-e cards for the Visual Drill only. They do not go on the blending board.
- Hold up the decorated Magic E card at the end of the blending board when appropriate.
  - Have students snap their fingers when Magic E appears and then read the word.
- Can revisit that y says /ī/ when used with Magic E (e.g., type, Skype). There is no card for this, but one can be created on an index card. Y with Magic E can also be practiced on the blending board by using the yellow y vowel card and the Magic E card.
- For dictation, use the extra visual cue for Magic E.

- Students should have short vowels mastered by this point if they weren't already mastered. Give an assessment with 20 CVC syllables (not real words). If students pass with 80% accuracy or better, discontinue the Vowel Intensive.

Reviewing Magic E

Three-Part Drill (Review)

1. **Visual:**   (T) Flashes cards | a - e |
   (S) a Magic E says /ā/

2. **Aud/Kin.:**   (T) Uses phoneme/grapheme chart
   (T) "You know two ways to spell this. Spell /ā/. Repeat."
   (S) Repeat and write in sand or on appropriate paper:
   "/ā/, a says /ā/; a Magic E says /ā/" | a || a - e |

3. **Blending:** | a - e | not used on blending board - use Magic E card
   Example: | b | a | k | e*** |
   (S) Read
   (T) Can snap fingers as a cue to read

- The "are," "ere," "ire," "ore," and "ure" combinations are listed under the "R-Controlled/Bossy-R" column of the Phoneme/Grapheme Chart. These combinations can be taught with this lesson and highlighted on the chart, but they don't need to be written in the sand during the Auditory/Kinesthetic Drill. (This is why there is a diagonal slash in these boxes on the Phoneme/Grapheme Chart.) Exposing students to these combinations is important; the combinations can be tricky because the liquid /r/ skews the vowel sound a little (e.g., bare, here, tire, sore, pure).

Phonological Awareness:

Materials Needed:
tokens, sound boxes, one-minute activities, or Zgonc PA book

Use the PAST assessment to determine a starting point for instruction. Incorporate daily phonological awareness activities by using Zgonc's tiered activities and/or Kilpatrick's One-Minute Activities in *Equipped for Reading Success*.

Phonemic awareness warm-up: Use tokens (or letter tiles once concepts have been taught) and sound boxes to do a quick phonemic awareness activity that ties in with the new concept, if appropriate.

Three-Part Drill

Materials Needed:
review cards, sand, blending board, vowel tents or sticks

Do this at least 3x per week. Use the Flip Chart for steps. Include the new concept after Day 1.

- Vowel Intensive: Use the Flip Chart for steps.
  - Do the Vowel Intensive with all 5 vowels.

V	VC	CVC
a	ag, ap, ab	lat, cad, zan
e	et, en, eb	zeg, ren, med
i	ig, ib, im	lin, hib, fid
o	ob, ot, oz	rom, hob, cog
u	un, ud, ub	sup, pum, dut

  - **NOTE:** If students are doing well with the Vowel Intensive, (T) give an assessment with 20 CVC syllables (not real words). If students pass with 80% accuracy or better, discontinue the Vowel Intensive.

- Below is a sample script. Remember to use review concepts only.

---

1. **Visual:**
   (T) Tell me the sounds you know for these letters.
   (S) /m/, /l/, etc.

2. **Auditory/Kinesthetic:**
   (T) You know three ways to spell this. (S) split trays. (T) Eyes on me.
   Spell /k/. Repeat.
   (S) /k/ c says /k/; k says /k/; ck says /k/

3. **Blending:**
   (T) Tell me the sound for each letter as I point. Then blend the sounds together to read the word or syllable. Give me a thumbs up if it is a real word.
   (S) /mmm/ /ŏŏŏ/ /mmm/ *mom* (thumbs up)
   Alternative:
   (T) Watch me first. /mmm/ /ŏŏŏ/ /mmm/ *mom*
   (T) Do it with me. (T&S) /mmm/ /ŏŏŏ/ /mmm/ *mom*
   (T) Your turn. (S) /mmm/ /ŏŏŏ/ /mmm/ *mom* (thumbs up)

Vowel Intensive: Model the visual cue while calling out the sound. Students will do the visual cue as they repeat the sound. Students will then hold up the vowel tent while stating the letter name and sound.

- (T): Eyes on me. The sound is /ă/. Repeat.
- (S): /ă/ a says /ă/

Teaching a New Concept

Materials Needed:
concept card, screen, green crayon, object, sand, decodable readers, literature, P/G chart

Introduce on Monday, and practice daily.

1. (T) Shows the new concept card(s).
   a. (T) Tells students that they will learn another way to spell the long vowel sounds.
   b. (T) Tells students that "a magic e" says /ā/. (S) Repeat. Repeat this process for all 5 Magic E cards.
   c. (T) Tells students that Magic E uses its powers to make the vowel say its name.
2. (T) Shows an object.
   a. (T) Allows students to manipulate the object and discuss prior knowledge. Reminds (S) that the object has the target sound(s) spelled with the target letter(s).
3. (S) Brainstorm to help establish a spelling rule, if applicable.
   a. (T) Create a human blending board with 4 students. Have 3 students each hold a card in CVC order. Have the class read the word. Then have the 4th student, who will play the role of Magic E, bring the Magic E card to the end of the word. Explain to students that Magic E gives the vowel strength to say its own name. Have the class read the new word. Continue this with several examples (e.g., cap/cape, pin/pine, kit/kite, tap/tape).
   b. Brainstorm words that have the target sound(s) or rule. The brainstorming can be a teacher-directed activity if students need extra support.
4. (T) Teaches Letter Formation, if needed. Can teach cursive writing.
   a. Use the steps for teaching letter formation on the Flip Chart.
   b. Use house paper to teach lowercase letters.
   c. Teach capital letters throughout the week. Capital letters go outside the house.
5. (T) Dictates target sound(s). (S) Practice all known spellings in the sand or other medium.
6. (T) Connects with literature.
   a. Read for language comprehension.
   b. Continue to work on language comprehension with rich literature throughout the week.
7. (S) Use decodable readers to practice the concepts learned.
   a. (S) Highlight words with the new concept. Read those words.
   b. (S) Highlight Red Words. Read those words.
   c. (S) Start reading the decodable reader.
   d. (S) Continue reading throughout the week.
   e. (S) Read a clean copy on Friday.
8. (T&S) Mark the Phoneme/Grapheme (P/G) chart by highlighting the target sound(s).

© IMSE 2022

Word Dictation

Materials Needed:
fingertapping hand, dictation paper, pencil

Practice daily. Use the Flip Chart to follow the steps for word dictation.

Day 1:	1. shape	2. cute	3. broke	4. cupcake	5. athlete
Day 2:	1. concrete	2. froze	3. gave	4. include	5. quite
Day 3:	1. stone	2. escape	3. excuse	4. invite	5. Pete
Days 4-5:	Review prior words. Optional additional words: ate, bake, became, bike, bite, bone, byte*, cake, care, chase, choke, compensate, cube, dime, dispute, drive, dude, fine, five, fume, game, glare, grade, here, hide, hole, home, hope, hype*, inhale, insane, inside, joke, late, like, made, make, male, mandate, maze, mine, mule, mute, nine, poke, pole, pride, prime, quote, reptile, robe, rude, safe, same, save, shake, size, Skype*, slime, smile, smoke, stampede, stole, style, tape, theme, time, tube, tyke*, type*, vote, wide, wife, wipe				
	*Please note: These words have "y-e" as /ī/. Teachers should consider students' age and experience level when selecting words for this concept.				

- Below is a sample script for one-syllable word dictation.

  1. (T) States word: *boss*. Uses it in a sentence: My *boss* is kind and fair. (Pounds) *boss*. (T) Models fingertapping if needed: /b/ /ŏ/ /s/. (Pounds) *boss*.
  2. (S) State while pounding: *boss*. (Fingertap) /b/ /ŏ/ /s/. (Pound) *boss*. Write the letters known for the sounds.
  3. (T) When yours looks like mine, rewrite the word.
  4. (S) Rewrite.
  5. Repeat the process for each word.
  6. (S) Read the list of words multiple times to build automaticity.

- Below is a sample script for multisyllabic word dictation.

  1. (T) States word: *bathtub*. Uses it in a sentence: Clean out the *bathtub*. (Pounds each syllable) *bath/tub*.
  2. (S) State while pounding each syllable: *bath/tub*.
  3. (T) Models fingertapping, if needed. First syllable: (Pounds) *bath*. (Fingertaps) /b/ /ă/ /th/. (Pounds) *bath*.
  4. (S) State first syllable while pounding: *bath*. (Fingertap) /b/ /ă/ /th/. (Pound) *bath*. Write the letters known for the sounds.

5. (T) Second syllable: (Pounds) *tub*. (Fingertaps) /t/ /ŭ/ /b/. (Pounds) *tub*.

6. (S) State second syllable while pounding: *tub*. (Fingertap) /t/ /ŭ/ /b/. (Pound) *tub*. Write the letters known for the sounds.

7. (T) When yours looks like mine, rewrite the word.

8. (S) Rewrite.

9. Repeat the process for each word.

10. (S) Read the list of words multiple times to build automaticity.

Sentence Dictation

Red Words are underlined. Students can fingertap the green words. Use the Flip Chart to follow the steps for sentence dictation.

1. Pete ate cake at the lake.
2. Will you put the pole in the tube?
3. He gave me a dime to give to his wife.
4. That robe was not mine to take.
5. She said she will bake a cupcake for me!
6. The athlete will take the first prize in the contest.
7. The vote will be cast.
8. We saw a snake around the lake.
9. Pete froze the ice in the same shape.
10. His wife will save the cake for him.
11. She is going to take the robe home.
12. Tim can fix the pipe with some tape.
13. The kite came from a kit.
14. The athlete made an excuse.
15. Jane fell on the concrete step.
16. Should we hide from the reptile?
17. I will vacate my home if a snake is inside!
18. The judge will mandate a vote.
19. Frank will not dispute the fact.
20. Kate will invite Jake to ride the mule.

- Below is a sample script for sentence dictation.

> 1. (T): Listen to the sentence. *The bedbug bit Pam.*
> 2. (T): Listen while I pound the syllables. *The bedbug bit Pam.* (Make sure to pound *bedbug* twice because it has two syllables.)
> 3. (T): Pound it with me. (T&S): *The bedbug bit Pam.*
> 4. (T): You pound the sentence. (S): *The bedbug bit Pam.*
> 5. (T): Watch me as I point to the lines while stating the sentence. (Tap the line for *bedbug* twice because it has two syllables.) *The bedbug bit Pam.*
> 6. (T): You point to the lines while stating the sentence.
> 7. (S): *The bedbug bit Pam.*
> 8. (T): Now write the sentence. Fingertap if needed.

- Below is a sample script to check CUPS.*

> 1. (T): C stands for capitalization. Did you remember a capital letter at the beginning of your sentence? Did you remember a capital letter for *Pam*? It is a name. If you forgot, fix it. If you remembered, put a tally mark above each capital letter. Add a mark in the box for C.
> 2. (T): U stands for understanding. Is your sentence neat? Reread it to yourself. Does it make sense? Could someone else understand it? If not, fix it. Add a mark in the box for U.
> 3. (T): P stands for punctuation. Did you remember a period at the end? If not, fix it. If you remembered, put a tally mark above the period. Add a mark in the box for P.
> 4. (T): S stands for spelling. Did you spell your words correctly? Check them. Now, check yours with mine (shows the teacher's copy). Fix any words you spelled incorrectly. Put a tally mark above the words you spelled correctly. Add a mark in the box for S.
> 5. (T): Rewrite your sentence with all of the corrections.
> 6. (T): Check for CUPS again. Put another mark in the boxes.
> 7. (T): Let's read the sentences.
> 8. (S) Read the sentences for fluency and automaticity.
>
> *__Please note:__ Once students understand how to use CUPS, transition to letting them check their sentence independently before showing the teacher's copy.

Weekly Red Words

Materials Needed:
screen, red crayon, red word paper

Introduce on Tuesday, and practice daily. Use the Flip Chart for steps.

New:	Review:	New Read-Only:	Review Read-Only:
first, around, going	were, does, some, good, there, done, her, under, down, onto, people, saw, both, should, could, would, over, love, live, out, day, too, eye, all, again, boy, girl, sign, your, which, look, also, use, today, yesterday		our, oven, park, play, way, chair

Steps for Teaching a New Red Word:

1. (T) States the word. (*first*)
2. (T&S) Use tokens to determine how many sounds are in the word. (/f/ /er/ /s/ /t/; 4)
3. (T&S) Discuss how we would expect to spell each sound as the teacher writes the grapheme(s) correctly. Identify what is unexpected or irregular about the spelling of the word. It could also be expected, but the concept hasn't been taught yet.
4. (T&S) Discuss the etymology of the word, if appropriate (lexical words). Visit www. etymonline.com for more information on the word.
5. (T) Defines the word, and writes a sentence using the word.
6. (T) Writes the word on Red Word paper with the screen underneath, using red crayon.
7. (S) Write the word on Red Word paper with the screen underneath, using red crayon. (S) Show the word to the teacher.
   (**NOTE:** The teacher should have students chunk the word if it has more than four letters.)
8. (T&S) Stand up, holding the Red Word in the nondominant hand. Armtap word while naming each letter. Then "underline" the word by sweeping left to right while stating the word, 3x. (**NOTE:** Left-handed students will place their left hand on their right wrist. They tap to their right shoulder. Underline from wrist to shoulder. Right-handed students place their right hand on their left shoulder. They tap to their left wrist. Underline shoulder to wrist.)
9. (T&S) Trace crayon bumps with the pointer finger while naming the letters, 3x.

10. (T&S) Place the screen over the paper and trace the word with the pointer finger while naming the letters, 3x.

11. (S) Turn paper over. With red crayon, write the word without the screen one time, and hold up the word for the teacher to check. (S) Write the word two more times.

12. (S) Write an original sentence in pencil and underline the Red Word with a red crayon. (**NOTE:** The sentence can also be dictated by the teacher while the student writes or dictated by the student while the teacher writes it.)

13. Repeat the steps for *around* (/ə/ /r/ /ou/ /n/ /d/; 5), *going* (/g/ /ō/ /ĭ/ /ŋ/; 4).

Review Ideas for Red Words:

- Sculpt the word using red Play-Doh or clay. Have students spell the word as they smash each letter.
- Print flashcards from IOG, and practice reading.
- Armtap the word to review.
- Cross-clap the word to review.
- Stomp the letters to review.
- Use a voice jar with popsicle sticks that have a different voice (e.g., robot, baby, cheerleader, monster) listed on each stick. Have a student draw a stick from the jar. The class armtaps the word using the voice selected. (Another option is to have an electronic spinning wheel with the voices listed on the wheel.)

Syllabication (Decoding)

Materials Needed:
IMSE Syllable Division Word Book, Pencil, Highlighter, Syllable Division Posters

Introduce on Wednesday with the new concept. Practice regularly.

1. Choose 6 or more words with the new concept from the *IMSE Syllable Division Word Book* for syllabication.

2. Introduce the third syllable type: Magic E.

3. Introduce the third syllable pattern: VC/V. Have students try the V/CV pattern first, as it is more common. If they do not recognize the word, try the VC/V pattern. If they still do not recognize the word, look it up in the dictionary.
   - The determination between V/CV and VC/V is most impactful when there is a single vowel before the consonant. This is because the placement of the syllable wall determines whether the syllable is closed or open (i.e., a long or short vowel sound). When the vowel is part of a combination (e.g., er, ea, oi), students can simply divide the word using the more common syllable pattern (V/CV), as the vowel sound will not be affected by the placement of the syllable wall.

4. Use the steps on the Flip Chart and the Syllable Division Posters.

Syllable Division Patterns

1. vc|cv

2. v|cv

3. vc|v

4. v|v

1. Closed Syllable (Cl)
short vowel sound

mag|net

ten|nis

tip|top

tom|tom

up|set

2. Open Syllable (O)
long vowel sound

ra|ven

I|rish

o|pen

e|ven

hu|mid

ju|do

3. Magic E (ME)

cup|cake

stam|pede

rep|tile

tad|pole

im|mune

Nep|tune

- Below is a sample script for syllabication.

1. Find the first two vowels or vowel units. Underline and label with a "v."
2. Draw the bridge. Underline the consonants or consonant units and label with a "c."
3. Find the pattern and divide the word.
4. Is there another vowel (other than an "e" at the end)? If so, repeat steps 1-3. If not, go to step 5.
5. Label each syllable.
6. Read the word.

NOTE: If there are two consonants in the middle of a word, split the word between the two consonants. (Exception: If the two consonants are a digraph [sh, ch, th] they cannot be split.) If there are three or more consonants, some letters go together as one consonant unit (look for known digraphs or blends).

Fluency, Vocabulary, and Comprehension

- Incorporate fluency into your literacy lessons daily/weekly (minimum 30 min/week) by using Rapid Word Charts, IMSE Decodable Readers, words and sentences, Acadience Reading K-6 or DIBELS 8th Edition, repeated reading, and other activities.
- Incorporate vocabulary into your literacy lessons daily/weekly (minimum 50 min/week) by choosing 3-5 appropriate tier two words (can pull from rich literature or decodable readers). Teach the words through explicit, direct instruction using student-friendly definitions, word webs, vocabulary charts, illustrations, and other activities.
- Incorporate oral language comprehension into your literacy lessons daily/weekly (approximately 100 min/week). Comprehension instruction should be explicit, direct instruction that includes teacher modeling, guided practice, and independent practice. Plan ahead to build on students' background knowledge, language structures, verbal reasoning, and literacy knowledge.

Extension Activity Ideas

- Continue to create human blending boards throughout the week. Take turns playing the role of Magic E.
- Create a tachistoscope for students to practice reading CVC and CVCe (Magic E) words.
- Glue Magic E onto popsicle sticks. (A color copy of the Magic E shown below is in the Masters.) Each student can take a turn being Magic E. Have a list of CVC words available. Have students use the stick to turn the CVC word into a CVCe word.
- Visit IMSE's Orton-Gillingham's Pinterest page for more ideas.

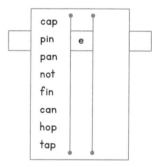

Weekly Lesson Reminders

- Daily practice with writing the weekly Red Word(s)
- Kilpatrick's "One-Minute Activities" for daily phonological awareness practice
- Zgonc's phonological awareness activities
- Listen to rich literature to work on oral language comprehension.
- Target concept practice sheets from IMSE's practice books
- Practice test on Thursday and test on Friday

Notes:

_____

_____

_____

_____

_____

_____

_____

_____

_____

_____

_____

_____

_____

_____

_____

_____

_____

_____

_____

_____

y as a vowel /ē/ (baby)

Card Pack #39 Decodable Reader #42	
Object Ideas:	**Literature Ideas:**
baby, candy, puppy, mommy, daddy, lady, jelly, family	<ul><li>*Mirandy and Brother Wind* by Patricia McKissack</li><li>*John Henry* by Julius Lester</li><li>*Minty: A Story of Young Harriet Tubman* by Alan Schroeder</li><li>*Roger, the Jolly Pirate* by Brett Helquist</li><li>*The Tiny Seed* by Eric Carle</li><li>*Julius's Candy Corn* by Kevin Henkes</li><li>*I Spy a Candy Cane* by Jean Marzollo</li><li>*I Am Every Good Thing* by Derrick Barnes</li><li>*My Daddy Rules the World: Poems About Dads* by Hope Anita Smith</li><li>*Baby Goes to Market* by Atinuke</li></ul>

Notes

- Use the Comprehensive Flip Chart for the steps on how to teach each part of IMSE's Lesson Plan.
- Use www.etymonline.com to help establish why a word might not follow the expected rules or patterns.
- Y says /ē/ at the end of an open, unstressed syllable (e.g., baby, mystery).
  - For younger students, you can start by telling them that when y comes at the end of a two-syllable word, it usually says /ē/.
- After the /ē/ sound for y is introduced, students will then begin providing both learned vowel sounds when the yellow y card is shown in the Visual Drill. (The students' response during the Visual Drill will be: /ī/, /ē/.)
- In the Auditory/Kinesthetic Drill, students know three ways to spell the /ē/ sound: e, e-e, y.
- Because this sound for y occurs at the end of a multisyllabic word, it will not be practiced on the blending board. When the y card is in the middle pile on the blending board, continue to remove the final pile to create an open syllable to practice the /ī/ sound (e.g., sky).

Phonological Awareness:

Materials Needed:
tokens, sound boxes, one-minute activities, or Zgonc PA book

Use the PAST assessment to determine a starting point for instruction. Incorporate daily phonological awareness activities by using Zgonc's tiered activities and/or Kilpatrick's One-Minute Activities in *Equipped for Reading Success.*

Phonemic awareness warm-up: Use tokens (or letter tiles once concepts have been taught) and sound boxes to do a quick phonemic awareness activity that ties in with the new concept, if appropriate.

 # Three-Part Drill

Materials Needed:
review cards, sand, blending board, vowel tents or sticks

Do this at least 3x per week. Use the Flip Chart for steps. Include the new concept after Day 1.

- Vowel Intensive: Use the Flip Chart for steps.
  - Do the Vowel Intensive with all 5 vowels.

V	VC	CVC
a	ag, ap, ab	lat, cad, zan
e	et, en, eb	zeg, ren, med
i	ig, ib, im	lin, hib, fid
o	ob, ot, oz	rom, hob, cog
u	un, ud, ub	sup, pum, dut

  - **NOTE:** If students are doing well with the Vowel Intensive, (T) give an assessment with 20 CVC syllables (not real words). If students pass with 80% accuracy or better, discontinue the Vowel Intensive.
- Below is a sample script. Remember to use review concepts only.

1. **Visual:**
   (T) Tell me the sounds you know for these letters.
   (S) /m/, /l/, etc.
2. **Auditory/Kinesthetic:**
   (T) You know three ways to spell this. (S) split trays. (T) Eyes on me.
   Spell /k/. Repeat.
   (S) /k/ c says /k/; k says /k/; ck says /k/

3. **Blending:**

(T) Tell me the sound for each letter as I point. Then blend the sounds together to read the word or syllable. Give me a thumbs up if it is a real word.

(S) /mmm/ /ŏŏŏ/ /mmm/ *mom* (thumbs up)

Alternative:

(T) Watch me first. /mmm/ /ŏŏŏ/ /mmm/ *mom*

(T) Do it with me. (T&S) /mmm/ /ŏŏŏ/ /mmm/ *mom*

(T) Your turn. (S) /mmm/ /ŏŏŏ/ /mmm/ *mom* (thumbs up)

*Vowel Intensive: Model the visual cue while calling out the sound. Students will do the visual cue as they repeat the sound. Students will then hold up the vowel tent while stating the letter name and sound.

- (T): Eyes on me. The sound is /ă/. Repeat.

- (S): /ă/ a says /ă/

 ## Teaching a New Concept

Materials Needed:
concept card, screen, green crayon, object, sand, decodable readers, literature, P/G chart

Introduce on Monday, and practice daily.

1. (T) Shows the new concept card(s).
    a. (T) Tells students that we will learn a new concept today.
    b. (T) Tells students that they know y is a consonant that says /y/ and a vowel that says /ī/. Today they will learn that sometimes y is a vowel that says /ē/.
    c. (T) States "y" says /ē/. (S) Repeat.
2. (T) Shows an object.
    a. (T) Allows students to manipulate the object and discuss prior knowledge. Reminds (S) that the object has the target sound(s) spelled with the target letter(s).
3. (S) Brainstorm to help establish a spelling rule, if applicable.
    a. Brainstorm words that have the target sound(s) or rule. The brainstorming can be a teacher-directed activity if students need extra support.
4. (T) Teaches Letter Formation, if needed. Can teach cursive writing.
    a. Use the steps for teaching letter formation on the Flip Chart.
    b. Use house paper to teach lowercase letters.
    c. Teach capital letters throughout the week. Capital letters go outside the house.
5. (T) Dictates target sound(s). (S) Practice all known spellings in the sand or other medium.
6. (T) Connects with literature.
    a. Read for language comprehension.
    b. Continue to work on language comprehension with rich literature throughout the week.

7. (S) Use decodable readers to practice the concepts learned.
   a. (S) Highlight words with the new concept. Read those words.
   b. (S) Highlight Red Words. Read those words.
   c. (S) Start reading the decodable reader.
   d. (S) Continue reading throughout the week.
   e. (S) Read a clean copy on Friday.
8. (T&S) Mark the Phoneme/Grapheme (P/G) chart by highlighting the target sound(s).

 ## Word Dictation

Materials Needed:
fingertapping hand, dictation paper, pencil

Practice daily. Use the Flip Chart to follow the steps for word dictation.

Day 1:	1. body	2. empty	3. daddy	4. lazy	5. penny
Day 2:	1. happy	2. baby	3. study	4. silly	5. copy
Day 3:	1. candy	2. lady	3. hobby	4. jelly	5. pity
Days 4-5:	Review prior words. Optional additional words: crazy, mommy, puppy, tummy				

- Below is a sample script for one-syllable word dictation.

1. (T) States word: *boss*. Uses it in a sentence: My *boss* is kind and fair. (Pounds) *boss*. (T) Models fingertapping if needed: /b/ /ŏ/ /s/. (Pounds) *boss*.
2. (S) State while pounding: *boss*. (Fingertap) /b/ /ŏ/ /s/. (Pound) *boss*. Write the letters known for the sounds.
3. (T) When yours looks like mine, rewrite the word.
4. (S) Rewrite.
5. Repeat the process for each word.
6. (S) Read the list of words multiple times to build automaticity.

- Below is a sample script for multisyllabic word dictation.

1. (T) States word: *bathtub*. Uses it in a sentence: Clean out the *bathtub*. (Pounds each syllable) *bath/tub*.
2. (S) State while pounding each syllable: *bath/tub*.
3. (T) Models fingertapping, if needed. First syllable: (Pounds) *bath*. (Fingertaps) /b/ /ă/ /th/. (Pounds) *bath*.
4. (S) State first syllable while pounding: *bath*. (Fingertap) /b/ /ă/ /th/. (Pound) *bath*. Write the letters known for the sounds.
5. (T) Second syllable: (Pounds) *tub*. (Fingertaps) /t/ /ŭ/ /b/. (Pounds) *tub*.
6. (S) State second syllable while pounding: *tub*. (Fingertap) /t/ /ŭ/ /b/. (Pound) *tub*. Write the letters known for the sounds.

7. (T) When yours looks like mine, rewrite the word.

8. (S) Rewrite.

9. Repeat the process for each word.

10. (S) Read the list of words multiple times to build automaticity.

Sentence Dictation

Red Words are underlined. Students can fingertap the green words. Use the Flip Chart to follow the steps for sentence dictation.

1. My puppy sat on my tummy.

2. The fig jelly made my tummy happy.

3. She got a penny from the bank.

4. My hobby is to pet the puppy.

5. The walk will make me happy.

6. The kid gave me a copy of the joke.

7. The judge made me a copy of the will.

8. The robot had a stiff body.

9. Mommy and Daddy went to get some candy or gum.

10. The lady had a baby.

- Below is a sample script for sentence dictation.

1. (T): Listen to the sentence. *The bedbug bit Pam.*

2. (T): Listen while I pound the syllables. *The bedbug bit Pam.* (Make sure to pound *bedbug* twice because it has two syllables.)

3. (T): Pound it with me. (T&S): *The bedbug bit Pam.*

4. (T): You pound the sentence. (S): *The bedbug bit Pam.*

5. (T): Watch me as I point to the lines while stating the sentence. (Tap the line for *bedbug* twice because it has two syllables.) *The bedbug bit Pam.*

6. (T): You point to the lines while stating the sentence.

7. (S): *The bedbug bit Pam.*

8. (T): Now write the sentence. Fingertap if needed.

- Below is a sample script to check CUPS.*

1. (T): C stands for capitalization. Did you remember a capital letter at the beginning of your sentence? Did you remember a capital letter for *Pam*? It is a name. If you forgot, fix it. If you remembered, put a tally mark above each capital letter. Add a mark in the box for C.

2. (T): U stands for understanding. Is your sentence neat? Reread it to yourself. Does it make sense? Could someone else understand it? If not, fix it. Add a mark in the box for U.

3. (T): P stands for punctuation. Did you remember a period at the end? If not, fix it. If you remembered, put a tally mark above the period. Add a mark in the box for P.

4. (T): S stands for spelling. Did you spell your words correctly? Check them. Now, check yours with mine (shows the teacher's copy). Fix any words you spelled incorrectly. Put a tally mark above the words you spelled correctly. Add a mark in the box for S.

5. (T): Rewrite your sentence with all of the corrections.

6. (T): Check for CUPS again. Put another mark in the boxes.

7. (T): Let's read the sentences.

8. (S) Read the sentences for fluency and automaticity.

*Please note:** Once students understand how to use CUPS, transition to letting them check their sentence independently before showing the teacher's copy.

Weekly Red Words

Materials Needed:
screen, red crayon, red word paper

Introduce on Tuesday, and practice daily. Use the Flip Chart for steps.

New:	Review:	New Read-Only:	Review Read-Only:
walk	were, does, some, good, there, done, her, under, down, onto, people, saw, both, should, could, would, over, love, live, out, day, too, eye, all, again, boy, girl, sign, your, which, look, also, use, today, yesterday, first, around, going		our, oven, park, play, way, chair

Steps for Teaching a New Red Word:

1. (T) States the word. (*walk*)

2. (T&S) Use tokens to determine how many sounds are in the word. (/w/ /aw/ /k/; 3)

3. (T&S) Discuss how we would expect to spell each sound as the teacher writes the grapheme(s) correctly. Identify what is unexpected or irregular about the spelling of the word. It could also be expected, but the concept hasn't been taught yet.

© IMSE 2022

4. (T&S) Discuss the etymology of the word, if appropriate (lexical words). Visit www.etymonline.com for more information on the word.

5. (T) Defines the word, and writes a sentence using the word.

6. (T) Writes the word on Red Word paper with the screen underneath, using red crayon.

7. (S) Write the word on Red Word paper with the screen underneath, using red crayon. (S) Show the word to the teacher.
(**NOTE:** The teacher should have students chunk the word if it has more than four letters.)

8. (T&S) Stand up, holding the Red Word in the nondominant hand. Armtap word while naming each letter. Then "underline" the word by sweeping left to right while stating the word, 3x. (**NOTE:** Left-handed students will place their left hand on their right wrist. They tap to their right shoulder. Underline from wrist to shoulder. Right-handed students place their right hand on their left shoulder. They tap to their left wrist. Underline shoulder to wrist.)

9. (T&S) Trace crayon bumps with the pointer finger while naming the letters, 3x.

10. (T&S) Place the screen over the paper and trace the word with the pointer finger while naming the letters, 3x.

11. (S) Turn paper over. With red crayon, write the word without the screen one time, and hold up the word for the teacher to check. (S) Write the word two more times.

12. (S) Write an original sentence in pencil and underline the Red Word with a red crayon. (**NOTE:** The sentence can also be dictated by the teacher while the student writes or dictated by the student while the teacher writes it.)

Review Ideas for Red Words:

- Sculpt the word using red Play-Doh or clay. Have students spell the word as they smash each letter.
- Print flashcards from IOG, and practice reading.
- Armtap the word to review.
- Cross-clap the word to review.
- Stomp the letters to review.
- Use a voice jar with popsicle sticks that have a different voice (e.g., robot, baby, cheerleader, monster) listed on each stick. Have a student draw a stick from the jar. The class armtaps the word using the voice selected. (Another option is to have an electronic spinning wheel with the voices listed on the wheel.)

 ## Syllabication (Decoding)

Materials Needed:
IMSE Syllable Division Word Book, Pencil, Highlighter, Syllable Division Posters

Introduce on Wednesday with the new concept. Practice regularly.

1. Choose 6 or more words with the new concept in the *IMSE Syllable Division Word Book* for syllabication.

2. Use the steps on the Flip Chart and the Syllable Division Posters.

Syllable Division Patterns

1. vc|cv
2. v|cv
3. vc|v
4. v|v

1. Closed Syllable (Cl)
short vowel sound

mag|net

ten|nis

tip|top

tom|tom

up|set

2. Open Syllable (O)
long vowel sound

ra|ven

I|rish

o|pen

e|ven

hu|mid

ju|do

3. Magic E (ME)

cup|cake

stam|pede

rep|tile

tad|pole

im|mune

Nep|tune

- Below is a sample script for syllabication.

1. Find the first two vowels or vowel units. Underline and label with a "v."
2. Draw the bridge. Underline the consonants or consonant units and label with a "c."
3. Find the pattern and divide the word.
4. Is there another vowel (other than an "e" at the end)? If so, repeat steps 1-3. If not, go to step 5.
5. Label each syllable.
6. Read the word.

NOTE: If there are two consonants in the middle of a word, split the word between the two consonants. (Exception: If the two consonants are a digraph [sh, ch, th] they cannot be split.) If there are three or more consonants, some letters go together as one consonant unit (look for known digraphs or blends).

Fluency, Vocabulary, and Comprehension

- Incorporate fluency into your literacy lessons daily/weekly (minimum 30 min/week) by using Rapid Word Charts, IMSE Decodable Readers, words and sentences, Acadience Reading K-6 or DIBELS 8th Edition, repeated reading, and other activities.

- Incorporate vocabulary into your literacy lessons daily/weekly (minimum 50 min/week) by choosing 3-5 appropriate tier two words (can pull from rich literature or decodable readers). Teach the words through explicit, direct instruction using student-friendly definitions, word webs, vocabulary charts, illustrations, and other activities.

- Incorporate oral language comprehension into your literacy lessons daily/weekly (approximately 100 min/week). Comprehension instruction should be explicit, direct instruction that includes teacher modeling, guided practice, and independent practice. Plan ahead to build on students' background knowledge, language structures, verbal reasoning, and literacy knowledge.

Extension Activity Ideas

- Add to the sounds of "y" bulletin board.
- Visit IMSE's Orton-Gillingham's Pinterest page for more ideas.

Weekly Lesson Reminders

- Daily practice with writing the weekly Red Word(s)
- Kilpatrick's "One-Minute Activities" for daily phonological awareness practice
- Zgonc's phonological awareness activities
- Listen to rich literature to work on oral language comprehension.
- Target concept practice sheets from IMSE's practice books
- Practice test on Thursday and test on Friday

Notes:

© IMSE 2022

Soft C /s/ and G /j/

(city, giraffe)

Card Pack #6 and 7, plus 45	Decodable Reader #43
Object Ideas:	**Literature Ideas:**

Gentle Cindy*

giraffe, city, cyclone, ice, dance, mice, face, pencil, prince, ice, lace, magic, gem (*A color copy is located in the Masters.)

- *Malala's Magic Pencil* by Malala Yousafzai
- *The Rough-Face Girl* by Rafe Martin
- *Book Fiesta!: Celebrate Children's Day/Book Day* by Pat Mora
- *Everybody Cooks Rice* by Norah Dooley
- *City Dog, Country Frog* by Mo Willems
- *Giraffes Can't Dance* by Giles Andreae
- *The City Mouse and the Country Mouse* by Aesop

Notes

- Use the Comprehensive Flip Chart for the steps on how to teach each part of IMSE's Lesson Plan.
- Use www.etymonline.com to help establish why a word might not follow the expected rules or patterns.
- C says /k/ next to a, o, u, and consonants. C says /s/ next to e, i, and y.
- G says /g/ next to a, o, u, and consonants. G says /j/ next to e, i, and y.
- Draw Gentle Cindy to help teach the spelling rule.
- Use card numbers 6 and 7 to introduce this concept.
- When the c card is shown during the Visual Drill, students will say /k/, /s/. When the g card is shown, students will say /g/, /j/.
- In the Auditory/Kinesthetic Drill, students will know 3 ways to spell the /s/ sound: s, -ss, c. Students will know 3 ways to spell the /j/ sound: j, -dge, g.

- For Blending, "c" and "g" can go with any vowel. Students will provide the sound for "c" or "g" based on the vowel that follows and will sound out the word accordingly.
- Use card pack number 45 as a separate drill after the Three-Part Drill. Students will only state the sound of "c" or "g" based on the vowel that is next to it (e.g., cy /s/, ga /g/).
- Some exceptions include *give, get, gift, girl.*
- Sometimes a word ends with a silent e only to make a c or g soft, and the preceding vowel is not a long vowel sound. This happens when there is more than one consonant between the vowel and the silent e at the end. For example, the "e" at the end of *fence* is a silent e to make the c soft, but it is not working as a Magic E. The preceding vowel sound is short. In the word *hinge*, the silent "e" is at the end to make the g soft, but it does not affect the preceding vowel.

Phonological Awareness:

Materials Needed:
tokens, sound boxes, one-minute activities, or Zgonc PA book

Use the PAST assessment to determine a starting point for instruction. Incorporate daily phonological awareness activities by using Zgonc's tiered activities and/or Kilpatrick's One-Minute Activities in *Equipped for Reading Success.*

Phonemic awareness warm-up: Use tokens (or letter tiles once concepts have been taught) and sound boxes to do a quick phonemic awareness activity that ties in with the new concept, if appropriate.

Three-Part Drill

Materials Needed:
review cards, sand, blending board, vowel tents or sticks

Do this at least 3x per week. Use the Flip Chart for steps. Include the new concept after Day 1.

- Vowel Intensive: Use the Flip Chart for steps.
  - Do the Vowel Intensive with all 5 vowels.

V	VC	CVC
a	ag, ap, ab	lat, cad, zan
e	et, en, eb	zeg, ren, med
i	ig, ib, im	lin, hib, fid
o	ob, ot, oz	rom, hob, cog
u	un, ud, ub	sup, pum, dut

  - **NOTE:** If students are doing well with the Vowel Intensive, (T) give an assessment with 20 CVC syllables (not real words). If students pass with 80% accuracy or better, discontinue the Vowel Intensive.

- Below is a sample script. Remember to use review concepts only.

> 1. **Visual:**
>   (T) Tell me the sounds you know for these letters.
>   (S) /m/, /l/, etc.
> 2. **Auditory/Kinesthetic:**
>   (T) You know three ways to spell this. (S) split trays. (T) Eyes on me.
>   Spell /k/. Repeat.
>   (S) /k/ c says /k/; k says /k/; ck says /k/
> 3. **Blending:**
>   (T) Tell me the sound for each letter as I point. Then blend the sounds together
>   to read the word or syllable. Give me a thumbs up if it is a real word.
>   (S) /mmm/ /ŏŏŏ/ /mmm/ *mom* (thumbs up)
>   *Alternative:*
>   (T) Watch me first. /mmm/ /ŏŏŏ/ /mmm/ *mom*
>   (T) Do it with me. (T&S) /mmm/ /ŏŏŏ/ /mmm/ *mom*
>   (T) Your turn. (S) /mmm/ /ŏŏŏ/ /mmm/ *mom* (thumbs up)
>
> ***Vowel Intensive:** Model the visual cue while calling out the sound. Students will
> do the visual cue as they repeat the sound. Students will then hold up the vowel
> tent while stating the letter name and sound.
> - (T): Eyes on me. The sound is /ă/. Repeat.
> - (S): /ă/ a says /ă/

 Teaching a New Concept

Materials Needed:
concept card, screen, green crayon, object, sand, decodable readers, literature, P/G chart

Introduce on Monday, and practice daily.

1. (T) Shows the new concept card(s).
   a. (T) Tells students that we will learn a new concept today.
   b. (T) Tells students that they know c says /k/. Today they will learn that sometimes c says /s/. (S) Repeat ("c" says /s/).
   c. (T) Tells students that they know g says /g/. Today they will learn that sometimes g says /j/. (S) Repeat ("g" says /j/).
   d. (T) Reminds students that c says /k/ next to a, o, and u (and consonants). C says /s/ next to e, i, and y.
   e. (T) Tells students that g says /g/ next to a, o, and u (and consonants). G says /j/ next to e, i, and y.
2. (T) Shows an object.
   a. (T) Allows students to manipulate the object and discuss prior knowledge. Reminds (S) that the object has the target sound(s) spelled with the target letter(s).
3. (S) Brainstorm to help establish a spelling rule, if applicable.
   a. Brainstorm words that have the target sound(s) or rule. The brainstorming can be a teacher-directed activity if students need extra support.

4. (T) Teaches Letter Formation, if needed. Can teach cursive writing.
   a. Use the steps for teaching letter formation on the Flip Chart.
   b. Use house paper to teach lowercase letters.
   c. Teach capital letters throughout the week. Capital letters go outside the house.
5. (T) Dictates target sound(s). (S) Practice all known spellings in the sand or other medium.
6. (T) Connects with literature.
   a. Read for language comprehension.
   b. Continue to work on language comprehension with rich literature throughout the week.
7. (S) Use decodable readers to practice the concepts learned.
   a. (S) Highlight words with the new concept. Read those words.
   b. (S) Highlight Red Words. Read those words.
   c. (S) Start reading the decodable reader.
   d. (S) Continue reading throughout the week.
   e. (S) Read a clean copy on Friday.
8. (T&S) Mark the Phoneme/Grapheme (P/G) chart by highlighting the target sound(s).

 ## Word Dictation

Materials Needed:
fingertapping hand, dictation paper, pencil

Practice daily. Use the Flip Chart to follow the steps for word dictation.

Day 1:	1. cent	2. page	3. place	4. decide	5. agent
Day 2:	1. stage	2. lunge	3. race	4. digest	5. fancy
Day 3:	1. engage	2. dance	3. price	4. advice	5. huge
Days 4-5:	Review prior words. Optional additional words: accent, accept, age, brace, cage, cell, chance, cinch, city, digit, enrage, face, fence, gem, gin, glance, grace (Grace), hinge, ice, lace, legend, magic, mice, nice, pace, prince, rage, rancid, sage, since, slice, space, suggest, twice, wage, wince				

- Below is a sample script for one-syllable word dictation.

1. (T) States word: *boss*. Uses it in a sentence: My *boss* is kind and fair. (Pounds) *boss*. (T) Models fingertapping if needed: /b/ /ŏ/ /s/. (Pounds) *boss*.
2. (S) State while pounding: *boss*. (Fingertap) /b/ /ŏ/ /s/. (Pound) *boss*. Write the letters known for the sounds.
3. (T) When yours looks like mine, rewrite the word.
4. (S) Rewrite.
5. Repeat the process for each word.
6. (S) Read the list of words multiple times to build automaticity.

- Below is a sample script for multisyllabic word dictation.

1. (T) States word: *bathtub*. Uses it in a sentence: Clean out the *bathtub*. (Pounds each syllable) *bath/tub*.
2. (S) State while pounding each syllable: *bath/tub*.
3. (T) Models fingertapping, if needed. First syllable: (Pounds) *bath*. (Fingertaps) */b/ /ă/ /th/*. (Pounds) *bath*.
4. (S) State first syllable while pounding: *bath*. (Fingertap) */b/ /ă/ /th/*. (Pound) *bath*. Write the letters known for the sounds.
5. (T) Second syllable: (Pounds) *tub*. (Fingertaps) */t/ /ŭ/ /b/*. (Pounds) *tub*.
6. (S) State second syllable while pounding: *tub*. (Fingertap) */t/ /ŭ/ /b/*. (Pound) *tub*. Write the letters known for the sounds.
7. (T) When yours looks like mine, rewrite the word.
8. (S) Rewrite.
9. Repeat the process for each word.
10. (S) Read the list of words multiple times to build automaticity.

Sentence Dictation

Red Words are underlined. Students can fingertap the green words. Use the Flip Chart to follow the steps for sentence dictation.

1. Grace will trim her dress with lace.
2. The ten mice made me wince!
3. She was so nice to send the gift to Kim.
4. The mice in the cage did a funny trick.
5. Their happy puppy gave me a kiss on my face.
6. The ring had a red gem.
7. Did you decide where we should go?
8. They say the judge was a legend to the people.
9. On stage, she became a legend.
10. Send me the page to copy.
11. Grace will go to the dance with the prince.
12. An ice cube will melt in the drink.
13. The agent at the gate gave us a pass.

- Below is a sample script for sentence dictation.

1. (T): Listen to the sentence. *The bedbug bit Pam.*
2. (T): Listen while I pound the syllables. *The bedbug bit Pam.* (Make sure to pound *bedbug* twice because it has two syllables.)
3. (T): Pound it with me. (T&S): *The bedbug bit Pam.*
4. (T): You pound the sentence. (S): *The bedbug bit Pam.*

5. (T): Watch me as I point to the lines while stating the sentence. (Tap the line for *bedbug* twice because it has two syllables.) *The bedbug bit Pam.*

6. (T): You point to the lines while stating the sentence.

7. (S): *The bedbug bit Pam.*

8. (T): Now write the sentence. Fingertap if needed.

- Below is a sample script to check CUPS.*

1. (T): C stands for capitalization. Did you remember a capital letter at the beginning of your sentence? Did you remember a capital letter for *Pam*? It is a name. If you forgot, fix it. If you remembered, put a tally mark above each capital letter. Add a mark in the box for C.

2. (T): U stands for understanding. Is your sentence neat? Reread it to yourself. Does it make sense? Could someone else understand it? If not, fix it. Add a mark in the box for U.

3. (T): P stands for punctuation. Did you remember a period at the end? If not, fix it. If you remembered, put a tally mark above the period. Add a mark in the box for P.

4. (T): S stands for spelling. Did you spell your words correctly? Check them. Now, check yours with mine (shows the teacher's copy). Fix any words you spelled incorrectly. Put a tally mark above the words you spelled correctly. Add a mark in the box for S.

5. (T): Rewrite your sentence with all of the corrections.

6. (T): Check for CUPS again. Put another mark in the boxes.

7. (T): Let's read the sentences.

8. (S) Read the sentences for fluency and automaticity.

*Please note: Once students understand how to use CUPS, transition to letting them check their sentence independently before showing the teacher's copy.

 ## Weekly Red Words

Materials Needed:
screen, red crayon, red word paper

Introduce on Tuesday, and practice daily. Use the Flip Chart for steps.

New:	Review:	New Read-Only:	Review Read-Only:
say, their	were, does, some, good, there, done, her, under, down, onto, people, saw, both, should, could, would, over, love, live, out, day, too, eye, all, again, boy, girl, sign, your, which, look, also, use, today, yesterday, first, around, going, walk	center	our, oven, park, play, way, chair

Steps for Teaching a New Red Word:

1. (T) States the word. (*say*)

2. (T&S) Use tokens to determine how many sounds are in the word. (/s/ /ā/; 2)

3. (T&S) Discuss how we would expect to spell each sound as the teacher writes the grapheme(s) correctly. Identify what is unexpected or irregular about the spelling of the word. It could also be expected, but the concept hasn't been taught yet.

4. (T&S) Discuss the etymology of the word, if appropriate (lexical words). Visit www. etymonline.com for more information on the word.

5. (T) Defines the word, and writes a sentence using the word.

6. (T) Writes the word on Red Word paper with the screen underneath, using red crayon.

7. (S) Write the word on Red Word paper with the screen underneath, using red crayon. (S) Show the word to the teacher.
   (**NOTE:** The teacher should have students chunk the word if it has more than four letters.)

8. (T&S) Stand up, holding the Red Word in the nondominant hand. Armtap word while naming each letter. Then "underline" the word by sweeping left to right while stating the word, 3x. (**NOTE:** Left-handed students will place their left hand on their right wrist. They tap to their right shoulder. Underline from wrist to shoulder. Right-handed students place their right hand on their left shoulder. They tap to their left wrist. Underline shoulder to wrist.)

9. (T&S) Trace crayon bumps with the pointer finger while naming the letters, 3x.

10. (T&S) Place the screen over the paper and trace the word with the pointer finger while naming the letters, 3x.

11. (S) Turn paper over. With red crayon, write the word without the screen one time, and hold up the word for the teacher to check. (S) Write the word two more times.

12. (S) Write an original sentence in pencil and underline the Red Word with a red crayon. (**NOTE:** The sentence can also be dictated by the teacher while the student writes or dictated by the student while the teacher writes it.)

13. Repeat the steps for *their*. (/TH/ /ā/ /r/; 3)

Review Ideas for Red Words:

- Sculpt the word using red Play-Doh or clay. Have students spell the word as they smash each letter.

- Print flashcards from IOG, and practice reading.

- Armtap the word to review.

- Cross-clap the word to review.

- Stomp the letters to review.

- Use a voice jar with popsicle sticks that have a different voice (e.g., robot, baby, cheerleader, monster) listed on each stick. Have a student draw a stick from the jar. The class armtaps the word using the voice selected. (Another option is to have an electronic spinning wheel with the voices listed on the wheel.)

Syllabication (Decoding)

Materials Needed:
IMSE Syllable Division Word Book, Pencil, Highlighter, Syllable Division Posters

Introduce on Wednesday with the new concept. Practice regularly.

1. Choose 6 or more words with the new concept in the *IMSE Syllable Division Word Book* for syllabication.

2. Use the steps on the Flip Chart and the Syllable Division Posters.

<table>
<tr><td>

Syllable Division Patterns

1. vc|cv

2. v|cv

3. vc|v

4. v|v

</td><td>

1. Closed Syllable (Cl)
short vowel sound

mag|net

ten|nis

tip|top

tom|tom

up|set

</td></tr>
<tr><td>

2. Open Syllable (O)
long vowel sound

ra|ven

I|rish

o|pen

e|ven

hu|mid

ju|do

</td><td>

3. Magic E (ME)

cup|cake

stam|pede

rep|tile

tad|pole

im|mune

Nep|tune

</td></tr>
</table>

- Below is a sample script for syllabication.

> 1. Find the first two vowels or vowel units. Underline and label with a "v."
> 2. Draw the bridge. Underline the consonants or consonant units and label with a "c."
> 3. Find the pattern and divide the word.
> 4. Is there another vowel (other than an "e" at the end)? If so, repeat steps 1-3. If not, go to step 5.
> 5. Label each syllable.
> 6. Read the word.

> **NOTE:** If there are two consonants in the middle of a word, split the word between the two consonants. (Exception: If the two consonants are a digraph [sh, ch, th] they cannot be split.) If there are three or more consonants, some letters go together as one consonant unit (look for known digraphs or blends).

 ## Fluency, Vocabulary, and Comprehension

- Incorporate fluency into your literacy lessons daily/weekly (minimum 30 min/week) by using Rapid Word Charts, IMSE Decodable Readers, words and sentences, Acadience Reading K-6 or DIBELS 8th Edition, repeated reading, and other activities.

- Incorporate vocabulary into your literacy lessons daily/weekly (minimum 50 min/week) by choosing 3-5 appropriate tier two words (can pull from rich literature or decodable readers). Teach the words through explicit, direct instruction using student-friendly definitions, word webs, vocabulary charts, illustrations, and other activities.

- Incorporate oral language comprehension into your literacy lessons daily/weekly (approximately 100 min/week). Comprehension instruction should be explicit, direct instruction that includes teacher modeling, guided practice, and independent practice. Plan ahead to build on students' background knowledge, language structures, verbal reasoning, and literacy knowledge.

Extension Activity Ideas

- Have students create a story or news article with the titles "Gyles the Gentle Giraffe" and "Cyclone Hits Center City." (A color copy of each poster is located in the Masters.)

Gyles the Gentle Giraffe

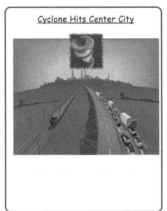

Cyclone Hits Center City

- Use the following song with students:

Soft c and g (to the tune of Old MacDonald):

Sometimes the c makes the /s/ sound: eieiy

Sometimes the g makes the /j/ sound: eieiy

When you see an e, when you see an i, when you see a y

These are the letters that change the sound: eieiy.

(A color copy is located in the Masters.)

- Continue to use Card Pack number 45 for practice with the hard and soft c and g. Students just state the sound c or g is making based on the vowel that lives next to it.
- Extend the -dge rule. Have words with the /j/ sound at the end that are missing either a "ge" or "-dge." Have students fill in the blank with the correct grapheme (-ge or -dge).
- Visit IMSE's Orton-Gillingham's Pinterest page for more ideas.

Weekly Lesson Reminders

- Daily practice with writing the weekly Red Word(s)
- Kilpatrick's "One-Minute Activities" for daily phonological awareness practice
- Zgonc's phonological awareness activities
- Listen to rich literature to work on oral language comprehension.
- Target concept practice sheets from IMSE's practice books
- Practice test on Thursday and test on Friday

Review for Concepts m-soft c and g

After teaching the first 50 concepts, the following words and sentences may be utilized for review. Teachers can dictate a different list (A, B, C, or D) and three sentences each day of the review. Teachers can spend up to a week on review *if needed*. If a review is not needed, this page can be skipped or partially utilized. Students can use IMSE workbooks or age-appropriate paper for recording their answers.

List A	List B	List C	List D
1. shy	1. smudge	1. crisp	1. thick
2. dodge	2. mustang	2. athlete	2. my
3. brunch	3. lazy	3. truck	3. snatch
4. include	4. pumpkin	4. agent	4. belong
5. clock	5. stitch	5. sibling	5. empty
6. broke	6. dry	6. badge	6. cupcake
7. chipmunk	7. concrete	7. patch	7. fancy
8. place	8. shack	8. copy	8. intend
9. switch	9. choke	9. shape	9. trudge
10. candy	10. stage	10. cry	10. drive

Sentences:

1. A duck was stuck in the pond.
2. The agent at the gate gave us a pass.
3. The camp had a blue tent.
4. The cat and dog ran to the hedge and hid.
5. I do not wish to fly.
6. Should we hide from the reptile?
7. Kate will invite Jake to ride the mule.
8. Honk if you open the trunk.
9. An ice cube will melt in the drink.
10. I will vacate my home if a snake is inside!
11. He will use a hitch on the truck.
12. The lady had a baby.

Notes:

_____

_____

_____

_____

_____

_____

_____

_____

_____

_____

_____

_____

_____

_____

_____

_____

_____

_____

Suffix -ed: /id/, /d/, /t/

(folded, soared, crashed)

Card Pack #46 Decodable Reader #44	
Object Ideas:	**Literature Ideas:**
paper airplane (folded, soared, crashed), pictures of action verbs	▪ *She Persisted: 13 American Women Who Changed the World* by Chelsea Clinton ▪ *The Undefeated* by Kwame Alexander ▪ *More! Phonics Through Poetry* by Babs Bell Hajdusiewicz ▪ *It's Hard to Be a Verb!* by Julia Cook ▪ *To Root, to Toot, to Parachute: What Is a Verb?* by Brian P. Cleary ▪ *Slide and Slurp, Scratch and Burp: More About Verbs* by Brian P. Cleary ▪ *If You Were a Verb* by Michael Dahl

Notes

- Use the Comprehensive Flip Chart for the steps on how to teach each part of IMSE's Lesson Plan.
- Use www.etymonline.com to help establish why a word might not follow the expected rules or patterns.
- Suffix -ed says /id/ when the base word ends with /d/ or /t/ (e.g., hun**t**ed, ja**d**ed).
- Suffix -ed says /d/ when the base word ends with a voiced sound other than /d/ (e.g., spe**ll**ed, bu**zz**ed).
- Suffix -ed says /t/ when the base word ends with an unvoiced sound other than /t/ (e.g., ru**sh**ed, ki**ss**ed).
- As an object idea, have students make paper airplanes. Brainstorm words on the airplane. (A color copy of this activity is located in the Masters.)

> 1. Fold the paper airplane.
> 2. Throw the planes.
> 3. Collect your plane. Write -ed /id/, /d/, /t/ on it. Let's brainstorm words.
>   a. We FOLDED the paper into a plane.
>   b. We SOARED the planes into the air.
>   c. They CRASHED onto the floor.
> 4. Can you think of other past tense verbs?

- In the Visual Drill, students will say, "Suffix -ed says /id/, /d/, /t/."
- In the Auditory/Kinesthetic Drill, students will know two ways to spell /d/ (d, -ed), two ways to spell /t/ (t, -ed), and one way to spell /id/ (-ed).
- In the Blending Drill, pull up -ed next to the end of the blending board when it is appropriate. (Remember that the Three Great Rules haven't been taught yet. Therefore, only put -ed next to double consonants, such as a blend or digraph.)
- For word dictation, students should only fingertap the base word. Then they add the suffix.

$$\underline{\text{cr}} \quad \underline{a} \quad \underline{\text{sh}} + \left(\text{ed}\right) = \underline{\text{crashed}}$$

- For syllabication, encourage students to circle any known prefixes or suffixes. Then look at the rest of the word and divide it into syllables. Determine what suffix -ed says based on the last sound in the base word. This will lay a foundation for word sums, which can be utilized when students have a deeper understanding of morphology.

Phonological Awareness:

Materials Needed:
tokens, sound boxes, one-minute activities, or Zgonc PA book

Use the PAST assessment to determine a starting point for instruction. Incorporate daily phonological awareness activities by using Zgonc's tiered activities and/or Kilpatrick's One-Minute Activities in *Equipped for Reading Success*.

Phonemic awareness warm-up: Use tokens (or letter tiles once concepts have been taught) and sound boxes to do a quick phonemic awareness activity that ties in with the new concept, if appropriate.

Three-Part Drill

Materials Needed:
review cards, sand, blending board, vowel tents or sticks

Do this at least 3x per week. Use the Flip Chart for steps. Include the new concept after Day 1.

1. Can do the hard/soft c/g drill after the Three-Part Drill
2. Can do the -ed tents activity after the Three-Part Drill (see *Extension Activity Ideas*)

- Below is a sample script. Remember to use review concepts only.

> 1. **Visual:**
>   (T) Tell me the sounds you know for these letters.
>   (S) /m/, /l/, etc.
> 2. **Auditory/Kinesthetic:**
>   (T) You know three ways to spell this. (S) split trays. (T) Eyes on me.
>   Spell /k/. Repeat.
>   (S) /k/ c says /k/; k says /k/; ck says /k/

3. **Blending:**

(T) Tell me the sound for each letter as I point. Then blend the sounds together to read the word or syllable. Give me a thumbs up if it is a real word.

(S) /mmm/ /ŏŏŏ/ /mmm/ *mom* (thumbs up)

Alternative:

(T) Watch me first. /mmm/ /ŏŏŏ/ /mmm/ *mom*

(T) Do it with me. (T&S) /mmm/ /ŏŏŏ/ /mmm/ *mom*

(T) Your turn. (S) /mmm/ /ŏŏŏ/ /mmm/ *mom* (thumbs up)

Optional: Once students have mastered their short vowel sounds, you can choose another drill to take the place of the Vowel Intensive, such as:

a. Use Card Pack Number 45 to do the hard/soft c/g drill.

b. Do the -ed tents activity (see *Extension Activity Ideas*).

Teaching a New Concept

Materials Needed:
concept card, screen, green crayon, object, sand, decodable readers, literature, P/G chart

Introduce on Monday, and practice daily.

1. (T) Shows the new concept card(s).

    a. (T) Tells students that we will learn about the suffix -ed. -Ed makes verbs past tense.

    b. (T) Tells students that suffix -ed says /id/, /d/, /t/. (S) Repeat (suffix -ed says /id/, /d/, /t/).

    c. (T) Tells students that they need to learn when suffix -ed says each sound.

    d. (T) Tells students that we will learn the spelling rule as we look at our object (paper airplanes). (See the directions in the Notes section regarding how to use the paper airplanes as the object and for brainstorming [Steps 2 and 3].)

2. (T) Shows an object. The paper airplane can also serve as the object.

    a. (T) Allows students to manipulate the object and discuss prior knowledge. Reminds (S) that the object has the target sound(s) spelled with the target letter(s).

3. (S) Brainstorm to help establish a spelling rule, if applicable.

    a. Brainstorm words that have the target sound(s) or rule. The brainstorming can be a teacher-directed activity if students need extra support.

4. (T) Teaches Letter Formation, if needed. Can teach cursive writing.

    a. Use the steps for teaching letter formation on the Flip Chart.

    b. Use house paper to teach lowercase letters.

    c. Teach capital letters throughout the week. Capital letters go outside the house.

5. (T) Dictates target sound(s). (S) Practice all known spellings in the sand or other medium.

6. (T) Connects with literature.
   a. Read for language comprehension.
   b. Continue to work on language comprehension with rich literature throughout the week.
7. (S) Use decodable readers to practice the concepts learned.
   a. (S) Highlight words with the new concept. Read those words.
   b. (S) Highlight Red Words. Read those words.
   c. (S) Start reading the decodable reader.
   d. (S) Continue reading throughout the week.
   e. (S) Read a clean copy on Friday.
8. (T&S) Mark the Phoneme/Grapheme (P/G) chart by highlighting the target sound(s).

Word Dictation

Materials Needed:
fingertapping hand, dictation paper, pencil

Practice daily. Use the Flip Chart to follow the steps for word dictation.

Day 1:	1. bumped	2. smelled	3. grilled	4. handed	5. erupted
Day 2:	1. acted	2. disgusted	3. crashed	4. relaxed	5. landed
Day 3:	1. spilled	2. rushed	3. projected	4. thanked	5. commented
Days 4-5:	Review prior words. Optional additional words: asked, banded, belonged, buzzed, camped, clenched, cranked, crusted, dished, drafted, drenched, drilled, dunked, dwelled, ended, famished, filled, granted, happened, helped, hunted, insisted, insulted, jumped, kissed, lasted, lifted, melted, milled, mulled, nested, packed, pinched, planted, printed, rented, rested, sifted, sniffed, spelled, stamped, swelled, tested, tossed, tricked, winked, yanked, yelled				

- Below is a sample script for one-syllable word dictation.

> 1. (T) States word: *boss*. Uses it in a sentence: My *boss* is kind and fair. (Pounds) *boss*. (T) Models fingertapping if needed: /b/ /ŏ/ /s/. (Pounds) *boss*.
> 2. (S) State while pounding: *boss*. (Fingertap) /b/ /ŏ/ /s/. (Pound) *boss*. Write the letters known for the sounds.
> 3. (T) When yours looks like mine, rewrite the word.
> 4. (S) Rewrite.
> 5. Repeat the process for each word.
> 6. (S) Read the list of words multiple times to build automaticity.

- Below is a sample script for multisyllabic word dictation.

> 1. (T) States word: *bathtub*. Uses it in a sentence: Clean out the *bathtub*. (Pounds each syllable) *bath/tub*.
> 2. (S) State while pounding each syllable: *bath/tub*.
> 3. (T) Models fingertapping, if needed. First syllable: (Pounds) *bath*. (Fingertaps) */b/ /ă/ /th/*. (Pounds) *bath*.
> 4. (S) State first syllable while pounding: *bath*. (Fingertap) */b/ /ă/ /th/*. (Pound) *bath*. Write the letters known for the sounds.
> 5. (T) Second syllable: (Pounds) *tub*. (Fingertaps) */t/ /ŭ/ /b/*. (Pounds) *tub*.
> 6. (S) State second syllable while pounding: *tub*. (Fingertap) */t/ /ŭ/ /b/*. (Pound) *tub*. Write the letters known for the sounds.
> 7. (T) When yours looks like mine, rewrite the word.
> 8. (S) Rewrite.
> 9. Repeat the process for each word.
> 10. (S) Read the list of words multiple times to build automaticity.

Sentence Dictation

Red Words are underlined. Students can fingertap the green words. Use the Flip Chart to follow the steps for sentence dictation.

1. The plane landed late yesterday.
2. The duck nested close to the lake.
3. Kate asked her mom for some cake.
4. Bob rented a place for his kid to dwell.
5. How was the copy of the test printed?
6. The lady yelled when she crashed her bike.
7. Once the puppy jumped up, he sniffed the cage.
8. He kissed his wife as she got out of the truck.
9. I planted it in the pot.
10. She thanked me and winked as she went into the class.
11. Fred handed me the test, and I mulled it over.
12. I filled the cup and then spilled it.
13. My red vest was drenched.
14. The ice cube melted in the hot sun.
15. I was disgusted when I saw the slimy bug!

- Below is a sample script for sentence dictation.

  1. (T): Listen to the sentence. *The bedbug bit Pam.*
  2. (T): Listen while I pound the syllables. *The bedbug bit Pam.* (Make sure to pound *bedbug* twice because it has two syllables.)
  3. (T): Pound it with me. (T&S): *The bedbug bit Pam.*
  4. (T): You pound the sentence. (S): *The bedbug bit Pam.*
  5. (T): Watch me as I point to the lines while stating the sentence. (Tap the line for *bedbug* twice because it has two syllables.) *The bedbug bit Pam.*
  6. (T): You point to the lines while stating the sentence.
  7. (S): *The bedbug bit Pam.*
  8. (T): Now write the sentence. Fingertap if needed.

- Below is a sample script to check CUPS.*

  1. (T): C stands for capitalization. Did you remember a capital letter at the beginning of your sentence? Did you remember a capital letter for *Pam*? It is a name. If you forgot, fix it. If you remembered, put a tally mark above each capital letter. Add a mark in the box for C.
  2. (T): U stands for understanding. Is your sentence neat? Reread it to yourself. Does it make sense? Could someone else understand it? If not, fix it. Add a mark in the box for U.
  3. (T): P stands for punctuation. Did you remember a period at the end? If not, fix it. If you remembered, put a tally mark above the period. Add a mark in the box for P.
  4. (T): S stands for spelling. Did you spell your words correctly? Check them. Now, check yours with mine (shows the teacher's copy). Fix any words you spelled incorrectly. Put a tally mark above the words you spelled correctly. Add a mark in the box for S.
  5. (T): Rewrite your sentence with all of the corrections.
  6. (T): Check for CUPS again. Put another mark in the boxes.
  7. (T): Let's read the sentences.
  8. (S) Read the sentences for fluency and automaticity.

  ***Please note:** Once students understand how to use CUPS, transition to letting them check their sentence independently before showing the teacher's copy.

Weekly Red Words

Materials Needed:
screen, red crayon, red word paper

Introduce on Tuesday, and practice daily. Use the Flip Chart for steps.

New:	Review:	New Read-Only:	Review Read-Only:
how, once	were, does, some, good, there, done, her, under, down, onto, people, saw, both, should, could, would, over, love, live, out, day, too, eye, all, again, boy, girl, sign, your, which, look, also, use, today, yesterday, first, around, going, walk, say, their		our, oven, park, play, way, chair, center

Steps for Teaching a New Red Word:

1. (T) States the word. (*how*)
2. (T&S) Use tokens to determine how many sounds are in the word. (/h/ /ou/; 2)
3. (T&S) Discuss how we would expect to spell each sound as the teacher writes the grapheme(s) correctly. Identify what is unexpected or irregular about the spelling of the word. It could also be expected, but the concept hasn't been taught yet.
4. (T&S) Discuss the etymology of the word, if appropriate (lexical words). Visit www.etymonline.com for more information on the word.
5. (T) Defines the word, and writes a sentence using the word.
6. (T) Writes the word on Red Word paper with the screen underneath, using red crayon.
7. (S) Write the word on Red Word paper with the screen underneath, using red crayon. (S) Show the word to the teacher.
(**NOTE:** The teacher should have students chunk the word if it has more than four letters.)

8. (T&S) Stand up, holding the Red Word in the nondominant hand. Armtap word while naming each letter. Then "underline" the word by sweeping left to right while stating the word, 3x. (**NOTE:** Left-handed students will place their left hand on their right wrist. They tap to their right shoulder. Underline from wrist to shoulder. Right-handed students place their right hand on their left shoulder. They tap to their left wrist. Underline shoulder to wrist.)

9. (T&S) Trace crayon bumps with the pointer finger while naming the letters, 3x.

10. (T&S) Place the screen over the paper and trace the word with the pointer finger while naming the letters, 3x.

11. (S) Turn paper over. With red crayon, write the word without the screen one time, and hold up the word for the teacher to check. (S) Write the word two more times.

12. (S) Write an original sentence in pencil and underline the Red Word with a red crayon. (**NOTE:** The sentence can also be dictated by the teacher while the student writes or dictated by the student while the teacher writes it.)

13. Repeat the steps for *once*. (/w/ /ŭ/ /n/ /s/; 4)

Review Ideas for Red Words:

- Sculpt the word using red Play-Doh or clay. Have students spell the word as they smash each letter.
- Print flashcards from IOG, and practice reading.
- Armtap the word to review.
- Cross-clap the word to review.
- Stomp the letters to review.
- Use a voice jar with popsicle sticks that have a different voice (e.g., robot, baby, cheerleader, monster) listed on each stick. Have a student draw a stick from the jar. The class armtaps the word using the voice selected. (Another option is to have an electronic spinning wheel with the voices listed on the wheel.)

Syllabication (Decoding)

Materials Needed:
IMSE Syllable Division Word Book, Pencil, Highlighter, Syllable Division Posters

Introduce on Wednesday with the new concept. Practice regularly.

1. Choose 6 or more words with the new concept from the *IMSE Syllable Division Word Book* for syllabication.

2. Remember to have students circle any known prefixes or suffixes. Then divide the rest of the word. For suffix -ed, students will have to determine what sound -ed is making based on the base word.

3. Use the steps on the Flip Chart and the Syllable Division Posters.

Syllable Division Patterns

1. vc|cv

2. v|cv

3. vc|v

4. v|v

1. Closed Syllable (Cl)
short vowel sound

mag|net

ten|nis

tip|top

tom|tom

up|set

2. Open Syllable (O)
long vowel sound

ra|ven

I|rish

o|pen

e|ven

hu|mid

ju|do

3. Magic E (ME)

cup|cake

stam|pede

rep|tile

tad|pole

im|mune

Nep|tune

- Below is a sample script for syllabication.

1. Find the first two vowels or vowel units. Underline and label with a "v."
2. Draw the bridge. Underline the consonants or consonant units and label with a "c."
3. Find the pattern and divide the word.
4. Is there another vowel (other than an "e" at the end)? If so, repeat steps 1-3. If not, go to step 5.
5. Label each syllable.
6. Read the word.

NOTE: If there are two consonants in the middle of a word, split the word between the two consonants. (Exception: If the two consonants are a digraph [sh, ch, th] they cannot be split.) If there are three or more consonants, some letters go together as one consonant unit (look for known digraphs or blends).

Fluency, Vocabulary, and Comprehension

- Incorporate fluency into your literacy lessons daily/weekly (minimum 30 min/week) by using Rapid Word Charts, IMSE Decodable Readers, words and sentences, Acadience Reading K-6 or DIBELS 8th Edition, repeated reading, and other activities.

- Incorporate vocabulary into your literacy lessons daily/weekly (minimum 50 min/week) by choosing 3-5 appropriate tier two words (can pull from rich literature or decodable readers). Teach the words through explicit, direct instruction using student-friendly definitions, word webs, vocabulary charts, illustrations, and other activities.

- Incorporate oral language comprehension into your literacy lessons daily/weekly (approximately 100 min/week). Comprehension instruction should be explicit, direct instruction that includes teacher modeling, guided practice, and independent practice. Plan ahead to build on students' background knowledge, language structures, verbal reasoning, and literacy knowledge.

Extension Activity Ideas

- Create a list of several past tense verbs (jumped, smiled, rested, etc.). Pass out the words to students. Have students perform the past tense verb as you take a picture of them. Show the pictures to the students to see if they can figure out the past tense verb that the picture represents. Discuss the sound of -ed and why -ed is making that sound.

- Give students 3 different colored index cards. On one card students write, "I hear /id/, but I write -ed." On the second card, students write, "I hear /d/, but I write -ed." On the last card, students write, "I hear /t/, but I write -ed." Make sure all students write the same information on each of the colors (e.g., if you choose pink for /id/, all students should have /id/ on the pink card). This drill can be implemented after the Three-Part Drill.
  - (T) States a past tense verb. *(hunted)*
  - (S) Repeat the word. *(hunted)* Then hold up the correct card while stating the sentence on the card. *(I hear /id/, but I write -ed.)*

    OR

  - (T) States a sentence with a past tense verb. *(The child <u>spelled</u> the word correctly.)*
  - (S) Identify the verb. *(spelled)* Then hold up the correct card while stating the sentence. *(I hear /d/, but I write -ed.)*

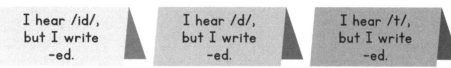

- Provide students with a list of past-tense verbs with -ed and a template for a timeline. Have students create an individual or class timeline of the previous day's activities using -ed verbs (e.g., 7:00 a.m. - jumped out of bed; 8:00 a.m. - traveled to school; 1:30 p.m. - worked on math).

- Visit IMSE's Orton-Gillingham's Pinterest page for more ideas.

Weekly Lesson Reminders

- Daily practice with writing the weekly Red Word(s)
- Kilpatrick's "One-Minute Activities" for daily phonological awareness practice
- Zgonc's phonological awareness activities
- Listen to rich literature to work on oral language comprehension.
- Target concept practice sheets from IMSE's practice books
- Practice test on Thursday and test on Friday

Notes:

_____

_____

_____

_____

_____

_____

_____

_____

_____

_____

_____

_____

_____

_____

_____

_____

_____

_____

_____

_____

_____

Plural Suffixes: -s /s/ or /z/, -es /iz/ (cats, dogs, dishes)

Card Pack #47 Decodable Reader #45	
Object Ideas:	**Literature Ideas:**
cats, cupcakes, bats, bears, socks, dogs, dishes	▪ *Pete the Cat and the Missing Cupcakes* by Kimberly and James Dean ▪ *Bats* by Gail Gibbons ▪ *Parts* by Tedd Arnold ▪ *More Parts* by Tedd Arnold ▪ *The Three Snow Bears* by Jan Brett ▪ *Smelly Socks* by Robert Munsch

Notes

- Use the Comprehensive Flip Chart for the steps on how to teach each part of IMSE's Lesson Plan.
- Use www.etymonline.com to help establish why a word might not follow the expected rules or patterns.
- Suffix -s says /s/ when the base word ends in a voiceless sound (e.g., ca**t**s). It says /z/ when the word ends in a voiced sound (e.g., do**g**s).
- Suffix -es says /ĭz/ and comes after words that end with /ch/, /j/, /s/, /sh/, /z/, or the letter "x" (e.g., ma**tch**es, wi**sh**es, bo**x**es).
- In the Visual Drill, when the "-s" card is shown, students will say, "Suffix -s says /s/ or /z/." When the "-es" card is shown, students will say, "Suffix -es says /ĭz/."
- In the Auditory/Kinesthetic Drill, students will know three ways to spell /z/ sounds (z, -zz, s) and one way to spell /iz/ (-es).
- In the Blending Drill, pull up -s/-es next to the end of the blending board when it is appropriate. Students will decide which spelling to use and the sound it makes. (Note: Do not put -s/-es next to -dge until the drop rule has been taught. Do not put -s/-es next to a word ending with y until the change rule has been taught.)
- For word dictation, students should only fingertap the base word. Then they add the suffix.

$$\underline{h} \quad \underline{a} \quad \underline{t} \; + \; \boxed{\underline{s}} \; = \underline{hats}$$

$$\underline{f} \quad \underline{o} \quad \underline{x} \; + \; \boxed{\underline{es}} \; = \underline{foxes}$$

- For syllabication, encourage students to circle any known prefixes or suffixes. Then look at the rest of the word and divide it into syllables. Determine what suffix -s/-es says based on the last sound in the base word. This will lay a foundation for word sums, which can be utilized when students have a deeper understanding of morphology.

Phonological Awareness:

Materials Needed:
tokens, sound boxes, one-minute activities, or Zgonc PA book

Use the PAST assessment to determine a starting point for instruction. Incorporate daily phonological awareness activities by using Zgonc's tiered activities and/or Kilpatrick's One-Minute Activities in *Equipped for Reading Success*.

Phonemic awareness warm-up: Use tokens (or letter tiles once concepts have been taught) and sound boxes to do a quick phonemic awareness activity that ties in with the new concept, if appropriate.

Three-Part Drill

Materials Needed:
review cards, sand, blending board, vowel tents or sticks

Do this at least 3x per week. Use the Flip Chart for steps. Include the new concept after Day 1.

1. Can do the hard/soft c/g drill after the Three-Part Drill
2. Can do the -ed tents activity after the Three-Part Drill (see *Extension Activity Ideas*)
3. Can do the -s/-es tents activity after the Three-Part Drill (see *Extension Activity Ideas*)

- Below is a sample script. Remember to use review concepts only.

---

1. **Visual:**
   (T) Tell me the sounds you know for these letters.
   (S) /m/, /l/, etc.

2. **Auditory/Kinesthetic:**
   (T) You know three ways to spell this. (S) split trays. (T) Eyes on me.
   Spell /k/. Repeat.
   (S) /k/ c says /k/; k says /k/; ck says /k/

3. **Blending:**
   (T) Tell me the sound for each letter as I point. Then blend the sounds together to read the word or syllable. Give me a thumbs up if it is a real word.
   (S) /mmm/ /ŏŏŏ/ /mmm/ *mom* (thumbs up)
   Alternative:
   (T) Watch me first. /mmm/ /ŏŏŏ/ /mmm/ *mom*
   (T) Do it with me. (T&S) /mmm/ /ŏŏŏ/ /mmm/ *mom*
   (T) Your turn. (S) /mmm/ /ŏŏŏ/ /mmm/ *mom* (thumbs up)

Optional: Once students have mastered their short vowel sounds, you can choose another drill to take the place of the Vowel Intensive, such as:

    a. Use Card Pack Number 45 to do the hard/soft c/g drill.

    b. Do the -ed tents activity (see *Extension Activity Ideas*).

    c. Do the -s/-es tents activity (see *Extension Activity Ideas*).

 ## Teaching a New Concept

Materials Needed:
concept card, screen, green crayon, object, sand, decodable readers, literature, P/G chart

Introduce on Monday, and practice daily.

1. (T) Shows the new concept card(s).

    a. (T) Tells students that we will learn about the suffixes -s and -es. Suffix -s/-es makes nouns plural (more than one) or verbs present tense.

    b. (T) Tells students that suffix -s says /s/ or /z/. Suffix -es says /iz/. (S) Repeat (suffix -s says /s/ or /z/; suffix -es says /iz/).

    c. (T) Tells students that they need to learn when the suffix -s/-es says each sound.

    d. (T) Tells students the spelling rule.

2. (T) Shows an object.

    a. (T) Allows students to manipulate the object and discuss prior knowledge. Reminds (S) that the object has the target sound(s) spelled with the target letter(s).

3. (S) Brainstorm to help establish a spelling rule, if applicable.

    a. Brainstorm words that have the target sound(s) or rule. The brainstorming can be a teacher-directed activity if students need extra support.

4. (T) Teaches Letter Formation, if needed. Can teach cursive writing.

    a. Use the steps for teaching letter formation on the Flip Chart.

    b. Use house paper to teach lowercase letters.

    c. Teach capital letters throughout the week. Capital letters go outside the house.

5. (T) Dictates target sound(s). (S) Practice all known spellings in the sand or other medium.

6. (T) Connects with literature.

    a. Read for language comprehension.

    b. Continue to work on language comprehension with rich literature throughout the week.

7. (S) Use decodable readers to practice the concepts learned.

    a. (S) Highlight words with the new concept. Read those words.

    b. (S) Highlight Red Words. Read those words.

    c. (S) Start reading the decodable reader.

    d. (S) Continue reading throughout the week.

    e. (S) Read a clean copy on Friday.

8. (T&S) Mark the Phoneme/Grapheme (P/G) chart by highlighting the target sound(s).

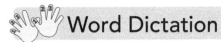 Word Dictation

Materials Needed:
fingertapping hand, dictation paper, pencil

Practice daily. Use the Flip Chart to follow the steps for word dictation.

Day 1:	1. chips	2. swings	3. glasses	4. contests	5. menus
Day 2:	1. cribs	2. plates	3. acrobats	4. songs	5. radishes
Day 3:	1. robots	2. brushes	3. twigs	4. pumpkins	5. matches
Days 4-5:	Review prior words. Optional additional words: baskets, bells, blemishes, boxes, cakes, cats, clams, crutches, cupcakes, dishes, dishpans, dogs, dolls, drops, fangs, fetches, foxes, frogs, hands, hats, itches, kids, kisses, lashes, legs, lips, mistakes, passes, pens, pills, puffs, rings, rinks, rushes, socks, stops, suffixes, swims, taps, ticks, trashes, wings, wishes				

- Below is a sample script for one-syllable word dictation.

1. (T) States word: *boss*. Uses it in a sentence: My *boss* is kind and fair. (Pounds) *boss*. (T) Models fingertapping if needed: /b/ /ŏ/ /s/. (Pounds) *boss*.
2. (S) State while pounding: *boss*. (Fingertap) /b/ /ŏ/ /s/. (Pound) *boss*. Write the letters known for the sounds.
3. (T) When yours looks like mine, rewrite the word.
4. (S) Rewrite.
5. Repeat the process for each word.
6. (S) Read the list of words multiple times to build automaticity.

- Below is a sample script for multisyllabic word dictation.

1. (T) States word: *bathtub*. Uses it in a sentence: Clean out the *bathtub*. (Pounds each syllable) *bath/tub*.
2. (S) State while pounding each syllable: *bath/tub*.
3. (T) Models fingertapping, if needed. First syllable: (Pounds) *bath*. (Fingertaps) /b/ /ă/ /th/. (Pounds) *bath*.
4. (S) State first syllable while pounding: *bath*. (Fingertap) /b/ /ă/ /th/. (Pound) *bath*. Write the letters known for the sounds.
5. (T) Second syllable: (Pounds) *tub*. (Fingertaps) /t/ /ŭ/ /b/. (Pounds) *tub*.
6. (S) State second syllable while pounding: *tub*. (Fingertap) /t/ /ŭ/ /b/. (Pound) *tub*. Write the letters known for the sounds.
7. (T) When yours looks like mine, rewrite the word.
8. (S) Rewrite.
9. Repeat the process for each word.
10. (S) Read the list of words multiple times to build automaticity.

Sentence Dictation

Red Words are underlined. Students can fingertap the green words. Use the Flip Chart to follow the steps for sentence dictation.

1. The bells will ring at ten.
2. The cats swim with the frogs.
3. Ten frogs jumped into the pond.
4. The foxes had huge fangs!
5. Mom gave Kim five rings.
6. Pam has another six cakes.
7. Ken broke the dishes when he got mad.
8. My legs had scabs from the huge cuts.
9. When she fell, she broke her glasses.
10. Her lashes are so long!
11. Who do you think will win the contests?
12. The rash on my skin itches.
13. Is Greg on crutches?

- Below is a sample script for sentence dictation.

> 1. (T): Listen to the sentence. *The bedbug bit Pam.*
> 2. (T): Listen while I pound the syllables. *The bedbug bit Pam.* (Make sure to pound *bedbug* twice because it has two syllables.)
> 3. (T): Pound it with me. (T&S): *The bedbug bit Pam.*
> 4. (T): You pound the sentence. (S): *The bedbug bit Pam.*
> 5. (T): Watch me as I point to the lines while stating the sentence. (Tap the line for *bedbug* twice because it has two syllables.) *The bedbug bit Pam.*
> 6. (T): You point to the lines while stating the sentence.
> 7. (S): *The bedbug bit Pam.*
> 8. (T): Now write the sentence. Fingertap if needed.

- Below is a sample script to check CUPS.*

> 1. (T): C stands for capitalization. Did you remember a capital letter at the beginning of your sentence? Did you remember a capital letter for *Pam*? It is a name. If you forgot, fix it. If you remembered, put a tally mark above each capital letter. Add a mark in the box for C.
> 2. (T): U stands for understanding. Is your sentence neat? Reread it to yourself. Does it make sense? Could someone else understand it? If not, fix it. Add a mark in the box for U.

3. (T): P stands for punctuation. Did you remember a period at the end? If not, fix it. If you remembered, put a tally mark above the period. Add a mark in the box for P.

4. (T): S stands for spelling. Did you spell your words correctly? Check them. Now, check yours with mine (shows the teacher's copy). Fix any words you spelled incorrectly. Put a tally mark above the words you spelled correctly. Add a mark in the box for S.

5. (T): Rewrite your sentence with all of the corrections.

6. (T): Check for CUPS again. Put another mark in the boxes.

7. (T): Let's read the sentences.

8. (S) Read the sentences for fluency and automaticity.

*Please note: Once students understand how to use CUPS, transition to letting them check their sentence independently before showing the teacher's copy.

Weekly Red Words

Materials Needed:
screen, red crayon, red word paper

Introduce on Tuesday, and practice daily. Use the Flip Chart for steps.

New:	Review:	New Read-Only:	Review Read-Only:
another	were, does, some, good, there, done, her, under, down, onto, people, saw, both, should, could, would, over, love, live, out, day, too, eye, all, again, boy, girl, sign, your, which, look, also, use, today, yesterday, first, around, going, walk, say, their, how, once		our, oven, park, play, way, chair, center

Steps for Teaching a New Red Word:

1. (T) States the word. (*another*)
2. (T&S) Use tokens to determine how many sounds are in the word. (/ə/ /n/ /ə/ /TH/ /er/; 5)
3. (T&S) Discuss how we would expect to spell each sound as the teacher writes the grapheme(s) correctly. Identify what is unexpected or irregular about the spelling of the word. It could also be expected, but the concept hasn't been taught yet.
4. (T&S) Discuss the etymology of the word, if appropriate (lexical words). Visit www.etymonline.com for more information on the word.
5. (T) Defines the word, and writes a sentence using the word.
6. (T) Writes the word on Red Word paper with the screen underneath, using red crayon.
7. (S) Write the word on Red Word paper with the screen underneath, using red crayon. (S) Show the word to the teacher.
   (**NOTE:** The teacher should have students chunk the word if it has more than four letters.)
8. (T&S) Stand up, holding the Red Word in the nondominant hand. Armtap word while naming each letter. Then "underline" the word by sweeping left to right while stating the word, 3x. (**NOTE:** Left-handed students will place their left hand on their right wrist. They tap to their right shoulder. Underline from wrist to shoulder. Right-handed students place their right hand on their left shoulder. They tap to their left wrist. Underline shoulder to wrist.)
9. (T&S) Trace crayon bumps with the pointer finger while naming the letters, 3x.
10. (T&S) Place the screen over the paper and trace the word with the pointer finger while naming the letters, 3x.
11. (S) Turn paper over. With red crayon, write the word without the screen one time, and hold up the word for the teacher to check. (S) Write the word two more times.
12. (S) Write an original sentence in pencil and underline the Red Word with a red crayon. (**NOTE:** The sentence can also be dictated by the teacher while the student writes or dictated by the student while the teacher writes it.)

Review Ideas for Red Words:

- Sculpt the word using red Play-Doh or clay. Have students spell the word as they smash each letter.
- Print flashcards from IOG, and practice reading.
- Armtap the word to review.
- Cross-clap the word to review.
- Stomp the letters to review.
- Use a voice jar with popsicle sticks that have a different voice (e.g., robot, baby, cheerleader, monster) listed on each stick. Have a student draw a stick from the jar. The class armtaps the word using the voice selected. (Another option is to have an electronic spinning wheel with the voices listed on the wheel.)

Syllabication (Decoding)

Materials Needed:
IMSE Syllable Division Word Book, Pencil, Highlighter, Syllable Division Posters

Introduce on Wednesday with the new concept. Practice regularly.

1. Choose 6 or more words with the new concept from the *IMSE Syllable Division Word Book* for syllabication.

2. Remember to have students circle any known prefixes or suffixes. Then divide the rest of the word. For suffix -s, students will have to determine what sound -s is making based on the base word.

3. Use the steps on the Flip Chart and the Syllable Division Posters.

<table>
<tr><td>

Syllable Division Patterns

1. vc|cv

2. v|cv

3. vc|v

4. v|v

</td><td>

1. Closed Syllable (Cl)
short vowel sound

mag|net

ten|nis

tip|top

tom|tom

up|set

</td></tr>
<tr><td>

2. Open Syllable (O)
long vowel sound

ra|ven

I|rish

o|pen

e|ven

hu|mid

ju|do

</td><td>

3. Magic E (ME)

cup|cake

stam|pede

rep|tile

tad|pole

im|mune

Nep|tune

</td></tr>
</table>

- Below is a sample script for syllabication.

1. Find the first two vowels or vowel units. Underline and label with a "v."

2. Draw the bridge. Underline the consonants or consonant units and label with a "c."

3. Find the pattern and divide the word.

4. Is there another vowel (other than an "e" at the end)? If so, repeat steps 1-3. If not, go to step 5.

5. Label each syllable.

6. Read the word.

> **NOTE:** If there are two consonants in the middle of a word, split the word between the two consonants. (Exception: If the two consonants are a digraph [sh, ch, th] they cannot be split.) If there are three or more consonants, some letters go together as one consonant unit (look for known digraphs or blends).

Fluency, Vocabulary, and Comprehension

- Incorporate fluency into your literacy lessons daily/weekly (minimum 30 min/week) by using Rapid Word Charts, IMSE Decodable Readers, words and sentences, Acadience Reading K-6 or DIBELS 8th Edition, repeated reading, and other activities.

- Incorporate vocabulary into your literacy lessons daily/weekly (minimum 50 min/week) by choosing 3-5 appropriate tier two words (can pull from rich literature or decodable readers). Teach the words through explicit, direct instruction using student-friendly definitions, word webs, vocabulary charts, illustrations, and other activities.

- Incorporate oral language comprehension into your literacy lessons daily/weekly (approximately 100 min/week). Comprehension instruction should be explicit, direct instruction that includes teacher modeling, guided practice, and independent practice. Plan ahead to build on students' background knowledge, language structures, verbal reasoning, and literacy knowledge.

Extension Activity Ideas

- Give students 3 different colored index cards. On one card students write, "I hear /s/, and I write -s." On the second card, students write, "I hear /z/, but I write -s." On the last card, students write, "I hear /iz/, but I write -es." Make sure all students write the same information on each of the colors (e.g., if you choose pink for /s/, all students should have /s/ on the pink card).

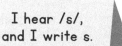 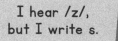 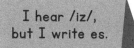

This drill can be implemented after the Three-Part Drill.
- (T) States a plural noun. *(cats)*
- (S) Repeat the word. *(cats)* Then hold up the correct card while stating the sentence on the card. *(I hear /s/, and I write -s.)*

OR

- (T) States a sentence with a plural noun. *(The bushes need to be trimmed.)*
- (S) Identify the noun. *(bushes)* Then hold up the correct card while stating the sentence. *(I hear /iz/, but I write -es.)*
- Visit IMSE's Orton-Gillingham's Pinterest page for more ideas.

Weekly Lesson Reminders

- Daily practice with writing the weekly Red Word(s)
- Kilpatrick's "One-Minute Activities" for daily phonological awareness practice
- Zgonc's phonological awareness activities
- Listen to rich literature to work on oral language comprehension.
- Target concept practice sheets from IMSE's practice books
- Practice test on Thursday and test on Friday

Vowel Team: ea and ee /ē/

(treat, bee)
Syllable Type 4 (VT)

Card Pack #48 Decodable Reader #46	
Object Ideas:	**Literature Ideas:**
beach theme, meal theme, sheep, bee, tree	▪ *Tar Beach* by Faith Ringgold ▪ *Dreamers* by Yuyi Morales ▪ *Freedom Summer* by Deborah Wiles ▪ *Juneteenth for Mazie* by Floyd Cooper ▪ *Sweet Clara and the Freedom Quilt* by Deborah Hopkinson ▪ *Mike Mulligan and His Steam Shovel* by Virginia Lee Burton ▪ *James and the Giant Peach* by Roald Dahl ▪ *How Are You Peeling?: Foods With Moods* by Saxton Freymann and Joost Elffers ▪ *The Giving Tree* by Shel Silverstein ▪ *Henry's Freedom Box: A True Story From the Underground Railroad* by Ellen Levine ▪ *Sheep in a Jeep* by Nancy Shaw ▪ *The Tiny Seed* by Eric Carle

Notes

▪ Use the Comprehensive Flip Chart for the steps on how to teach each part of IMSE's Lesson Plan.

▪ Use www.etymonline.com to help establish why a word might not follow the expected rules or patterns.

▪ A Vowel Team (VT) is two, three, or four letters that work together to produce a vowel sound. The vowel sound may be long, short, or a diphthong (gliding, monosyllabic speech sound).

▪ In the Auditory/Kinesthetic Drill, students will know 5 ways to spell the /ē/ sound: e, e-e, y, ea, ee.

- Use the Vowel Team Placement Chart to teach students where "ea" and "ee" typically live in a word. This can serve as the brainstorming activity for the new concept lesson. Exposure to words with each spelling and learning rules about the placement of these vowel teams within a word will help students know which spelling to use.

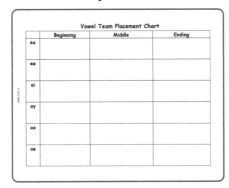

- Students now know multiple ways to spell long vowels (i.e., a single vowel in an open syllable, a Magic E combination, and vowel teams). Use the Multiple Spellings Practice Sheet to help students narrow down the options for the correct spelling based on the spelling rules they have learned.

- "Wet words" and "dinner words" with the /ē/ sound are often spelled with the "ea" spelling (e.g., beach, sea, tea, treat, meat).

(A color copy of each of these visuals is located in the Masters.)

- "Nature words" with the /ē/ sound are often spelled with the "ee" spelling (e.g., beetle, tree, bee). (A color copy of this visual is located in the Masters.)

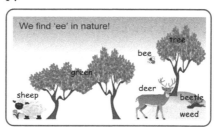

- "Ear" and "eer" (/eer/) are listed under "Other Combinations" in the "R-Controlled/ Bossy-R" column of the Phoneme/Grapheme Chart. These combinations can be taught with this lesson and highlighted on the chart, but they don't need to be written in the sand during the Auditory/Kinesthetic Drill. (This is why there is a diagonal slash in these boxes on the Phoneme/Grapheme Chart.) Exposing students to these combinations is important; the combinations can be tricky because the liquid /r/ skews the vowel sound a little (e.g., clear, steer).

Phonological Awareness:

Materials Needed:
tokens, sound boxes, one-minute activities, or Zgonc PA book

Use the PAST assessment to determine a starting point for instruction. Incorporate daily phonological awareness activities by using Zgonc's tiered activities and/or Kilpatrick's One-Minute Activities in *Equipped for Reading Success*.

Phonemic awareness warm-up: Use tokens (or letter tiles once concepts have been taught) and sound boxes to do a quick phonemic awareness activity that ties in with the new concept, if appropriate.

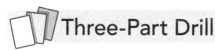

Three-Part Drill

Materials Needed:
review cards, sand, blending board, vowel tents or sticks

Do this at least 3x per week. Use the Flip Chart for steps. Include the new concept after Day 1.

1. Can do the hard/soft c/g drill after the Three-Part Drill
2. Can do the -ed tents activity after the Three-Part Drill (see *Extension Activity Ideas*)
3. Can do the -s/-es tents activity after the Three-Part Drill (see *Extension Activity Ideas*)

- Below is a sample script. Remember to use review concepts only.

> 1. **Visual:**
>   (T) Tell me the sounds you know for these letters.
>   (S) /m/, /l/, etc.

2. **Auditory/Kinesthetic:**
(T) You know three ways to spell this. (S) split trays. (T) Eyes on me.
Spell /k/. Repeat.
(S) /k/ c says /k/; k says /k/; ck says /k/

3. **Blending:**
(T) Tell me the sound for each letter as I point. Then blend the sounds together
to read the word or syllable. Give me a thumbs up if it is a real word.
(S) /mmm/ /ŏŏŏ/ /mmm/ *mom* (thumbs up)
Alternative:
(T) Watch me first. /mmm/ /ŏŏŏ/ /mmm/ *mom*
(T) Do it with me. (T&S) /mmm/ /ŏŏŏ/ /mmm/ *mom*
(T) Your turn. (S) /mmm/ /ŏŏŏ/ /mmm/ *mom* (thumbs up)

Optional: Once students have mastered their short vowel sounds, you can choose
another drill to take the place of the Vowel Intensive, such as:
  a. Use Card Pack Number 45 to do the hard/soft c/g drill.
  b. Do the -ed tents activity (see *Extension Activity Ideas*).
  c. Do the -s/-es tents activity (see *Extension Activity Ideas*).

Teaching a New Concept

Materials Needed:
concept card, screen, green crayon, object, sand, decodable readers, literature, P/G chart

Introduce on Monday, and practice daily.

1. (T) Shows the new concept card(s).
   a. (T) Tells students that we will learn about the first set of vowel teams. A vowel
   team is 2-4 letters that work together to make one vowel sound.
   b. (T) Tells students that ea says /ē/, and ee says /ē/. (S) Repeat (ea says /ē/, and ee says
   /ē/).
   c. (T) Tells students that they need to learn when to use each spelling.
   d. (T) Tells students there isn't a specific rule for these, but we can learn where "ea"
   and "ee" live in a word. We can also look at a few "tricks."

2. (T) Shows an object.
   a. (T) Allows students to manipulate the object and discuss prior knowledge.
   Reminds (S) that the object has the target sound(s) spelled with the target letter(s).

3. (S) Brainstorm to help establish a spelling rule, if applicable.
   a. Brainstorm words that have the target sound(s) or rule. The brainstorming can be
   a teacher-directed activity if students need extra support.

4. (T) Teaches Letter Formation, if needed. Can teach cursive writing.
   a. Use the steps for teaching letter formation on the Flip Chart.
   b. Use house paper to teach lowercase letters.
   c. Teach capital letters throughout the week. Capital letters go outside the house.

5. (T) Dictates target sound(s). (S) Practice all known spellings in the sand or other
   medium.

6. (T) Connects with literature.

    a. Read for language comprehension.

    b. Continue to work on language comprehension with rich literature throughout the week.

7. (S) Use decodable readers to practice the concepts learned.

    a. (S) Highlight words with the new concept. Read those words.

    b. (S) Highlight Red Words. Read those words.

    c. (S) Start reading the decodable reader.

    d. (S) Continue reading throughout the week.

    e. (S) Read a clean copy on Friday.

8. (T&S) Mark the Phoneme/Grapheme (P/G) chart by highlighting the target sound(s).

 ## Word Dictation

Materials Needed:
fingertapping hand, dictation paper, pencil

Practice daily. Use the Flip Chart to follow the steps for word dictation.

Day 1:	1. bee	2. cheap	3. read	4. fifteen	5. meantime
Day 2:	1. green	2. mean	3. peanut	4. sweet	5. indeed
Day 3:	1. beneath	2. dream	3. keep	4. chimpanzee	5. east
Days 4-5:	Review prior words. Optional additional words: beach, bead, beak, bean, beast, beat, beef, beet, bleach, bleed, breed, cheat, cheek, cheep, cheer, clean, cream, creep, deal, deep, deer, ear, eat, eel, feast, fee, feed, feel, feet, flea, gleam, glee, greet, heal, heat, heel, leaf, lean, leap, leek, meal, meat, meet, near, neat, need, peach, peek, peel, preach, queen, redeem, reef, reel, repeat, seat, see, seed, seek, seen, sheep, sheet, sleep, sneak, speech, steal, steep, tea, teach, team, teapot, tee, teen, teeth, tepee, three, weak, weed, week, wheat, wheel, year, yeast				

- Below is a sample script for one-syllable word dictation.

> 1. (T) States word: *boss*. Uses it in a sentence: My *boss* is kind and fair. (Pounds) *boss*. (T) Models fingertapping if needed: /b/ /ŏ/ /s/. (Pounds) *boss*.
>
> 2. (S) State while pounding: *boss*. (Fingertap) /b/ /ŏ/ /s/. (Pound) *boss*. Write the letters known for the sounds.
>
> 3. (T) When yours looks like mine, rewrite the word.
>
> 4. (S) Rewrite.
>
> 5. Repeat the process for each word.
>
> 6. (S) Read the list of words multiple times to build automaticity.

- Below is a sample script for multisyllabic word dictation.

1. (T) States word: *bathtub*. Uses it in a sentence: Clean out the *bathtub*. (Pounds each syllable) *bath/tub*.
2. (S) State while pounding each syllable: *bath/tub*.
3. (T) Models fingertapping, if needed. First syllable: (Pounds) *bath*. (Fingertaps) */b/ /ă/ /th/*. (Pounds) *bath*.
4. (S) State first syllable while pounding: *bath*. (Fingertap) */b/ /ă/ /th/*. (Pound) *bath*. Write the letters known for the sounds.
5. (T) Second syllable: (Pounds) *tub*. (Fingertaps) */t/ /ŭ/ /b/*. (Pounds) *tub*.
6. (S) State second syllable while pounding: *tub*. (Fingertap) */t/ /ŭ/ /b/*. (Pound) *tub*. Write the letters known for the sounds.
7. (T) When yours looks like mine, rewrite the word.
8. (S) Rewrite.
9. Repeat the process for each word.
10. (S) Read the list of words multiple times to build automaticity.

Sentence Dictation

Red Words are underlined. Students can fingertap the green words. Use the Flip Chart to follow the steps for sentence dictation.

1. We ate the meal at the beach.
2. Take a peek at that green eel!
3. Jean will treat me to the lean meat.
4. The deer will feed by the sheep.
5. She will wash the teacup.
6. The teen drank some sweet green tea.
7. The queen gave a speech on the beach.
8. The beak on the chick is on the mend.
9. At my meal, I had a peach and some meat.
10. I need wheat and yeast to bake.
11. Pull the flea from the sheep.
12. She ate the peach and drank the tea.
13. She did not eat, so she felt weak.
14. Today the reef can be seen from the beach.
15. I will teach him to read.

- Below is a sample script for sentence dictation.

> 1. (T): Listen to the sentence. *The bedbug bit Pam.*
> 2. (T): Listen while I pound the syllables. *The bedbug bit Pam.* (Make sure to pound *bedbug* twice because it has two syllables.)
> 3. (T): Pound it with me. (T&S): *The bedbug bit Pam.*
> 4. (T): You pound the sentence. (S): *The bedbug bit Pam.*
> 5. (T): Watch me as I point to the lines while stating the sentence. (Tap the line for *bedbug* twice because it has two syllables.) *The bedbug bit Pam.*
> 6. (T): You point to the lines while stating the sentence.
> 7. (S): *The bedbug bit Pam.*
> 8. (T): Now write the sentence. Fingertap if needed.

- Below is a sample script to check CUPS.*

> 1. (T): C stands for capitalization. Did you remember a capital letter at the beginning of your sentence? Did you remember a capital letter for *Pam*? It is a name. If you forgot, fix it. If you remembered, put a tally mark above each capital letter. Add a mark in the box for C.
> 2. (T): U stands for understanding. Is your sentence neat? Reread it to yourself. Does it make sense? Could someone else understand it? If not, fix it. Add a mark in the box for U.
> 3. (T): P stands for punctuation. Did you remember a period at the end? If not, fix it. If you remembered, put a tally mark above the period. Add a mark in the box for P.
> 4. (T): S stands for spelling. Did you spell your words correctly? Check them. Now, check yours with mine (shows the teacher's copy). Fix any words you spelled incorrectly. Put a tally mark above the words you spelled correctly. Add a mark in the box for S.
> 5. (T): Rewrite your sentence with all of the corrections.
> 6. (T): Check for CUPS again. Put another mark in the boxes.
> 7. (T): Let's read the sentences.
> 8. (S) Read the sentences for fluency and automaticity.
>
> ***Please note:*** Once students understand how to use CUPS, transition to letting them check their sentence independently before showing the teacher's copy.

Weekly Red Words

Materials Needed:
screen, red crayon, red word paper

Introduce on Tuesday, and practice daily. Use the Flip Chart for steps.

New:	Review:	New Read-Only:	Review Read-Only:
pull, wash	were, does, some, good, there, done, her, under, down, onto, people, saw, both, should, could, would, over, love, live, out, day, too, eye, all, again, boy, girl, sign, your, which, look, also, use, today, yesterday, first, around, going, walk, say, their, how, once, another		our, oven, park, play, way, chair, center

Steps for Teaching a New Red Word:

1. (T) States the word. (*pull*)
2. (T&S) Use tokens to determine how many sounds are in the word. (/p/ /o͞o/ /l/; 3)
3. (T&S) Discuss how we would expect to spell each sound as the teacher writes the grapheme(s) correctly. Identify what is unexpected or irregular about the spelling of the word. It could also be expected, but the concept hasn't been taught yet.
4. (T&S) Discuss the etymology of the word, if appropriate (lexical words). Visit www.etymonline.com for more information on the word.
5. (T) Defines the word, and writes a sentence using the word.
6. (T) Writes the word on Red Word paper with the screen underneath, using red crayon.
7. (S) Write the word on Red Word paper with the screen underneath, using red crayon. (S) Show the word to the teacher.
   (**NOTE:** The teacher should have students chunk the word if it has more than four letters.)

8. (T&S) Stand up, holding the Red Word in the nondominant hand. Armtap word while naming each letter. Then "underline" the word by sweeping left to right while stating the word, 3x. (**NOTE:** Left-handed students will place their left hand on their right wrist. They tap to their right shoulder. Underline from wrist to shoulder. Right-handed students place their right hand on their left shoulder. They tap to their left wrist. Underline shoulder to wrist.)

9. (T&S) Trace crayon bumps with the pointer finger while naming the letters, 3x.

10. (T&S) Place the screen over the paper and trace the word with the pointer finger while naming the letters, 3x.

11. (S) Turn paper over. With red crayon, write the word without the screen one time, and hold up the word for the teacher to check. (S) Write the word two more times.

12. (S) Write an original sentence in pencil and underline the Red Word with a red crayon. (**NOTE:** The sentence can also be dictated by the teacher while the student writes or dictated by the student while the teacher writes it.)

13. Repeat the steps for *wash*. (/w/ /ŏ/ /sh/; 3) (**NOTE:** There may be some dialect differences depending on where you live. This could be /w/ /aw/ /sh/.)

Review Ideas for Red Words:

- Sculpt the word using red Play-Doh or clay. Have students spell the word as they smash each letter.
- Print flashcards from IOG, and practice reading.
- Armtap the word to review.
- Cross-clap the word to review.
- Stomp the letters to review.
- Use a voice jar with popsicle sticks that have a different voice (e.g., robot, baby, cheerleader, monster) listed on each stick. Have a student draw a stick from the jar. The class armtaps the word using the voice selected. (Another option is to have an electronic spinning wheel with the voices listed on the wheel.)

 ## Syllabication (Decoding)

Materials Needed:
IMSE Syllable Division Word Book, Pencil, Highlighter, Syllable Division Posters

Introduce on Wednesday with the new concept. Practice regularly.

1. Choose 6 or more words with the new concept from the *IMSE Syllable Division Word Book* for syllabication.

2. Remember to have students circle any known prefixes or suffixes. Then divide the rest of the word.

3. Introduce the fourth syllable type: Vowel Team.

4. Use the steps on the Flip Chart and the Syllable Division Posters.

Syllable Division Patterns	1. Closed Syllable (Cl) short vowel sound	2. Open Syllable (O) long vowel sound
1. vc|cv	mag|net	ra|ven
2. v|cv	ten|nis	I|rish
3. vc|v	tip|top	o|pen
4. v|v	tom|tom	e|ven
	up|set	hu|mid
		ju|do

3. Magic E (ME)	4. Vowel Teams (VT)	
cup|cake	ea	leaf|let
	ee	sea|weed
stam|pede	ai	sail|boat
	ay	play|time
rep|tile	oa	oat|meal
	oe	tip|toe
tad|pole	oi	tin|foil
	oy	en|joy
im|mune	ou	out|line
	ow	pow|er
Nep|tune	igh	high|way
	au	au|dit
	aw	jig|saw
	o͞o	car|toon
	o͝o	book|case

- Below is a sample script for syllabication.

1. Find the first two vowels or vowel units. Underline and label with a "v."

2. Draw the bridge. Underline the consonants or consonant units and label with a "c."

3. Find the pattern and divide the word.

4. Is there another vowel (other than an "e" at the end)? If so, repeat steps 1-3. If not, go to step 5.

5. Label each syllable.

6. Read the word.

NOTE: If there are two consonants in the middle of a word, split the word between the two consonants. (Exception: If the two consonants are a digraph [sh, ch, th] they cannot be split.) If there are three or more consonants, some letters go together as one consonant unit (look for known digraphs or blends).

Fluency, Vocabulary, and Comprehension

- Incorporate fluency into your literacy lessons daily/weekly (minimum 30 min/week) by using Rapid Word Charts, IMSE Decodable Readers, words and sentences, Acadience Reading K-6 or DIBELS 8th Edition, repeated reading, and other activities.

- Incorporate vocabulary into your literacy lessons daily/weekly (minimum 50 min/week) by choosing 3-5 appropriate tier two words (can pull from rich literature or decodable readers). Teach the words through explicit, direct instruction using student-friendly definitions, word webs, vocabulary charts, illustrations, and other activities.

- Incorporate oral language comprehension into your literacy lessons daily/weekly (approximately 100 min/week). Comprehension instruction should be explicit, direct instruction that includes teacher modeling, guided practice, and independent practice. Plan ahead to build on students' background knowledge, language structures, verbal reasoning, and literacy knowledge.

Extension Activity Ideas

- Continue to add to the vowel team placement chart. Students can use this in an interactive notebook.
- Teachers could start to teach homophones with ea/ee spellings (e.g., sea/see, flea/flee).
- Visit IMSE's Orton-Gillingham's Pinterest page for more ideas.

Weekly Lesson Reminders

- Daily practice with writing the weekly Red Word(s)
- Kilpatrick's "One-Minute Activities" for daily phonological awareness practice
- Zgonc's phonological awareness activities
- Listen to rich literature to work on oral language comprehension.
- Target concept practice sheets from IMSE's practice books
- Practice test on Thursday and test on Friday

Notes:

_____

_____

_____

_____

_____

_____

_____

_____

_____

_____

_____

_____

_____

_____

_____

_____

_____

_____

Vowel Team: ai and ay /ā/

(sail, clay)

Card Pack #49 Decodable Reader #47	
Object Ideas:	**Literature Ideas:**
sail, clay, rain, day, rainbow, snail, crayon	<ul><li>*Hair Love* by Matthew A. Cherry</li><li>*Bringing the Rain to Kapiti Plain* by Verna Aardema</li><li>*I Love My Hair!* by Natasha Anastasia Tarpley</li><li>*The Snowy Day* by Ezra Jack Keats</li><li>*Saturday* by Oge Mora</li><li>*The Rainbow Fish* by Marcus Pfister</li><li>*Oh Say Can You Say?* by Dr. Seuss</li></ul>

Notes

- Use the Comprehensive Flip Chart for the steps on how to teach each part of IMSE's Lesson Plan.
- Use www.etymonline.com to help establish why a word might not follow the expected rules or patterns.
- In the Auditory/Kinesthetic Drill, students will know 4 ways to spell the /ā/ sound: a, a-e, ai, ay.
- Use the Vowel Team Placement Chart to teach students where "ai" and "ay" typically live in a word. This can serve as the brainstorming activity for the new concept lesson. Exposure to words with each spelling and learning rules about the placement of these vowel teams within a word will help students know which spelling to use.

Vowel Team Placement Chart

	Beginning	Middle	Ending
ea			
ee			
ai			
ay			
oa			
oe			

- "Ai" typically comes at the beginning or in the middle of a word or syllable (e.g., ail, sail).

- "Ay" typically comes at the end of a word or syllable (e.g., bay, crayon). (A color copy of this visual is located in the Masters.)

A tail comes at the end of a dog just like the ay comes at the end of a word or syllable.

- Students now know multiple ways to spell long vowels (i.e., a single vowel in an open syllable, a Magic E combination, and vowel teams). Use the Multiple Spellings Practice Sheet to help students narrow down the options for the correct spelling based on the spelling rules they have learned.

- "Air" is listed under "Other Combinations" in the "R-Controlled/Bossy-R" column of the Phoneme/Grapheme Chart. This combination can be taught with this lesson and highlighted on the chart, but it doesn't need to be written in the sand during the Auditory/Kinesthetic Drill. (This is why there is a diagonal slash in this box on the Phoneme/Grapheme Chart.) Exposing students to this combination is important; the combination can be tricky because the liquid /r/ skews the vowel sound a little (e.g., pair, stair).

 ## Phonological Awareness:

Materials Needed:
tokens, sound boxes, one-minute activities, or Zgonc PA book

Use the PAST assessment to determine a starting point for instruction. Incorporate daily phonological awareness activities by using Zgonc's tiered activities and/or Kilpatrick's One-Minute Activities in *Equipped for Reading Success*.

Phonemic awareness warm-up: Use tokens (or letter tiles once concepts have been taught) and sound boxes to do a quick phonemic awareness activity that ties in with the new concept, if appropriate.

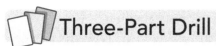

Three-Part Drill

Materials Needed:
review cards, sand, blending board, vowel tents or sticks

Do this at least 3x per week. Use the Flip Chart for steps. Include the new concept after Day 1.

1. Can do the hard/soft c/g drill after the Three-Part Drill
2. Can do the -ed tents activity after the Three-Part Drill (see *Extension Activity Ideas*)
3. Can do the -s/-es tents activity after the Three-Part Drill (see *Extension Activity Ideas*)

▪ Below is a sample script. Remember to use review concepts only.

---

1. **Visual:**
   (T) Tell me the sounds you know for these letters.
   (S) /m/, /l/, etc.
2. **Auditory/Kinesthetic:**
   (T) You know three ways to spell this. (S) split trays. (T) Eyes on me.
   Spell /k/. Repeat.
   (S) /k/ c says /k/; k says /k/; ck says /k/
3. **Blending:**
   (T) Tell me the sound for each letter as I point. Then blend the sounds together to read the word or syllable. Give me a thumbs up if it is a real word.
   (S) /mmm/ /ŏŏŏ/ /mmm/ *mom* (thumbs up)
   Alternative:
   (T) Watch me first. /mmm/ /ŏŏŏ/ /mmm/ *mom*
   (T) Do it with me. (T&S) /mmm/ /ŏŏŏ/ /mmm/ *mom*
   (T) Your turn. (S) /mmm/ /ŏŏŏ/ /mmm/ *mom* (thumbs up)

Optional: Once students have mastered their short vowel sounds, you can choose another drill to take the place of the Vowel Intensive, such as:

   a. Use Card Pack Number 45 to do the hard/soft c/g drill.
   b. Do the -ed tents activity (see *Extension Activity Ideas*).
   c. Do the -s/-es tents activity (see *Extension Activity Ideas*).

Teaching a New Concept

Materials Needed:
concept card, screen, green crayon, object, sand, decodable readers, literature, P/G chart

Introduce on Monday, and practice daily.

1. (T) Shows the new concept card(s).
   a. (T) Tells students that we will learn another vowel team. Reminds students that a vowel team is 2-4 letters that work together to make one vowel sound.
   b. (T) Tells students that ai says /ā/, and ay says /ā/. (S) Repeat (ai says /ā/, and ay says /ā/).

    c. (T) Tells students that they need to learn when to use each spelling.

    d. (T) Tells students the guidelines for when to use "ai" or "ay." "Ai" typically comes at the beginning or in the middle of a word or syllable. "Ay" typically comes at the end of a word or syllable.

2. (T) Shows an object.

    a. (T) Allows students to manipulate the object and discuss prior knowledge. Reminds (S) that the object has the target sound(s) spelled with the target letter(s).

3. (S) Brainstorm to help establish a spelling rule, if applicable.

    a. Brainstorm words that have the target sound(s) or rule. The brainstorming can be a teacher-directed activity if students need extra support.

4. (T) Teaches Letter Formation, if needed. Can teach cursive writing.

    a. Use the steps for teaching letter formation on the Flip Chart.

    b. Use house paper to teach lowercase letters.

    c. Teach capital letters throughout the week. Capital letters go outside the house.

5. (T) Dictates target sound(s). (S) Practice all known spellings in the sand or other medium.

6. (T) Connects with literature.

    a. Read for language comprehension.

    b. Continue to work on language comprehension with rich literature throughout the week.

7. (S) Use decodable readers to practice the concepts learned.

    a. (S) Highlight words with the new concept. Read those words.

    b. (S) Highlight Red Words. Read those words.

    c. (S) Start reading the decodable reader.

    d. (S) Continue reading throughout the week.

    e. (S) Read a clean copy on Friday.

8. (T&S) Mark the Phoneme/Grapheme (P/G) chart by highlighting the target sound(s).

 ## Word Dictation

Materials Needed:
fingertapping hand, dictation paper, pencil

Practice daily. Use the Flip Chart to follow the steps for word dictation.

Day 1:	1. train	2. day	3. chain	4. explain	5. subway
Day 2:	1. stay	2. Friday	3. main	4. detail	5. play
Day 3:	1. stain	2. brain	3. may	4. hangnail	5. payment
Days 4-5:	Review prior words. Optional additional words: aid, ail, aim, air, bail, bait, bay, braid, claim, clay, crayon, delay, domain, drain, fail, faith, gain, gait, grain, gray, hail, hay, jail, Jay, laid, lay, maid, mail, maintain, nay, pail, paint, pay, plain, quail, rain, ray, sail, say, snail, sustain, sway, taint, trail, tray, vain, wait, way, yay				

■ Below is a sample script for one-syllable word dictation.

1. (T) States word: *boss*. Uses it in a sentence: My *boss* is kind and fair. (Pounds) *boss*. (T) Models fingertapping if needed: /b/ /ŏ/ /s/. (Pounds) *boss*.

2. (S) State while pounding: *boss*. (Fingertap) /b/ /ŏ/ /s/. (Pound) *boss*. Write the letters known for the sounds.

3. (T) When yours looks like mine, rewrite the word.

4. (S) Rewrite.

5. Repeat the process for each word.

6. (S) Read the list of words multiple times to build automaticity.

■ Below is a sample script for multisyllabic word dictation.

1. (T) States word: *bathtub*. Uses it in a sentence: Clean out the *bathtub*. (Pounds each syllable) *bath/tub*.

2. (S) State while pounding each syllable: *bath/tub*.

3. (T) Models fingertapping, if needed. First syllable: (Pounds) *bath*. (Fingertaps) /b/ /ă/ /th/. (Pounds) *bath*.

4. (S) State first syllable while pounding: *bath*. (Fingertap) /b/ /ă/ /th/. (Pound) *bath*. Write the letters known for the sounds.

5. (T) Second syllable: (Pounds) *tub*. (Fingertaps) /t/ /ŭ/ /b/. (Pounds) *tub*.

6. (S) State second syllable while pounding: *tub*. (Fingertap) /t/ /ŭ/ /b/. (Pound) *tub*. Write the letters known for the sounds.

7. (T) When yours looks like mine, rewrite the word.

8. (S) Rewrite.

9. Repeat the process for each word.

10. (S) Read the list of words multiple times to build automaticity.

Sentence Dictation

Red Words are underlined. Students can fingertap the green words. Use the Flip Chart to follow the steps for sentence dictation.

1. The green paint was in the pail.

2. We play with clay on a tray.

3. When will we go to the bay again?

4. Did he explain the test?

5. We paid the man to maintain the drain.

6. The sky was gray.

7. I need to maintain the hangnail.

8. The hay was dry.

9. Can you explain the details to everyone?

10. Jay will pay <u>the</u> maid.

11. Hail came <u>down</u> like rain.

12. <u>Every</u> train will gain speed on <u>the</u> track.

- Below is a sample script for sentence dictation.

  1. (T): Listen to the sentence. *The bedbug bit Pam.*
  2. (T): Listen while I pound the syllables. *The bedbug bit Pam.* (Make sure to pound *bedbug* twice because it has two syllables.)
  3. (T): Pound it with me. (T&S): *The bedbug bit Pam.*
  4. (T): You pound the sentence. (S): *The bedbug bit Pam.*
  5. (T): Watch me as I point to the lines while stating the sentence. (Tap the line for *bedbug* twice because it has two syllables.) *The bedbug bit Pam.*
  6. (T): You point to the lines while stating the sentence.
  7. (S): *The bedbug bit Pam.*
  8. (T): Now write the sentence. Fingertap if needed.

- Below is a sample script to check CUPS.*

  1. (T): C stands for capitalization. Did you remember a capital letter at the beginning of your sentence? Did you remember a capital letter for *Pam*? It is a name. If you forgot, fix it. If you remembered, put a tally mark above each capital letter. Add a mark in the box for C.
  2. (T): U stands for understanding. Is your sentence neat? Reread it to yourself. Does it make sense? Could someone else understand it? If not, fix it. Add a mark in the box for U.
  3. (T): P stands for punctuation. Did you remember a period at the end? If not, fix it. If you remembered, put a tally mark above the period. Add a mark in the box for P.
  4. (T): S stands for spelling. Did you spell your words correctly? Check them. Now, check yours with mine (shows the teacher's copy). Fix any words you spelled incorrectly. Put a tally mark above the words you spelled correctly. Add a mark in the box for S.
  5. (T): Rewrite your sentence with all of the corrections.
  6. (T): Check for CUPS again. Put another mark in the boxes.
  7. (T): Let's read the sentences.
  8. (S) Read the sentences for fluency and automaticity.

  ***Please note:** Once students understand how to use CUPS, transition to letting them check their sentence independently before showing the teacher's copy.

Weekly Red Words

Materials Needed:
screen, red crayon, red word paper

Introduce on Tuesday, and practice daily. Use the Flip Chart for steps.

New:	Review:	New Read-Only:	Review Read-Only:
every, everyone	were, does, some, good, there, done, her, under, down, onto, people, saw, both, should, could, would, over, love, live, out, too, eye, all, again, boy, girl, sign, your, which, look, also, use, today, yesterday, first, around, going, walk, their, how, once, another, pull, wash	school, tractor	our, oven, park, chair, center

Steps for Teaching a New Red Word:

1. (T) States the word. (*every*)
2. (T&S) Use tokens to determine how many sounds are in the word. (/ĕ/ /v/ /r/ /ē/; 4)
3. (T&S) Discuss how we would expect to spell each sound as the teacher writes the grapheme(s) correctly. Identify what is unexpected or irregular about the spelling of the word. It could also be expected, but the concept hasn't been taught yet.
4. (T&S) Discuss the etymology of the word, if appropriate (lexical words). Visit www.etymonline.com for more information on the word.
5. (T) Defines the word, and writes a sentence using the word.
6. (T) Writes the word on Red Word paper with the screen underneath, using red crayon.
7. (S) Write the word on Red Word paper with the screen underneath, using red crayon. (S) Show the word to the teacher.
(**NOTE:** The teacher should have students chunk the word if it has more than four letters.)

8. (T&S) Stand up, holding the Red Word in the nondominant hand. Armtap word while naming each letter. Then "underline" the word by sweeping left to right while stating the word, 3x. (**NOTE:** Left-handed students will place their left hand on their right wrist. They tap to their right shoulder. Underline from wrist to shoulder. Right-handed students place their right hand on their left shoulder. They tap to their left wrist. Underline shoulder to wrist.)

9. (T&S) Trace crayon bumps with the pointer finger while naming the letters, 3x.

10. (T&S) Place the screen over the paper and trace the word with the pointer finger while naming the letters, 3x.

11. (S) Turn paper over. With red crayon, write the word without the screen one time, and hold up the word for the teacher to check. (S) Write the word two more times.

12. (S) Write an original sentence in pencil and underline the Red Word with a red crayon. (**NOTE:** The sentence can also be dictated by the teacher while the student writes or dictated by the student while the teacher writes it.)

13. Repeat the steps for *everyone*. (/ĕ/ /v/ /r/ /ē/ /w/ /ŭ/ /n/; 7)

Review Ideas for Red Words:

- Sculpt the word using red Play-Doh or clay. Have students spell the word as they smash each letter.
- Print flashcards from IOG, and practice reading.
- Armtap the word to review.
- Cross-clap the word to review.
- Stomp the letters to review.
- Use a voice jar with popsicle sticks that have a different voice (e.g., robot, baby, cheerleader, monster) listed on each stick. Have a student draw a stick from the jar. The class armtaps the word using the voice selected. (Another option is to have an electronic spinning wheel with the voices listed on the wheel.)

Syllabication (Decoding)

Materials Needed:
IMSE Syllable Division Word Book, Pencil, Highlighter, Syllable Division Posters

Introduce on Wednesday with the new concept. Practice regularly.

1. Choose 6 or more words with the new concept from the *IMSE Syllable Division Word Book* for syllabication.

2. Remember to have students circle any known prefixes or suffixes. Then divide the rest of the word.

3. Use the steps on the Flip Chart and the Syllable Division Posters.

Syllable Division Patterns

1. vc|cv
2. v|cv
3. vc|v
4. v|v

1. Closed Syllable (Cl)
short vowel sound

mag|net

ten|nis

tip|top

tom|tom

up|set

2. Open Syllable (O)
long vowel sound

ra|ven

I|rish

o|pen

e|ven

hu|mid

ju|do

3. Magic E (ME)

cup|cake

stam|pede

rep|tile

tad|pole

im|mune

Nep|tune

4. Vowel Teams (VT)

ea	leaf|let
ee	sea|weed
ai	sail|boat
ay	play|time
oa	oat|meal
oe	tip|toe
oi	tin|foil
oy	en|joy
ou	out|line
ow	pow|er
igh	high|way
au	au|dit
aw	jig|saw
o͞o	car|toon
o͝o	book|case

- Below is a sample script for syllabication.

1. Find the first two vowels or vowel units. Underline and label with a "v."
2. Draw the bridge. Underline the consonants or consonant units and label with a "c."
3. Find the pattern and divide the word.
4. Is there another vowel (other than an "e" at the end)? If so, repeat steps 1-3. If not, go to step 5.
5. Label each syllable.
6. Read the word.

NOTE: If there are two consonants in the middle of a word, split the word between the two consonants. (Exception: If the two consonants are a digraph [sh, ch, th] they cannot be split.) If there are three or more consonants, some letters go together as one consonant unit (look for known digraphs or blends).

Fluency, Vocabulary, and Comprehension

- Incorporate fluency into your literacy lessons daily/weekly (minimum 30 min/week) by using Rapid Word Charts, IMSE Decodable Readers, words and sentences, Acadience Reading K-6 or DIBELS 8th Edition, repeated reading, and other activities.

- Incorporate vocabulary into your literacy lessons daily/weekly (minimum 50 min/week) by choosing 3-5 appropriate tier two words (can pull from rich literature or decodable readers). Teach the words through explicit, direct instruction using student-friendly definitions, word webs, vocabulary charts, illustrations, and other activities.

- Incorporate oral language comprehension into your literacy lessons daily/weekly (approximately 100 min/week). Comprehension instruction should be explicit, direct instruction that includes teacher modeling, guided practice, and independent practice. Plan ahead to build on students' background knowledge, language structures, verbal reasoning, and literacy knowledge.

Extension Activity Ideas

- Continue to add to the vowel team placement chart. Students can use this in an interactive notebook.
- Visit IMSE's Orton-Gillingham's Pinterest page for more ideas.

Weekly Lesson Reminders

- Daily practice with writing the weekly Red Word(s)
- Kilpatrick's "One-Minute Activities" for daily phonological awareness practice
- Zgonc's phonological awareness activities
- Listen to rich literature to work on oral language comprehension.
- Target concept practice sheets from IMSE's practice books
- Practice test on Thursday and test on Friday

Vowel Team: oa and oe /ō/

(boat/toe)

Card Pack #50 Decodable Reader #48	
Object Ideas:	**Literature Ideas:**
boat, toe, toenail, goat, cloak, soap, toad, doe	▪ *Martina the Beautiful Cockroach: A Cuban Folktale* by Carmen Agra Deedy ▪ *Rainbow Joe and Me* by Maria Diaz Strom ▪ Frog and Toad series by Arnold Lobel ▪ *The Three Billy Goats Gruff* by Peter Asbjornsen and Jorgen Moe ▪ *Charlie Needs a Cloak* by Tomie de Paola

 ## Notes

- Use the Comprehensive Flip Chart for the steps on how to teach each part of IMSE's Lesson Plan.
- Use www.etymonline.com to help establish why a word might not follow the expected rules or patterns.
- In the Auditory/Kinesthetic Drill, students will know 4 ways to spell the /ō/ sound: o, o-e, oa, oe.
- Use the Vowel Team Placement Chart to teach students where "oa" and "oe" typically live in a word. This can serve as the brainstorming activity for the new concept lesson. Exposure to words with each spelling and learning rules about the placement of these vowel teams within a word will help students know which spelling to use.

Vowel Team Placement Chart			
	Beginning	Middle	Ending
ea			
ee			
ai			
ay			
oa			
oe			

- "Oa" typically comes at the beginning or in the middle of a word or syllable (e.g., oat, boat).

- "Oe" typically comes at the end of a word or syllable (e.g., Joe, toenail). (A color copy of this visual is located in the Masters.)

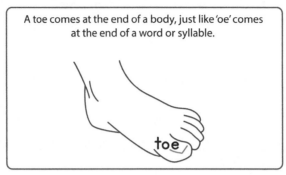

- Students now know multiple ways to spell long vowels (i.e., a single vowel in an open syllable, a Magic E combination, and vowel teams). Use the Multiple Spellings Practice Sheet to help students narrow down the options for the correct spelling based on the spelling rules they have learned.

- "Oar" is listed under the "R-Controlled/Bossy-R" column of the Phoneme/Grapheme Chart (next to /or/). This combination can be taught with this lesson and highlighted on the chart, but it doesn't need to be written in the sand during the Auditory/Kinesthetic Drill. (This is why there is a diagonal slash in this box on the Phoneme/Grapheme Chart.) Exposing students to this combination is important; the combination can be tricky because the liquid /r/ skews the vowel sound a little (e.g., boar, soar).

 ## Phonological Awareness:

Materials Needed:
tokens, sound boxes, one-minute activities, or Zgonc PA book

Use the PAST assessment to determine a starting point for instruction. Incorporate daily phonological awareness activities by using Zgonc's tiered activities and/or Kilpatrick's One-Minute Activities in *Equipped for Reading Success*.

Phonemic awareness warm-up: Use tokens (or letter tiles once concepts have been taught) and sound boxes to do a quick phonemic awareness activity that ties in with the new concept, if appropriate.

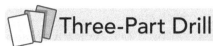

Three-Part Drill

Materials Needed:
review cards, sand, blending board, vowel tents or sticks

Do this at least 3x per week. Use the Flip Chart for steps. Include the new concept after Day 1.

1. Can do the hard/soft c/g drill after the Three-Part Drill
2. Can do the -ed tents activity after the Three-Part Drill (see *Extension Activity Ideas*)
3. Can do the -s/-es tents activity after the Three-Part Drill (see *Extension Activity Ideas*)

- Below is a sample script. Remember to use review concepts only.

> 1. **Visual:**
>   (T) Tell me the sounds you know for these letters.
>   (S) /m/, /l/, etc.
> 2. **Auditory/Kinesthetic:**
>   (T) You know three ways to spell this. (S) split trays. (T) Eyes on me.
>   Spell /k/. Repeat.
>   (S) /k/ c says /k/; k says /k/; ck says /k/
> 3. **Blending:**
>   (T) Tell me the sound for each letter as I point. Then blend the sounds together to read the word or syllable. Give me a thumbs up if it is a real word.
>   (S) /mmm/ /ŏŏŏ/ /mmm/ *mom* (thumbs up)
>   *Alternative:*
>   (T) Watch me first. /mmm/ /ŏŏŏ/ /mmm/ *mom*
>   (T) Do it with me. (T&S) /mmm/ /ŏŏŏ/ /mmm/ *mom*
>   (T) Your turn. (S) /mmm/ /ŏŏŏ/ /mmm/ *mom* (thumbs up)
>
> **Optional:** Once students have mastered their short vowel sounds, you can choose another drill to take the place of the Vowel Intensive, such as:
>   a. Use Card Pack Number 45 to do the hard/soft c/g drill.
>   b. Do the -ed tents activity (see *Extension Activity Ideas*).
>   c. Do the -s/-es tents activity (see *Extension Activity Ideas*).

Teaching a New Concept

Materials Needed:
concept card, screen, green crayon, object, sand, decodable readers, literature, P/G chart

Introduce on Monday, and practice daily.

1. (T) Shows the new concept card(s).
   a. (T) Tells students that we will learn another vowel team. Reminds students that a vowel team is 2-4 letters that work together to make one vowel sound.
   b. (T) Tells students that oa says /ō/, and oe says /ō/. (S) Repeat (oa says /ō/, and oe says /ō/).

  c. (T) Tells students that they need to learn when to use each spelling.

  d. (T) Tells students the guidelines for when to use "oa" or "oe." "Oa" typically comes at the beginning or in the middle of a word or syllable. "Oe" typically comes at the end of a word or syllable.

2. (T) Shows an object.

  a. (T) Allows students to manipulate the object and discuss prior knowledge. Reminds (S) that the object has the target sound(s) spelled with the target letter(s).

3. (S) Brainstorm to help establish a spelling rule, if applicable.

  a. Brainstorm words that have the target sound(s) or rule. The brainstorming can be a teacher-directed activity if students need extra support.

4. (T) Teaches Letter Formation, if needed. Can teach cursive writing.

  a. Use the steps for teaching letter formation on the Flip Chart.

  b. Use house paper to teach lowercase letters.

  c. Teach capital letters throughout the week. Capital letters go outside the house.

5. (T) Dictates target sound(s). (S) Practice all known spellings in the sand or other medium.

6. (T) Connects with literature.

  a. Read for language comprehension.

  b. Continue to work on language comprehension with rich literature throughout the week.

7. (S) Use decodable readers to practice the concepts learned.

  a. (S) Highlight words with the new concept. Read those words.

  b. (S) Highlight Red Words. Read those words.

  c. (S) Start reading the decodable reader.

  d. (S) Continue reading throughout the week.

  e. (S) Read a clean copy on Friday.

8. (T&S) Mark the Phoneme/Grapheme (P/G) chart by highlighting the target sound(s).

Word Dictation

Materials Needed:
fingertapping hand, dictation paper, pencil

Practice daily. Use the Flip Chart to follow the steps for word dictation.

Day 1:	1. float	2. coach	3. doe	4. tiptoe	5. steamboat
Day 2:	1. toe	2. roast	3. oatmeal	4. goat	5. aloe
Day 3:	1. toast	2. coat	3. toenail	4. coastline	5. Joe
Days 4-5:	Review prior words. Optional additional words: boast, boat, coal, coast, coat, crossroad, foam, foe, goal, hoe, load, loaf, loam, oak, oat, oath, oboe, pekoe, poach, roach, road, soak, soap, soapbox, toad, toadstone, woe				

■ Below is a sample script for one-syllable word dictation.

> 1. (T) States word: *boss*. Uses it in a sentence: My *boss* is kind and fair. (Pounds) *boss*. (T) Models fingertapping if needed: /b/ /ŏ/ /s/. (Pounds) *boss*.
> 2. (S) State while pounding: *boss*. (Fingertap) /b/ /ŏ/ /s/. (Pound) *boss*. Write the letters known for the sounds.
> 3. (T) When yours looks like mine, rewrite the word.
> 4. (S) Rewrite.
> 5. Repeat the process for each word.
> 6. (S) Read the list of words multiple times to build automaticity.

■ Below is a sample script for multisyllabic word dictation.

> 1. (T) States word: *bathtub*. Uses it in a sentence: Clean out the *bathtub*. (Pounds each syllable) *bath/tub*.
> 2. (S) State while pounding each syllable: *bath/tub*.
> 3. (T) Models fingertapping, if needed. First syllable: (Pounds) *bath*. (Fingertaps) /b/ /ă/ /th/. (Pounds) *bath*.
> 4. (S) State first syllable while pounding: *bath*. (Fingertap) /b/ /ă/ /th/. (Pound) *bath*. Write the letters known for the sounds.
> 5. (T) Second syllable: (Pounds) *tub*. (Fingertaps) /t/ /ŭ/ /b/. (Pounds) *tub*.
> 6. (S) State second syllable while pounding: *tub*. (Fingertap) /t/ /ŭ/ /b/. (Pound) *tub*. Write the letters known for the sounds.
> 7. (T) When yours looks like mine, rewrite the word.
> 8. (S) Rewrite.
> 9. Repeat the process for each word.
> 10. (S) Read the list of words multiple times to build automaticity.

 ## Sentence Dictation

Red Words are underlined. Students can fingertap the green words. Use the Flip Chart to follow the steps for sentence dictation.

1. Can you eat oatmeal?
2. Joe had a big nail on his toe.
3. The steamboat is not in the shed.
4. Jay drove up the coastline last week.
5. I knew the doe was on the road.
6. Pam held a toadstone in her hand.
7. Can you soak the green coat?
8. The soap will foam and get the job done.
9. I know that Mom will make a roast today.

10. She got on her soapbox in class!
11. The boat had a sail.
12. The goat will soak in the sun.

- Below is a sample script for sentence dictation.

  1. (T): Listen to the sentence. *The bedbug bit Pam.*
  2. (T): Listen while I pound the syllables. *The bedbug bit Pam.* (Make sure to pound *bedbug* twice because it has two syllables.)
  3. (T): Pound it with me. (T&S): *The bedbug bit Pam.*
  4. (T): You pound the sentence. (S): *The bedbug bit Pam.*
  5. (T): Watch me as I point to the lines while stating the sentence. (Tap the line for *bedbug* twice because it has two syllables.) *The bedbug bit Pam.*
  6. (T): You point to the lines while stating the sentence.
  7. (S): *The bedbug bit Pam.*
  8. (T): Now write the sentence. Fingertap if needed.

- Below is a sample script to check CUPS.*

  1. (T): C stands for capitalization. Did you remember a capital letter at the beginning of your sentence? Did you remember a capital letter for *Pam*? It is a name. If you forgot, fix it. If you remembered, put a tally mark above each capital letter. Add a mark in the box for C.
  2. (T): U stands for understanding. Is your sentence neat? Reread it to yourself. Does it make sense? Could someone else understand it? If not, fix it. Add a mark in the box for U.
  3. (T): P stands for punctuation. Did you remember a period at the end? If not, fix it. If you remembered, put a tally mark above the period. Add a mark in the box for P.
  4. (T): S stands for spelling. Did you spell your words correctly? Check them. Now, check yours with mine (shows the teacher's copy). Fix any words you spelled incorrectly. Put a tally mark above the words you spelled correctly. Add a mark in the box for S.
  5. (T): Rewrite your sentence with all of the corrections.
  6. (T): Check for CUPS again. Put another mark in the boxes.
  7. (T): Let's read the sentences.
  8. (S) Read the sentences for fluency and automaticity.

  *Please note:** Once students understand how to use CUPS, transition to letting them check their sentence independently before showing the teacher's copy.

Weekly Red Words

Materials Needed:
screen, red crayon, red word paper

Introduce on Tuesday, and practice daily. Use the Flip Chart for steps.

New:	Review:	New Read-Only:	Review Read-Only:
know, knew	were, does, some, good, there, done, her, under, down, onto, people, saw, both, should, could, would, over, love, live, out, too, eye, all, again, boy, girl, sign, your, which, look, also, use, today, yesterday, first, around, going, walk, their, how, once, another, pull, wash, every, everyone		our, oven, park, chair, center, school, tractor

Steps for Teaching a New Red Word:

1. (T) States the word. (*know*)
2. (T&S) Use tokens to determine how many sounds are in the word. (/n/ /ō/; 2)
3. (T&S) Discuss how we would expect to spell each sound as the teacher writes the grapheme(s) correctly. Identify what is unexpected or irregular about the spelling of the word. It could also be expected, but the concept hasn't been taught yet.
4. (T&S) Discuss the etymology of the word, if appropriate (lexical words). Visit www.etymonline.com for more information on the word.
5. (T) Defines the word, and writes a sentence using the word.
6. (T) Writes the word on Red Word paper with the screen underneath, using red crayon.
7. (S) Write the word on Red Word paper with the screen underneath, using red crayon. (S) Show the word to the teacher.
   (**NOTE:** The teacher should have students chunk the word if it has more than four letters.)
8. (T&S) Stand up, holding the Red Word in the nondominant hand. Armtap word while naming each letter. Then "underline" the word by sweeping left to right while stating the word, 3x. (**NOTE:** Left-handed students will place their left hand on their

right wrist. They tap to their right shoulder. Underline from wrist to shoulder. Right-handed students place their right hand on their left shoulder. They tap to their left wrist. Underline shoulder to wrist.)

9. (T&S) Trace crayon bumps with the pointer finger while naming the letters, 3x.

10. (T&S) Place the screen over the paper and trace the word with the pointer finger while naming the letters, 3x.

11. (S) Turn paper over. With red crayon, write the word without the screen one time, and hold up the word for the teacher to check. (S) Write the word two more times.

12. (S) Write an original sentence in pencil and underline the Red Word with a red crayon. (**NOTE:** The sentence can also be dictated by the teacher while the student writes or dictated by the student while the teacher writes it.)

13. Repeat the steps for *knew*. (/n/ /o͞o/; 2)

Review Ideas for Red Words:

- Sculpt the word using red Play-Doh or clay. Have students spell the word as they smash each letter.
- Print flashcards from IOG, and practice reading.
- Armtap the word to review.
- Cross-clap the word to review.
- Stomp the letters to review.
- Use a voice jar with popsicle sticks that have a different voice (e.g., robot, baby, cheerleader, monster) listed on each stick. Have a student draw a stick from the jar. The class armtaps the word using the voice selected. (Another option is to have an electronic spinning wheel with the voices listed on the wheel.)

Syllabication (Decoding)

Materials Needed:
IMSE Syllable Division Word Book, Pencil, Highlighter, Syllable Division Posters

Introduce on Wednesday with the new concept. Practice regularly.

1. Choose 6 or more words with the new concept from the *IMSE Syllable Division Word Book* for syllabication.

2. Remember to have students circle any known prefixes or suffixes. Then divide the rest of the word.

3. Use the steps on the Flip Chart and the Syllable Division Posters.

Syllable Division Patterns
1. vc|cv
2. v|cv
3. vc|v
4. v|v

1. Closed Syllable (Cl)
short vowel sound

mag\|net

ten\|nis

tip\|top

tom\|tom

up\|set

2. Open Syllable (O)
long vowel sound

ra\|ven

I\|rish

o\|pen

e\|ven

hu\|mid

ju\|do

3. Magic E (ME)

cup\|cake

stam\|pede

rep\|tile

tad\|pole

im\|mune

Nep\|tune

4. Vowel Teams (VT)

ea	leaf|let
ee	sea|weed
ai	sail|boat
ay	play|time
oa	oat|meal
oe	tip|toe
oi	tin|foil
oy	en|joy
ou	out|line
ow	pow|er
igh	high|way
au	au|dit
aw	jig|saw
ōō	car|toon
ŏŏ	book|case

- Below is a sample script for syllabication.

  1. Find the first two vowels or vowel units. Underline and label with a "v."
  2. Draw the bridge. Underline the consonants or consonant units and label with a "c."
  3. Find the pattern and divide the word.
  4. Is there another vowel (other than an "e" at the end)? If so, repeat steps 1-3. If not, go to step 5.
  5. Label each syllable.
  6. Read the word.

  NOTE: If there are two consonants in the middle of a word, split the word between the two consonants. (Exception: If the two consonants are a digraph [sh, ch, th] they cannot be split.) If there are three or more consonants, some letters go together as one consonant unit (look for known digraphs or blends).

Fluency, Vocabulary, and Comprehension

- Incorporate fluency into your literacy lessons daily/weekly (minimum 30 min/week) by using Rapid Word Charts, IMSE Decodable Readers, words and sentences, Acadience Reading K-6 or DIBELS 8th Edition, repeated reading, and other activities.
- Incorporate vocabulary into your literacy lessons daily/weekly (minimum 50 min/week) by choosing 3-5 appropriate tier two words (can pull from rich literature or decodable readers). Teach the words through explicit, direct instruction using student-friendly definitions, word webs, vocabulary charts, illustrations, and other activities.
- Incorporate oral language comprehension into your literacy lessons daily/weekly (approximately 100 min/week). Comprehension instruction should be explicit, direct instruction that includes teacher modeling, guided practice, and independent practice. Plan ahead to build on students' background knowledge, language structures, verbal reasoning, and literacy knowledge.

Extension Activity Ideas

- Continue to add to the vowel team placement chart. Students can use this in an interactive notebook.
- Visit IMSE's Orton-Gillingham's Pinterest page for more ideas.

Weekly Lesson Reminders

- Daily practice with writing the weekly Red Word(s)
- Kilpatrick's "One-Minute Activities" for daily phonological awareness practice
- Zgonc's phonological awareness activities
- Listen to rich literature to work on oral language comprehension.
- Target concept practice sheets from IMSE's practice books
- Practice test on Thursday and test on Friday

Suffix -ing (walking)

Card Pack #51   Decodable Reader #49

Object Ideas:	Literature Ideas:
walking, jumping, talking, crying, flying	▪ *Happy Endings: A Story About Suffixes* by Robin Pulver ▪ *The Kissing Hand* by Audrey Penn ▪ *Follow the Drinking Gourd* by Jeanette Winter ▪ *Harvesting Hope: The Story of Cesar Chavez* by Kathleen Krull ▪ *Coming on Home Soon* by Jacqueline Woodson

 ## Notes

- Use the Comprehensive Flip Chart for the steps on how to teach each part of IMSE's Lesson Plan.
- Use www.etymonline.com to help establish why a word might not follow the expected rules or patterns.
- Teach students the difference between suffix -ing and "ing" in a word (e.g, ring vs. ringing).
- The suffix -ing means the action or process of (verb), such as *playing*, or materials (noun), such as *bedding*.
- In the Blending Drill, pull up suffix -ing next to the end of the blending board when it is appropriate. (Remember that the Three Great Rules haven't been taught yet. Therefore, only put suffix -ing next to short-vowel words ending in double consonants, such as a blend or digraph, or next to a word with a vowel team.) **Note:** Remember that suffix -ing is represented on a white card. The yellow ing card represents sounds in a base word and not a suffix.
- For word dictation, when -ing is being used as a *suffix*, students should only fingertap the sounds in the base word. Then they add the suffix.

$$\underline{d} \quad \underline{a} \quad \underline{sh} + \left(\underline{ing}\right) = \underline{dashing}$$

- For syllabication, encourage students to circle any known prefixes or suffixes. Then look at the rest of the word and divide it into syllables. This will lay a foundation for word sums, which can be utilized when students have a deeper understanding of morphology.

Phonological Awareness:

Materials Needed:
tokens, sound boxes, one-minute activities, or Zgonc PA book

Use the PAST assessment to determine a starting point for instruction. Incorporate daily phonological awareness activities by using Zgonc's tiered activities and/or Kilpatrick's One-Minute Activities in *Equipped for Reading Success.*

Phonemic awareness warm-up: Use tokens (or letter tiles once concepts have been taught) and sound boxes to do a quick phonemic awareness activity that ties in with the new concept, if appropriate.

 # Three-Part Drill

Materials Needed:
review cards, sand, blending board, vowel tents or sticks

Do this at least 3x per week. Use the Flip Chart for steps. Include the new concept after Day 1.

1. Can do the hard/soft c/g drill after the Three-Part Drill
2. Can do the -ed tents activity after the Three-Part Drill (see *Extension Activity Ideas*)
3. Can do the -s/-es tents activity after the Three-Part Drill (see *Extension Activity Ideas*)

- Below is a sample script. Remember to use review concepts only.

1. **Visual:**
   (T) Tell me the sounds you know for these letters.
   (S) /m/, /l/, etc.

2. **Auditory/Kinesthetic:**
   (T) You know three ways to spell this. (S) split trays. (T) Eyes on me.
   Spell /k/. Repeat.
   (S) /k/ c says /k/; k says /k/; ck says /k/

3. **Blending:**
   (T) Tell me the sound for each letter as I point. Then blend the sounds together to read the word or syllable. Give me a thumbs up if it is a real word.
   (S) /mmm/ /ŏŏŏ/ /mmm/ *mom* (thumbs up)
   Alternative:
   (T) Watch me first. /mmm/ /ŏŏŏ/ /mmm/ *mom*
   (T) Do it with me. (T&S) /mmm/ /ŏŏŏ/ /mmm/ *mom*
   (T) Your turn. (S) /mmm/ /ŏŏŏ/ /mmm/ *mom* (thumbs up)

Optional: Once students have mastered their short vowel sounds, you can choose another drill to take the place of the Vowel Intensive, such as:
   a. Use Card Pack Number 45 to do the hard/soft c/g drill.
   b. Do the -ed tents activity (see *Extension Activity Ideas*).
   c. Do the -s/-es tents activity (see *Extension Activity Ideas*).

Teaching a New Concept

Materials Needed:
concept card, screen, green crayon, object, sand, decodable readers, literature, P/G chart

Introduce on Monday, and practice daily.

1. (T) Shows the new concept card(s).
   a. (T) Tells students that we will learn about the suffix -ing. Suffix -ing makes words present tense.
   b. (T) Tells students that suffix -ing says /ing/. (S) Repeat.
   c. (T) Teaches the meaning of -ing.
2. (T) Shows an object.
   a. (T) Allows students to manipulate the object and discuss prior knowledge. Reminds (S) that the object has the target sound(s) spelled with the target letter(s).
3. (S) Brainstorm to help establish a spelling rule, if applicable.
   a. Brainstorm words that have the target sound(s) or rule. The brainstorming can be a teacher-directed activity if students need extra support.
4. (T) Teaches Letter Formation, if needed. Can teach cursive writing.
   a. Use the steps for teaching letter formation on the Flip Chart.
   b. Use house paper to teach lowercase letters.
   c. Teach capital letters throughout the week. Capital letters go outside the house.
5. (T) Dictates target sound(s). (S) Practice all known spellings in the sand or other medium.
6. (T) Connects with literature.
   a. Read for language comprehension.
   b. Continue to work on language comprehension with rich literature throughout the week.
7. (S) Use decodable readers to practice the concepts learned.
   a. (S) Highlight words with the new concept. Read those words.
   b. (S) Highlight Red Words. Read those words.
   c. (S) Start reading the decodable reader.
   d. (S) Continue reading throughout the week.
   e. (S) Read a clean copy on Friday.
8. (T&S) Mark the Phoneme/Grapheme (P/G) chart by highlighting the target sound(s).

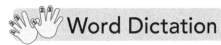 # Word Dictation

Materials Needed:
fingertapping hand, dictation paper, pencil

Practice daily. Use the Flip Chart to follow the steps for word dictation.

Day 1:	1. fishing	2. sniffing	3. sinking	4. delaying	5. impacting
Day 2:	1. crying	2. asking	3. emailing	4. handing	5. requesting
Day 3:	1. landing	2. finishing	3. bringing	4. depending	5. yelling
Days 4-5:	Review prior words. Optional additional words: brushing, camping, drinking, electing, flashing, grilling, helping, honking, jumping, listing, missing, mocking, opening, ringing, singing, spelling, stuffing, telling, unpacking, vanishing, wishing, yelling				

- Below is a sample script for one-syllable word dictation.

1. (T) States word: *boss.* Uses it in a sentence: My *boss* is kind and fair. (Pounds) *boss.* (T) Models fingertapping if needed: /b/ /ŏ/ /s/. (Pounds) *boss.*
2. (S) State while pounding: *boss.* (Fingertap) /b/ /ŏ/ /s/. (Pound) *boss.* Write the letters known for the sounds.
3. (T) When yours looks like mine, rewrite the word.
4. (S) Rewrite.
5. Repeat the process for each word.
6. (S) Read the list of words multiple times to build automaticity.

- Below is a sample script for multisyllabic word dictation.

1. (T) States word: *bathtub.* Uses it in a sentence: Clean out the *bathtub.* (Pounds each syllable) *bath/tub.*
2. (S) State while pounding each syllable: *bath/tub.*
3. (T) Models fingertapping, if needed. First syllable: (Pounds) *bath.* (Fingertaps) /b/ /ă/ /th/. (Pounds) *bath.*
4. (S) State first syllable while pounding: *bath.* (Fingertap) /b/ /ă/ /th/. (Pound) *bath.* Write the letters known for the sounds.
5. (T) Second syllable: (Pounds) *tub.* (Fingertaps) /t/ /ŭ/ /b/. (Pounds) *tub.*
6. (S) State second syllable while pounding: *tub.* (Fingertap) /t/ /ŭ/ /b/. (Pound) *tub.* Write the letters known for the sounds.
7. (T) When yours looks like mine, rewrite the word.
8. (S) Rewrite.
9. Repeat the process for each word.
10. (S) Read the list of words multiple times to build automaticity.

Sentence Dictation

Red Words are underlined. Students can fingertap the green words. Use the Flip Chart to follow the steps for sentence dictation.

1. Frogs were jumping into the pond.
2. The duck was honking at the people.
3. The bell was ringing when it was ten on the clock.
4. The kids were singing and yelling.
5. My friend asked me to bring the tent to go camping.
6. Bill and Ted went fishing for bass.
7. I was sniffing from all my crying.
8. I was missing my mom and dad.
9. Beth was wishing for a big red truck.
10. Ken was helping me give the cat a bath.
11. She was mocking me, and I did not like it.

- Below is a sample script for sentence dictation.

> 1. (T): Listen to the sentence. *The bedbug bit Pam.*
> 2. (T): Listen while I pound the syllables. *The bedbug bit Pam.* (Make sure to pound *bedbug* twice because it has two syllables.)
> 3. (T): Pound it with me. (T&S): *The bedbug bit Pam.*
> 4. (T): You pound the sentence. (S): *The bedbug bit Pam.*
> 5. (T): Watch me as I point to the lines while stating the sentence. (Tap the line for *bedbug* twice because it has two syllables.) *The bedbug bit Pam.*
> 6. (T): You point to the lines while stating the sentence.
> 7. (S): *The bedbug bit Pam.*
> 8. (T): Now write the sentence. Fingertap if needed.

- Below is a sample script to check CUPS.*

> 1. (T): C stands for capitalization. Did you remember a capital letter at the beginning of your sentence? Did you remember a capital letter for *Pam*? It is a name. If you forgot, fix it. If you remembered, put a tally mark above each capital letter. Add a mark in the box for C.
> 2. (T): U stands for understanding. Is your sentence neat? Reread it to yourself. Does it make sense? Could someone else understand it? If not, fix it. Add a mark in the box for U.
> 3. (T): P stands for punctuation. Did you remember a period at the end? If not, fix it. If you remembered, put a tally mark above the period. Add a mark in the box for P.

4. (T): S stands for spelling. Did you spell your words correctly? Check them. Now, check yours with mine (shows the teacher's copy). Fix any words you spelled incorrectly. Put a tally mark above the words you spelled correctly. Add a mark in the box for S.

5. (T): Rewrite your sentence with all of the corrections.

6. (T): Check for CUPS again. Put another mark in the boxes.

7. (T): Let's read the sentences.

8. (S) Read the sentences for fluency and automaticity.

*Please note:** Once students understand how to use CUPS, transition to letting them check their sentence independently before showing the teacher's copy.

Weekly Red Words

Materials Needed:
screen, red crayon, red word paper

Introduce on Tuesday, and practice daily. Use the Flip Chart for steps.

New:	Review:	New Read-Only:	Review Read-Only:
friend	were, does, some, good, there, done, her, under, down, onto, people, saw, both, should, could, would, over, love, live, out, too, eye, all, again, boy, girl, sign, your, which, look, also, use, today, yesterday, first, around, walk, their, how, once, another, pull, wash, every, everyone, know, knew		our, oven, park, chair, center, school, tractor

Steps for Teaching a New Red Word:

1. (T) States the word. (*friend*)
2. (T&S) Use tokens to determine how many sounds are in the word. (/f/ /r/ /ĕ/ /n/ /d/; 5)
3. (T&S) Discuss how we would expect to spell each sound as the teacher writes the grapheme(s) correctly. Identify what is unexpected or irregular about the spelling of the word. It could also be expected, but the concept hasn't been taught yet.
4. (T&S) Discuss the etymology of the word, if appropriate (lexical words). Visit www.etymonline.com for more information on the word.
5. (T) Defines the word, and writes a sentence using the word.
6. (T) Writes the word on Red Word paper with the screen underneath, using red crayon.
7. (S) Write the word on Red Word paper with the screen underneath, using red crayon. (S) Show the word to the teacher.
   (**NOTE:** The teacher should have students chunk the word if it has more than four letters.)
8. (T&S) Stand up, holding the Red Word in the nondominant hand. Armtap word while naming each letter. Then "underline" the word by sweeping left to right while stating the word, 3x. (**NOTE:** Left-handed students will place their left hand on their right wrist. They tap to their right shoulder. Underline from wrist to shoulder. Right-handed students place their right hand on their left shoulder. They tap to their left wrist. Underline shoulder to wrist.)
9. (T&S) Trace crayon bumps with the pointer finger while naming the letters, 3x.
10. (T&S) Place the screen over the paper and trace the word with the pointer finger while naming the letters, 3x.
11. (S) Turn paper over. With red crayon, write the word without the screen one time, and hold up the word for the teacher to check. (S) Write the word two more times.
12. (S) Write an original sentence in pencil and underline the Red Word with a red crayon. (**NOTE:** The sentence can also be dictated by the teacher while the student writes or dictated by the student while the teacher writes it.)

Review Ideas for Red Words:

- Sculpt the word using red Play-Doh or clay. Have students spell the word as they smash each letter.
- Print flashcards from IOG, and practice reading.
- Armtap the word to review.
- Cross-clap the word to review.
- Stomp the letters to review.
- Use a voice jar with popsicle sticks that have a different voice (e.g., robot, baby, cheerleader, monster) listed on each stick. Have a student draw a stick from the jar. The class armtaps the word using the voice selected. (Another option is to have an electronic spinning wheel with the voices listed on the wheel.)

Syllabication (Decoding)

Materials Needed:
IMSE Syllable Division Word Book, Pencil, Highlighter, Syllable Division Posters

Introduce on Wednesday with the new concept. Practice regularly.

1. Choose 6 or more words with the new concept from the *IMSE Syllable Division Word Book* for syllabication.

2. Remember to have students circle any known prefixes or suffixes. Then divide the rest of the word.

3. Use the steps on the Flip Chart and the Syllable Division Posters.

Syllable Division Patterns	1. Closed Syllable (Cl) short vowel sound	2. Open Syllable (O) long vowel sound
1. vc|cv	mag|net	ra|ven
2. v|cv	ten|nis	I|rish
3. vc|v	tip|top	o|pen
4. v|v	tom|tom	e|ven
	up|set	hu|mid
		ju|do

3. Magic E (ME)	4. Vowel Teams (VT)	
cup|cake	ea	leaf|let
stam|pede	ee	sea|weed
rep|tile	ai	sail|boat
tad|pole	ay	play|time
im|mune	oa	oat|meal
Nep|tune	oe	tip|toe
	oi	tin|foil
	oy	en|joy
	ou	out|line
	ow	pow|er
	igh	high|way
	au	au|dit
	aw	jig|saw
	ōō	car|toon
	ŏŏ	book|case

• Below is a sample script for syllabication.

1. Find the first two vowels or vowel units. Underline and label with a "v."

2. Draw the bridge. Underline the consonants or consonant units and label with a "c."

3. Find the pattern and divide the word.

4. Is there another vowel (other than an "e" at the end)? If so, repeat steps 1-3. If not, go to step 5.

5. Label each syllable.

6. Read the word.

NOTE: If there are two consonants in the middle of a word, split the word between the two consonants. (Exception: If the two consonants are a digraph [sh, ch, th] they cannot be split.) If there are three or more consonants, some letters go together as one consonant unit (look for known digraphs or blends).

Fluency, Vocabulary, and Comprehension

- Incorporate fluency into your literacy lessons daily/weekly (minimum 30 min/week) by using Rapid Word Charts, IMSE Decodable Readers, words and sentences, Acadience Reading K-6 or DIBELS 8th Edition, repeated reading, and other activities.
- Incorporate vocabulary into your literacy lessons daily/weekly (minimum 50 min/week) by choosing 3-5 appropriate tier two words (can pull from rich literature or decodable readers). Teach the words through explicit, direct instruction using student-friendly definitions, word webs, vocabulary charts, illustrations, and other activities.
- Incorporate oral language comprehension into your literacy lessons daily/weekly (approximately 100 min/week). Comprehension instruction should be explicit, direct instruction that includes teacher modeling, guided practice, and independent practice. Plan ahead to build on students' background knowledge, language structures, verbal reasoning, and literacy knowledge.

Extension Activity Ideas

- Create a center with -ed and -ing. Provide students with a list of base words, and have students add the suffixes to create new words. (Be careful not to choose base words that would follow rules involving doubling the final consonant, dropping a silent e, or changing a y.)
- Visit IMSE's Orton-Gillingham's Pinterest page for more ideas.

Weekly Lesson Reminders

- Daily practice with writing the weekly Red Word(s)
- Kilpatrick's "One-Minute Activities" for daily phonological awareness practice
- Zgonc's phonological awareness activities
- Listen to rich literature to work on oral language comprehension.
- Target concept practice sheets from IMSE's practice books
- Practice test on Thursday and test on Friday

Notes:

_____

_____

_____

_____

_____

_____

_____

_____

_____

_____

_____

_____

_____

_____

_____

_____

_____

_____

_____

_____

Contractions am, is, are, has, not (I'm, he's, we're, isn't)

Card Pack #None Decodable Reader #50	
Object Ideas:	**Literature Ideas:**
foldable strips of paper and Band-Aids® for "contraction surgery"	▪ *Alfie the Apostrophe* by Moira Rose Donohue ▪ *If You Were a Contraction* by Trisha Speed Shaskan

Notes

- Use the Comprehensive Flip Chart for the steps on how to teach each part of IMSE's Lesson Plan.
- Use www.etymonline.com to help establish why a word might not follow the expected rules or patterns.
- This concept will not be included in the Three-Part Drill. There are no cards for the Visual or Blending Drills. The contractions can be highlighted on the Phoneme/Grapheme Chart after they have been taught, but they do not need to be written in the sand during the Auditory/Kinesthetic Drill.
- When completing word dictation, students should not fingertap the contractions. Instead, students should spell contractions based on knowledge of the individual words and the rule for representing each contraction. Students can use one word line (rather than grapheme lines) when practicing these during dictation. See below:

isn't

- If students need extra support, another option is to have students represent each contraction as a word sum. See below:

is + not = isn't

Phonological Awareness:

Materials Needed:
tokens, sound boxes, one-minute activities, or Zgonc PA book

Use the PAST assessment to determine a starting point for instruction. Incorporate daily phonological awareness activities by using Zgonc's tiered activities and/or Kilpatrick's One-Minute Activities in *Equipped for Reading Success*.

Phonemic awareness warm-up: Use tokens (or letter tiles once concepts have been taught) and sound boxes to do a quick phonemic awareness activity that ties in with the new concept, if appropriate.

First Grade | 249

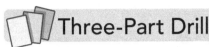

Three-Part Drill

Materials Needed:
review cards, sand, blending board, vowel tents or sticks

Do this at least 3x per week. Use the Flip Chart for steps.

1. Can do the hard/soft c/g drill after the Three-Part Drill
2. Can do the -ed tents activity after the Three-Part Drill (see *Extension Activity Ideas*)
3. Can do the -s/-es tents activity after the Three-Part Drill (see *Extension Activity Ideas*)

- Below is a sample script. Remember to use review concepts only.

---

1. **Visual:**
   (T) Tell me the sounds you know for these letters.
   (S) /m/, /l/, etc.

2. **Auditory/Kinesthetic:**
   (T) You know three ways to spell this. (S) split trays. (T) Eyes on me.
   Spell /k/. Repeat.
   (S) /k/ c says /k/; k says /k/; ck says /k/

3. **Blending:**
   (T) Tell me the sound for each letter as I point. Then blend the sounds together to read the word or syllable. Give me a thumbs up if it is a real word.
   (S) /mmm/ /ŏŏŏ/ /mmm/ *mom* (thumbs up)
   Alternative:
   (T) Watch me first. /mmm/ /ŏŏŏ/ /mmm/ *mom*
   (T) Do it with me. (T&S) /mmm/ /ŏŏŏ/ /mmm/ *mom*
   (T) Your turn. (S) /mmm/ /ŏŏŏ/ /mmm/ *mom* (thumbs up)

Optional: Once students have mastered their short vowel sounds, you can choose another drill to take the place of the Vowel Intensive, such as:

   a. Use Card Pack Number 45 to do the hard/soft c/g drill.
   b. Do the -ed tents activity (see *Extension Activity Ideas*).
   c. Do the -s/-es tents activity (see *Extension Activity Ideas*).

Teaching a New Concept

Materials Needed:
concept card, screen, green crayon, object, sand, decodable readers, literature, P/G chart

Introduce on Monday, and practice daily.

1. (T) Shows the new concept card(s). (no new card for this concept)
   a. (T) Tells students that we will learn about contractions. Contractions are words that use an apostrophe to put two words together.
   b. (T) Shows an example, such as *is* and *not*. When we combine these words, we have *isn't*. The "o" is removed, and the apostrophe takes its place.

© IMSE 2022

2. (T) Shows an object.
   a. (T) Allows students to manipulate the object and discuss prior knowledge. Reminds (S) that the object has the target sound(s) spelled with the target letter(s).

3. (S) Brainstorm to help establish a spelling rule, if applicable.
   a. Brainstorm words that have the target sound(s) or rule. The brainstorming can be a teacher-directed activity if students need extra support.

4. (T) Connects with literature.
   a. Read for language comprehension.
   b. Continue to work on language comprehension with rich literature throughout the week.

5. (S) Use decodable readers to practice the concepts learned.
   a. (S) Highlight words with the new concept. Read those words.
   b. (S) Highlight Red Words. Read those words.
   c. (S) Start reading the decodable reader.
   d. (S) Continue reading throughout the week.
   e. (S) Read a clean copy on Friday.

6. (T&S) Mark the Phoneme/Grapheme (P/G) chart by highlighting the target sound(s).

 ## Word Dictation

Materials Needed:
fingertapping hand, dictation paper, pencil

Practice daily. Students should not fingertap these words. Instead, these words will be spelled based on the combined knowledge of phonics, irregular words, and rules learned for each contraction.

Day 1:	1. we're	2. isn't	3. I'm	4. she's	5. wouldn't
Day 2:	1. he's	2. hasn't	3. they're	4. couldn't	5. when's
Day 3:	1. can't	2. shouldn't	3. you're	4. that's	5. didn't
Days 4-5:	Review prior words. Optional additional words: don't, hadn't, it's				

▪ Below is a sample script for one-syllable word dictation.

1. (T) States word: *boss*. Uses it in a sentence: My *boss* is kind and fair. (Pounds) *boss*. (T) Models fingertapping if needed: /b/ /ŏ/ /s/. (Pounds) *boss*.
2. (S) State while pounding: *boss*. (Fingertap) /b/ /ŏ/ /s/. (Pound) *boss*. Write the letters known for the sounds.
3. (T) When yours looks like mine, rewrite the word.
4. (S) Rewrite.
5. Repeat the process for each word.
6. (S) Read the list of words multiple times to build automaticity.

- Below is a sample script for multisyllabic word dictation.

> 1. (T) States word: *bathtub*. Uses it in a sentence: Clean out the *bathtub*. (Pounds each syllable) *bath/tub*.
> 2. (S) State while pounding each syllable: *bath/tub*.
> 3. (T) Models fingertapping, if needed. First syllable: (Pounds) *bath*. (Fingertaps) */b/ /ă/ /th/*. (Pounds) *bath*.
> 4. (S) State first syllable while pounding: *bath*. (Fingertap) */b/ /ă/ /th/*. (Pound) *bath*. Write the letters known for the sounds.
> 5. (T) Second syllable: (Pounds) *tub*. (Fingertaps) */t/ /ŭ/ /b/*. (Pounds) *tub*.
> 6. (S) State second syllable while pounding: *tub*. (Fingertap) */t/ /ŭ/ /b/*. (Pound) *tub*. Write the letters known for the sounds.
> 7. (T) When yours looks like mine, rewrite the word.
> 8. (S) Rewrite.
> 9. Repeat the process for each word.
> 10. (S) Read the list of words multiple times to build automaticity.

Sentence Dictation

Red Words are underlined. Students can fingertap the green words. Use the Flip Chart to follow the steps for sentence dictation.

1. I hadn't made a plan to stay for the day.
2. If it's too hot in July, we can swim in the lake.
3. Shouldn't we stay inside if it's raining?
4. I'm grilling a roast to eat with Pete.
5. She isn't happy with our test scores.
6. She's been ringing the bell to end the day.
7. He's upset from missing the race.
8. Why can't she go on the other bus?
9. It's not fun to play in the hay all day.
10. That's my red coat hanging on the ledge.
11. He can't tan in the sun today.
12. We're going to see the king.
13. They're here to help with the contest.

- Below is a sample script for sentence dictation.

> 1. (T): Listen to the sentence. *The bedbug bit Pam.*
> 2. (T): Listen while I pound the syllables. *The bedbug bit Pam.* (Make sure to pound *bedbug* twice because it has two syllables.)
> 3. (T): Pound it with me. (T&S): *The bedbug bit Pam.*
> 4. (T): You pound the sentence. (S): *The bedbug bit Pam.*
> 5. (T): Watch me as I point to the lines while stating the sentence. (Tap the line for *bedbug* twice because it has two syllables.) *The bedbug bit Pam.*
> 6. (T): You point to the lines while stating the sentence.
> 7. (S): *The bedbug bit Pam.*
> 8. (T): Now write the sentence. Fingertap if needed.

- Below is a sample script to check CUPS.*

> 1. (T): C stands for capitalization. Did you remember a capital letter at the beginning of your sentence? Did you remember a capital letter for *Pam*? It is a name. If you forgot, fix it. If you remembered, put a tally mark above each capital letter. Add a mark in the box for C.
> 2. (T): U stands for understanding. Is your sentence neat? Reread it to yourself. Does it make sense? Could someone else understand it? If not, fix it. Add a mark in the box for U.
> 3. (T): P stands for punctuation. Did you remember a period at the end? If not, fix it. If you remembered, put a tally mark above the period. Add a mark in the box for P.
> 4. (T): S stands for spelling. Did you spell your words correctly? Check them. Now, check yours with mine (shows the teacher's copy). Fix any words you spelled incorrectly. Put a tally mark above the words you spelled correctly. Add a mark in the box for S.
> 5. (T): Rewrite your sentence with all of the corrections.
> 6. (T): Check for CUPS again. Put another mark in the boxes.
> 7. (T): Let's read the sentences.
> 8. (S) Read the sentences for fluency and automaticity.
>
> **Please note:** Once students understand how to use CUPS, transition to letting them check their sentence independently before showing the teacher's copy.

 ## Weekly Red Words

Materials Needed:
screen, red crayon, red word paper

Introduce on Tuesday, and practice daily. Use the Flip Chart for steps.

New:	Review:	New Read-Only:	Review Read-Only:
been, our, other	were, does, some, good, there, done, her, under, down, onto, people, saw, both, should, could, would, over, love, live, out, too, eye, all, again, boy, girl, sign, your, which, look, also, use, today, yesterday, first, around, walk, their, how, once, another, pull, wash, every, everyone, know, knew, friend		oven, park, chair, center, school, tractor

Steps for Teaching a New Red Word:

1. (T) States the word. (*been*)
2. (T&S) Use tokens to determine how many sounds are in the word. (/b/ /ĭ/ /n/; 3)
3. (T&S) Discuss how we would expect to spell each sound as the teacher writes the grapheme(s) correctly. Identify what is unexpected or irregular about the spelling of the word. It could also be expected, but the concept hasn't been taught yet.
4. (T&S) Discuss the etymology of the word, if appropriate (lexical words). Visit www.etymonline.com for more information on the word.
5. (T) Defines the word, and writes a sentence using the word.
6. (T) Writes the word on Red Word paper with the screen underneath, using red crayon.

7. (S) Write the word on Red Word paper with the screen underneath, using red crayon. (S) Show the word to the teacher.
   (**NOTE:** The teacher should have students chunk the word if it has more than four letters.)

8. (T&S) Stand up, holding the Red Word in the nondominant hand. Armtap word while naming each letter. Then "underline" the word by sweeping left to right while stating the word, 3x. (**NOTE:** Left-handed students will place their left hand on their right wrist. They tap to their right shoulder. Underline from wrist to shoulder. Right-handed students place their right hand on their left shoulder. They tap to their left wrist. Underline shoulder to wrist.)

9. (T&S) Trace crayon bumps with the pointer finger while naming the letters, 3x.

10. (T&S) Place the screen over the paper and trace the word with the pointer finger while naming the letters, 3x.

11. (S) Turn paper over. With red crayon, write the word without the screen one time, and hold up the word for the teacher to check. (S) Write the word two more times.

12. (S) Write an original sentence in pencil and underline the Red Word with a red crayon. (**NOTE:** The sentence can also be dictated by the teacher while the student writes or dictated by the student while the teacher writes it.)

13. Repeat the steps for *our* (/ou/ /er/; 2), *other* (/ŭ/ /TH/ /er/; 3).

Review Ideas for Red Words:

- Sculpt the word using red Play-Doh or clay. Have students spell the word as they smash each letter.
- Print flashcards from IOG, and practice reading.
- Armtap the word to review.
- Cross-clap the word to review.
- Stomp the letters to review.
- Use a voice jar with popsicle sticks that have a different voice (e.g., robot, baby, cheerleader, monster) listed on each stick. Have a student draw a stick from the jar. The class armtaps the word using the voice selected. (Another option is to have an electronic spinning wheel with the voices listed on the wheel.)

Syllabication (Decoding)

Materials Needed:
IMSE Syllable Division Word Book, Pencil, Highlighter, Syllable Division Posters

Introduce on Wednesday with the new concept. Practice regularly.

1. Choose 6 or more words with the new concept from the *IMSE Syllable Division Word Book* for syllabication.

2. Remember to have students circle any known prefixes or suffixes. Then divide the rest of the word.

3. Use the steps on the Flip Chart and the Syllable Division Posters.

Syllable Division Patterns
1. vc|cv
2. v|cv
3. vc|v
4. v|v

1. Closed Syllable (Cl)
short vowel sound

mag\|net

ten\|nis

tip\|top

tom\|tom

up\|set

2. Open Syllable (O)
long vowel sound

ra\|ven

I\|rish

o\|pen

e\|ven

hu\|mid

ju\|do

3. Magic E (ME)

cup\|cake

stam\|pede

rep\|tile

tad\|pole

im\|mune

Nep\|tune

4. Vowel Teams (VT)

ea	leaf|let
ee	sea|weed
ai	sail|boat
ay	play|time
oa	oat|meal
oe	tip|toe
oi	tin|foil
oy	en|joy
ou	out|line
ow	pow|er
igh	high|way
au	au|dit
aw	jig|saw
ōo	car|toon
ŏo	book|case

- Below is a sample script for syllabication.

1. Find the first two vowels or vowel units. Underline and label with a "v."
2. Draw the bridge. Underline the consonants or consonant units and label with a "c."
3. Find the pattern and divide the word.
4. Is there another vowel (other than an "e" at the end)? If so, repeat steps 1-3. If not, go to step 5.
5. Label each syllable.
6. Read the word.

NOTE: If there are two consonants in the middle of a word, split the word between the two consonants. (Exception: If the two consonants are a digraph [sh, ch, th] they cannot be split.) If there are three or more consonants, some letters go together as one consonant unit (look for known digraphs or blends).

© IMSE 2022

Fluency, Vocabulary, and Comprehension

- Incorporate fluency into your literacy lessons daily/weekly (minimum 30 min/week) by using Rapid Word Charts, IMSE Decodable Readers, words and sentences, Acadience Reading K-6 or DIBELS 8th Edition, repeated reading, and other activities.
- Incorporate vocabulary into your literacy lessons daily/weekly (minimum 50 min/week) by choosing 3-5 appropriate tier two words (can pull from rich literature or decodable readers). Teach the words through explicit, direct instruction using student-friendly definitions, word webs, vocabulary charts, illustrations, and other activities.
- Incorporate oral language comprehension into your literacy lessons daily/weekly (approximately 100 min/week). Comprehension instruction should be explicit, direct instruction that includes teacher modeling, guided practice, and independent practice. Plan ahead to build on students' background knowledge, language structures, verbal reasoning, and literacy knowledge.

Extension Activity Ideas

- Contraction surgery: Have small Band-Aids® and strips of paper with two words written on each strip (e.g., *I am*). Have students fold the paper to "remove" the letter(s) that will be missing when a contraction is created (e.g., folding to "hide" the "a" in *am*). Add a Band-Aid® for the apostrophe as though you performed "surgery" on the word.
- Visit IMSE's Orton-Gillingham's Pinterest page for more ideas.

Weekly Lesson Reminders

- Daily practice with writing the weekly Red Word(s)
- Kilpatrick's "One-Minute Activities" for daily phonological awareness practice
- Zgonc's phonological awareness activities
- Listen to rich literature to work on oral language comprehension.
- Target concept practice sheets from IMSE's practice books
- Practice test on Thursday and test on Friday

Review for Concepts m-contractions with am, is, are, has, not

After teaching the first 57 concepts, the following words and sentences may be utilized for review. Teachers can dictate a different list (A, B, C, or D) and three sentences each day of the review. Teachers can spend up to a week on review *if needed*. If a review is not needed, this page can be skipped or partially utilized. Students can use IMSE workbooks or age-appropriate paper for recording their answers.

List A	List B	List C	List D
1. fifteen	1. tray	1. printed	1. foxes
2. planted	2. wishing	2. say	2. toenail
3. they're	3. meantime	3. rings	3. shouldn't
4. claim	4. asked	4. we're	4. chimpanzee
5. don't	5. speech	5. helping	5. mean
6. dolls	6. steamboat	6. teapot	6. Friday
7. drinking	7. I'm	7. hasn't	7. rushed
8. tiptoe	8. cupcakes	8. coastline	8. honking
9. oatmeal	9. toenail	9. aloe	9. snail
10. play	10. can't	10. feet	10. it's

Sentences:
1. She ate <u>the</u> peach and drank <u>the</u> tea.
2. Ken <u>was</u> helping me <u>give the</u> cat <u>a</u> bath.
3. I filled <u>the</u> cup and then spilled it.
4. <u>That's</u> my red coat hanging on <u>the</u> ledge.
5. Can <u>you</u> explain <u>the</u> details <u>to everyone</u>?
6. When she fell, she broke <u>her</u> glasses.
7. <u>The</u> hay <u>was</u> dry.
8. <u>Who do you</u> think will win <u>the</u> contests?
9. Beth <u>was</u> wishing <u>for a</u> big red truck.
10. <u>The</u> ice cube melted in <u>the</u> hot sun.
11. <u>We're</u> going <u>to</u> see <u>the</u> king.
12. I <u>know</u> that Mom will make <u>a</u> roast <u>today</u>.

Appendix

Page Intentionally Blank

Table of Contents
Appendix

THREE-PART DRILL

1. VISUAL
(T) Display cards one at a time in random order.

(S) Say sound(s) - if letter(s) represents more than one sound (or unit of sounds), **(S)** state first sound (or unit of sounds) learned, then next sound (or unit of sounds). (Can also name letter[s] and sound[s].)

2. AUDITORY
(T) Use phoneme/grapheme chart to dictate known sounds in random order.
(Eyes on me. Spell /b/. Repeat.)
Remind students if there is more than one way to spell a sound.
(You know two ways to spell this. Spell /k/.)

(S) Repeat (/b/).

(S) Using sand tray or other medium, **(S)** write the letter(s) while naming it and underlining L to R saying the sound(s). (Ex. /b/ b says /b/.)

3. BLENDING
(T) Separate cards into three piles: C/V/C.

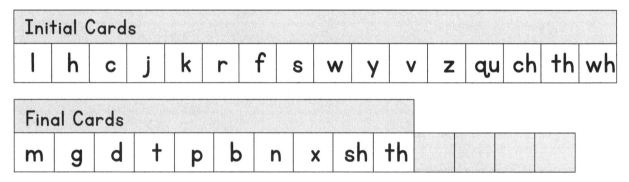

*Never use Magic E or hard and soft c & g cards on the blending board.

(S) Say sound for each letter and blend into syllable. Give thumbs up for real words. If the syllable is not a word, students can think of a multisyllabic word that has that syllable.
Ex: fam is a syllable for family.

VOWEL INTENSIVE

V The sound is ...	VC The syllable is ...	CVC The syllable is ...
a	ag, ap, ab	lat, cad, zan
e	et, en, ep	zeg, ren, med
i	ig, ib, im	lin, hib, fid
o	ob, ot, oz	rom, hob, cog
u	un, ug, ub	sup, pum, dut

(S) Place vowel sticks or tents in ABC order – use only those vowels previously taught.

(T) State vowel sound. (Eyes on me. The sound is /a/. Repeat.)

(S) Repeat vowel sound while doing the visual cue.

(S) Hold up appropriate vowel, naming the vowel and saying its sound.

(T) Progress into VC syllables and then into CVC syllables. (Eyes on me. The syllable is /ag/. Repeat.)

(S) Continue to listen for the correct vowel sound, naming the vowel and its sound.

**The chart represents some examples. (T) can create additional VC and CVC syllables.

/ă/: Place hand under the chin and drop your jaw.

/ĕ/: Pull corners of the mouth back with thumb and pointer finger.

/ĭ/: Scrunch nose and point to it.

/ŏ/: Circle your mouth with your finger.

/ŭ/: Push in on stomach.

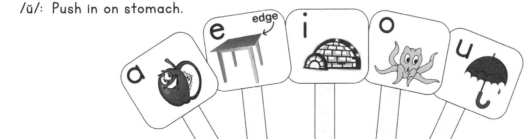

I. Review Using Three-Part Drill and Vowel Intensive (AFTER m-a-l-o HAVE BEEN TAUGHT)

II. TEACHING A NEW CONCEPT (m-wh)

A. MULTI-SENSORY EXPERIENCE

1. **(T)** Read **alliteration** sentences.
   (S) Identify target sound.
2. **(T)** Show new **card** and inform **(S)** of letter name(s) and sound(s).
   (S) Repeat (ex: "m says /m/") using a mirror to see and feel position of lips, teeth, and tongue. Discuss whether sound is voiced or unvoiced.
   (T) Show **position** of letter in the alphabet. Discuss whether the letter is a consonant or vowel.
3. **(T)** Show **object** (ex: marshmallow) to be used in an activity.
4. **(S)** **Brainstorm** words beginning with the letter and sound.
   (T) Write the brainstorm words on chart paper.
   *For short vowels, have students brainstorm word families or rhyming words containing the vowel sound.
5. **(T)** Teach **letter formation** – Use large house paper with directional arrows and starting points.
   *Use screen and green crayon.
   *You may progress to small house paper.
   *Teach capitals with lowercase if capitals are not yet learned.
6. **(T)** **Dictate** target sound(s).
   (S) **Practice** all known spellings in sand (or other medium) 3 times.
7. **(T)** **Read** book – ex: *Mixed Me* by Taye Diggs – Have **(S)** listen for words containing the new sound. Work on oral language comprehension skills.
8. **(S)** **Read** IMSE decodable reader.
9. **(T&S)** **Mark** Phoneme/Grapheme chart and **place** card in review deck.

> **Extension Activities**
> 1. Drawing
> 2. Collage
> 3. Alphabet Book
> 4. Multi-Sensory Activities
> 5. Supplemental workbook pages

B. APPLICATION OF NEW CONCEPT

One-Syllable Word Dictation

1. **(T)** State word: ex: "mom."
   (T) Use word in a sentence.
   (T) State word while pounding (ex: "mom"), model fingertapping (if appropriate), then pound word.
2. **(S)** State word while pounding (ex: "mom").
   (S) Fingertap word with off hand (/m/ /o/ /m/) and pound word.
   (S) Write word on appropriate paper.
3. **(S)** Check word and rewrite.
4. **(S)** Read all words to practice fluency.

Sentence Dictation: (Can also have **(S)** create their own sentences.)

1. **(T)** State the sentence: ex: "The lid is hot."
2. **(T)** Pound syllables in the sentence with off hand.
3. **(T&S)** Pound syllables in the sentence.
4. **(S)** Pound syllables without help from Teacher.
5. **(T)** Model pointing to word lines while saying sentence.
6. **(S)** Point to word lines while saying sentence. Write sentence, fingertap words (if necessary), check using **CUPS**. Rewrite sentence.
7. **(S)** Read all sentences to practice fluency.

TEACHING LETTER FORMATION
Steps for Letter Formation with House Paper

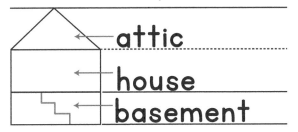

attic

house

basement

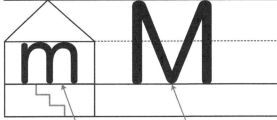

Write lowercase letters inside the house.

Write larger capital letters outside of the house.

Place screen under paper.

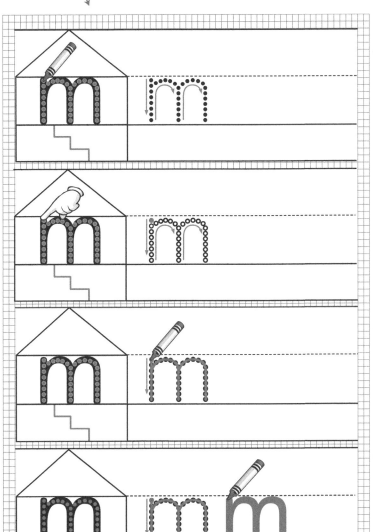

← Step 1:
(T) models "how to" with solid; (T&S) trace solid with crayon and screen 3x to create bumps-verbalizing while tracing (m says /m/).

← Step 2:
(T&S) trace crayon bumps 3x with finger-verbalizing while tracing (m says /m/).

← Step 3:
(S) trace dotted letter with crayon 1x.

← Step 4:
(S) create letter 1x independently.

Step 5: (not shown)
(S) move to smaller house, trace solid with screen and green crayon, and continue creating letter. (S) circle best example.

DECODABLE READER

MONDAY
1. (S) Highlight or underline words with the new concept in green. Read those words.
2. (S) Highlight or underline Red Words in red. Read those words.
3. If time allows, (S) start reading the decodable reader.

TUESDAY - THURSDAY
(S) Read the decodable reader.

NOTE: If a student makes an error on a phonetic word, have the student look at the letters, sound out the word, and read the word. If the student can't read the word or if the word is a Red Word, the teacher will state the word. Then the student should reread the sentence with automaticity.

FRIDAY
(S) Read a clean copy without pictures.

NOTES
- Comprehension questions are included with each decodable reader and can be incorporated throughout the week.
- A writing prompt is included with each decodable reader. The writing prompt can be incorporated at any time during the week.
- Decodable readers provide critical opportunities for students to apply the phonics skills that have been taught. They also help increase students' reading fluency. Decodable readers should be utilized *every week*.

I. Review With Three-Part Drill Before Teaching New Concept

II. TEACHING A NEW CONCEPT (ADVANCED)

A. MULTI-SENSORY EXPERIENCE

1. **(T)** Show new **card(s)**, inform **(S)** of letter name(s) and sound(s). Discuss spelling rule when applicable.
   (S) Repeat (ex: "ck says /k/").
2. **(T)** Show **object** (ex: backpack, clock) to be used later in follow-up activities.
3. **(S)** **Brainstorm** words when appropriate to establish spelling rules.
   (T) Write brainstorm words on chart paper.
   *Students can brainstorm word families or rhyming words, sort words, etc.
4. **(S)** **Handwriting practice**, if needed.
5. **(T)** **Dictate** sound(s).
   (S) **Practice** all known spellings in sand or on paper. (ex: "We know three ways to spell this. Spell /k/.")
6. **(T)** **Connect** concept with literature. Work on oral language comprehension skills.
7. **(S)** **Read** IMSE decodable reader.
8. **(T&S)** **Mark** Phoneme/Grapheme chart and **place** card(s) in review deck.

B. APPLICATION OF NEW CONCEPT

One-Syllable Word Dictation

1. **(T)** State word: ex: "mom."
   (T) Use word in a sentence.
   (T) State word while pounding (ex: "mom"), model fingertapping (if appropriate), then pound word.
2. **(S)** State word while pounding (ex: "mom").
   (S) Fingertap word with off hand (/m/ /o/ /m/) and pound word.
   (S) Write word on appropriate paper.
3. **(S)** Check word and rewrite.
4. **(S)** Read all words to practice fluency.

Multisyllabic Word Dictation

1. **(T)** State word: "sunset."
   (T) Use word in a sentence.
   (T) Repeat word while pounding each syllable: "sun," "set."
2. **(S)** State while pounding each syllable.
3. **(T&S)** Pound first syllable: "sun." Fingertap, pound, and write first syllable.
4. **(T&S)** Pound second syllable: "set." Fingertap, pound, and write second syllable.
5. **(S)** Check word and rewrite.
6. **(S)** Read all words to practice fluency.

Sentence Dictation (Can also have **(S)** create their own sentences.)

1. **(T)** State the sentence: ex: "The lid is hot."
2. **(T)** Pound syllables in the sentence with off hand.
3. **(T&S)** Pound syllables in the sentence.
4. **(S)** Pound syllables without help from Teacher.
5. **(T)** Model pointing to word lines while saying sentence.
6. **(S)** Point to word lines while saying sentence. Write sentence, fingertap words (if necessary), check using **CUPS**. Rewrite sentence.
7. **(S)** Read all sentences to practice fluency.

LEARNING A RED WORD

1. **(T)** State the word.
2. **(T&S)** Use tokens to determine how many sounds are in the word.
3. **(T&S)** Discuss how we would expect to spell each sound as the teacher writes the grapheme(s) correctly. Identify what is unexpected or irregular about the spelling of the word.
4. **(T&S)** Discuss the etymology of the word, if appropriate (lexical words).
5. **(T)** Define the word, and write a sentence using the word.
6. **(T)** Write word on Red Word paper with screen underneath, using red crayon.
7. **(S)** Write word on Red Word paper with screen underneath, using red crayon.
   (S) Show word to teacher.

> **For longer words, chunk groups of letters to facilitate memory.**
> **(T)** Scoop parts of word with red crayon.
> **(S)** Copy scooped word parts on their paper.

8. **(T&S)** Stand up, holding Red Word in nondominant hand. Armtap word while naming each letter. Then "underline" word by sweeping left to right while stating the word, 3 times.
   Left-Handed: Place left hand on right wrist, tap to right shoulder, underline from wrist to shoulder.
   Right-Handed: Place right hand on left shoulder, tap to left wrist, underline shoulder to wrist.
9. **(T&S)** Trace crayon bumps with finger while naming the letters, three times.
10. **(T&S)** Place screen over paper and trace word with the pointer finger while naming the letters, three times.
11. **(S)** Turn paper over. With red crayon, write word without screen one time, and hold up word for teacher to check.
    (S) Write word two more times.
12. **(S)** Write an original sentence in pencil and underline Red Word with red crayon.
    Once comfortable with the standard process, creative adaptations are encouraged.

> **Reviewing Red Words**
>
> Throughout the week, review Red Words by armtapping each Red Word once. Students may look at words while reviewing but should progress to spelling from memory. Red Word Activity Centers or extensions should be incorporated regularly for review.

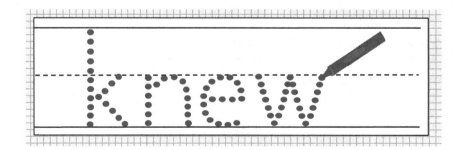

SYLLABICATION GUIDE

1. Use *The Syllable Division Word Book* to choose appropriate words.
2. Inform **(S)** that this is a strategy that will help them with vocabulary and word attack skills when they encounter an unfamiliar word.

How to Divide Two-Syllable Words:

1. Find the first two vowels (vowel sounds), underline them and label each with a V.
2. Draw a line (bridge) connecting the bottom of the two Vs, ex.: V__V.
3. Underline and label the letter(s) above the bridge with a C, ex.: <u>VCCV</u>.
4. Have **(S)** find pattern and divide word into syllables.
5. Have **(S)** label each syllable type (Cl, O, ME, VT, BR, C-le).
6. Have **(S)** read each syllable, then blend together into a word.
7. Check for comprehension or refer to dictionary for meaning.

How to Divide Words with Three or More Syllables:

1. Find the first two vowels (vowel sounds), underline them, and label with a V.
2. Draw a line (bridge) connecting the bottom of the two Vs, ex. V__V.
3. Underline and label each consonant with a C above the bridge. If there are three or more consonants, some consonants go together as one consonant unit (digraphs or blends).
   Example: b <u>a</u> <u>th</u> <u>t</u> <u>u</u> b
          V C C V
4. Have **(S)** find pattern and divide word into syllables.
5. Check to see if there is another vowel that is not an *e* at the end of the word.
6. If so, cover up the letters before the second labeled vowel, find the next vowel, and label with a V.
7. With off hand still covering up to the second labeled vowel, draw a bridge connecting the bottom of the vowels.
8. Label the consonant(s) above the bridge with a C, ex. <u>VCCV</u>.
9. Have **(S)** find pattern and divide word into syllables. If there is an additional vowel that is not an *e* at the end of the word, then go back to steps 6-8. If there are no additional vowels, then continue to steps 10-12.
10. Have **(S)** label each syllable type (Cl, O, ME, VT, BR, C-le).
11. Have **(S)** read each syllable, then blend together into a word.
12. Check for comprehension or refer to dictionary for meaning. Be sure **(S)** can write or say a sentence using the new word.

Remember

If two consonants are in the middle of a word, split the word between the two consonants. (Exception: If the two consonants are a digraph [sh, ch, th], they cannot be split.) If there are three or more consonants, some letters go together as one consonant unit (look for known digraphs or blends).

VISUAL CUES FOR WORDS AND SENTENCES

Words

——————	grapheme(s) line
qu	qu
sh	digraphs (sh, th)
b r	initial and final 2-letter blends
n ch	final digraph blends (-nch)
s t r	3-letter blends
sh r	initial digraph blends (shr-, thr-)
s qu	squ-
s m i l e ★★★	Magic E
+ed	suffix

Sentences*

——————	word line
══════	Red Word line
⛰	capital
☐	punctuation

*Remember not to use word visual cues for sentences.

Students should utilize CUPS to self-edit sentences.

Capitalization

Understanding

Punctuation

Spelling

Weekly Lesson Reminders (Comprehensive OG Plus)

Day	Components
Monday	☐ Phonological Awareness ☐ Three-Part Drill ☐ Teaching a New Concept: Multi-Sensory Experience ☐ Decodable Reader ☐ Language Comprehension with Rich Literature ☐ Teaching a New Concept: Application/Dictation of Words and Sentences
Tuesday	☐ PA Warm-Up or Activity ☐ Review Red Word(s) ☐ Introduce Weekly Red Word(s) ☐ Application/Dictation of Words and Sentences ☐ Decodable Reader ☐ Language Comprehension and Vocabulary ☐ Fluency (e.g., Rapid Word Chart) ☐ Written Expression
Wednesday	☐ PA Warm-Up or Activity ☐ Three-Part Drill (Include Monday's New Concept) ☐ Review Red Words ☐ Application/Dictation of Words and Sentences ☐ Decodable Readers ☐ Language Comprehension and Vocabulary ☐ Syllabication (after Concept 35)
Thursday	☐ PA Warm-Up or Activity ☐ Review Red Words ☐ Decodable Readers ☐ Syllabication (after Concept 35) ☐ Fluency (e.g., Rapid Word Chart) ☐ Language Comprehension and Vocabulary ☐ Written Expression ☐ Pretest or Additional Application/Dictation of Words and Sentences
Friday	☐ PA Warm-Up or Activity ☐ Three-Part Drill ☐ Review Red Words ☐ Decodable Readers (Clean One-Pager) ☐ Fluency Activity or Progress Monitoring ☐ Language Comprehension and Vocabulary ☐ Test with Green and Red Words

PHONEME/GRAPHEME CHART

Usage:
- Progress Reports
- Auditory/Kinesthetic Component of Drill

Consonants

#	Phoneme	Graphemes
1.	/b/	b
2.	/k/	c, k, -ck, ch, -que
3.	/d/	d, -ed
4.	/f/	f, -ff, ph, -gh
5.	/g/	g, gh
6.	/h/	h, -dge
7.	/j/	j
8.	/l/	l, -ll
9.	/m/	m, -mb, -mn
10.	/n/	n, kn, gn, mn
11.	/p/	p
12.	/kw/	qu
13.	/r/	r, wr, rh
14.	/s/	s, -ss, c, sc, ps, -se
15.	/t/	t, -ed, -bt, pt
16.	/v/	v, -ve
17.	/w/	w, wh
18.	/ks/	x
19.	/y/	y
20.	/z/	z, -zz, -s, -se

Consonant Digraphs

#	Phoneme	Graphemes
1.	/ch/	ch in chop, -tch e.g., latch
2.	/sh/	sh in shop, ch in chef, s in sure
3.	/TH/	th (voiced) e.g., this
4.	/th/	th (unvoiced) e.g., thimble
5.	/hw/	wh in whisper
6.	/zh/	s in treasure or in exclusion

Short Vowels

#	Phoneme	Graphemes
1.	/ă/	a
2.	/ĕ/	e, ea
3.	/ĭ/	i, y
4.	/ŏ/	o
5.	/ŭ/	u
6.	/aw/	au, aw, e.g., August
7.	/o͞o/	oo, u, e.g., look

Velar Nasal Units

#	Phoneme	Graphemes
1.	/ŋ/	-ang, -ing, -ong, -ung, -ank, -ink, -onk, -unk

Long Vowels

#	Phoneme	Graphemes
1.	/ā/	a, a-e, ai, ay, eigh, ei
2.	/ē/	e, e-e, y, ea, ee, ie, ei, ey
3.	/ī/	i, i-e, y, igh, ie, y-e
4.	/ō/	o, o-e, oa, oe, ow
5.	/yo͞o/	u, u-e, ew, ue, eu, e.g., cute, feud
6.	/o͞o/	u, u-e, oo, ew, ou, ue, ui, e.g., scoop

Kind Old Words

#	Phoneme	Graphemes
1.	/ī/	ild, ind
	/ō/	old, olt, ost

Diphthongs

#	Phoneme	Graphemes
1.	/oi/	oi, oy, e.g., coin
2.	/ou/	ou, ow, e.g., clown

R-Controlled Bossy-R

#	Phoneme	Graphemes
1.	/ar/	ar, ear, e.g., start, heart
2.	/er/	er, ir, ur, or, ar, ear, our, e.g., her, heard, onward, worthy
3.	/or/	ore, oar, or, ar, our, e.g., torn, war, quart

Other Combinations

#	Phoneme	Graphemes
1.	/air/	are, air, ar, ear, e.g., stair, arrow
2.	/eer/	ere, ear, eer, e.g., hear, steer
3.	/ire/	ire, e.g., tire
4.	/ure/	ure, e.g., cure

Consonant -le

1. -ble
2. -cle
3. -dle
4. -fle
5. -gle
6. -kle
7. -ple
8. -tle
9. -zle

Blends

Beginning
1. br, cr, dr, fr, gr, pr, tr
2. bl, cl, fl, gl, pl, sl
3. sc, sk, sm, sn, sp, st
4. dw, sw, tw
5. scr, shr, spl, spr, str, squ, thr

Ending
1. -ct, -ft, -lt, -nt, -pt, -xt
2. -st, -ld, -lf, -lk, -lp
3. -mp, -nch, -sk, -nd, -sp

Higher Level Concepts:

Suffixes:
1. /ĭd/: suffix -ed
2. /s/ and /z/: suffix -s
3. /ĭz/: suffix -es
4. /ĭŋ/: suffix -ing

NOTE: Do not use these for the Aud/Kin part of the Three-Part Drill:
1. Contractions: am, is, are, has, not, have, would, will
2. Schwa /ə/
3. Three Great Rules: Double, Drop, Change
4. Homophones: to, too, two, there, their, they're

Other:

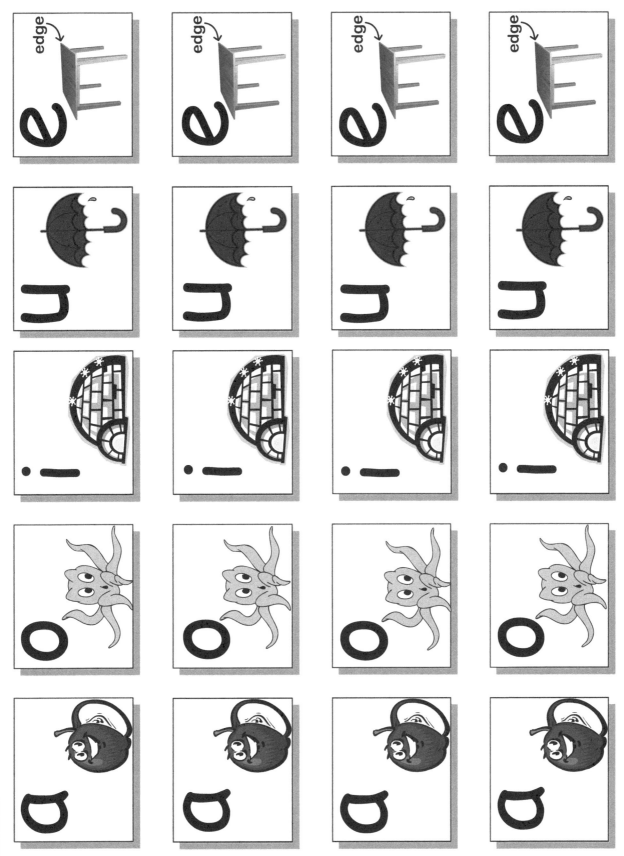

Appendix

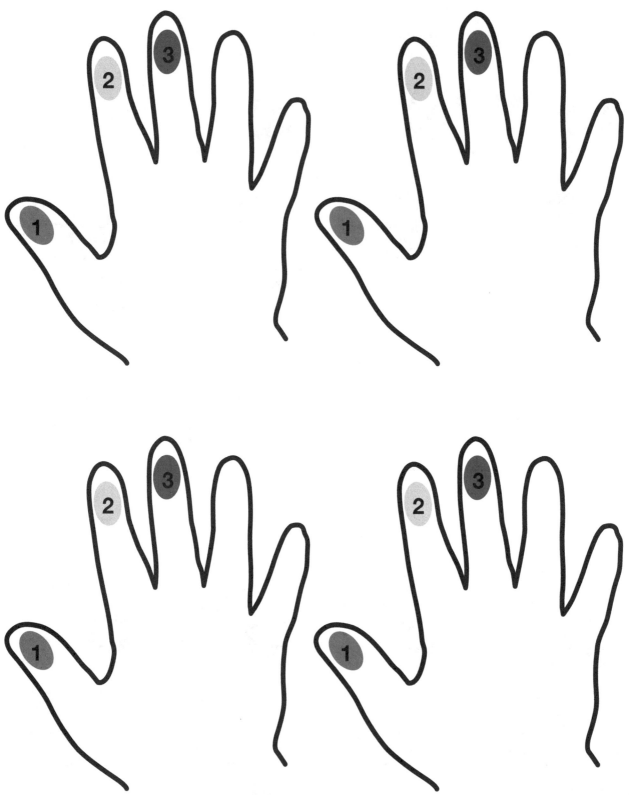

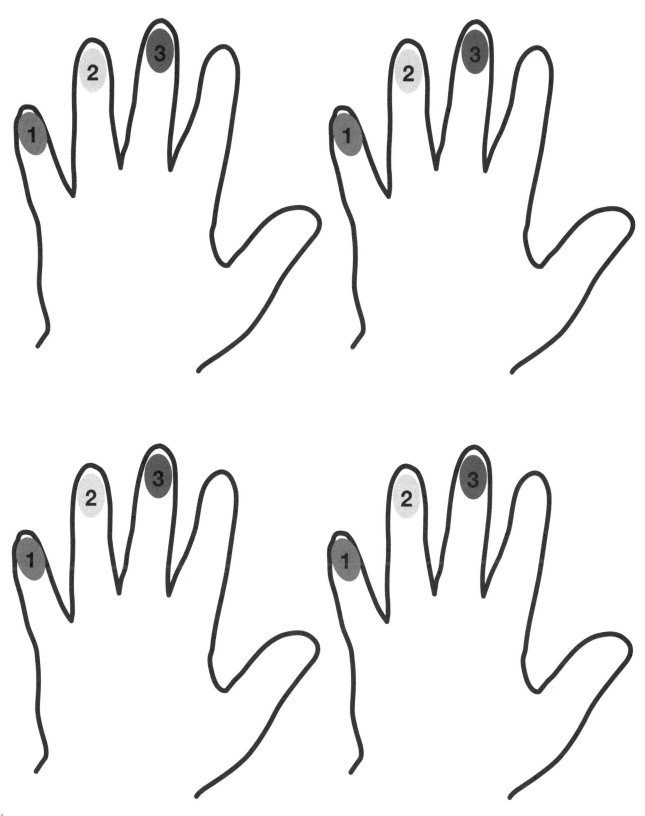

LESSON DICTATION (_____)

── WORDS ── ── REWRITE ──

WORDS	REWRITE
1.	1. _____
2.	2. _____
3.	3. _____
4.	4. _____
5.	5. _____

── SENTENCES ──

1.

1. _____

☐ C
☐ U
☐ P
☐ S

2.

2. _____

☐ C
☐ U
☐ P
☐ S

Capitalization

Understanding

Punctuation

Spelling

Page Intentionally Blank

SENTENCE:

SENTENCE:

Sammy – ss
Loves – ll
Friendly – ff
Zebras – zz

Spelling Rule: -ss, -ll, -ff, -zz
I syllable
I short vowel
ends with I s, I, f, or z
DOUBLE FINAL CONSONANT

-ss	-ll	-ff	-zz

-ss	-ll	-ff	-zz

-ss	-ll	-ff	-zz

-ss	-ll	-ff	-zz

-ss	-ll	-ff	-zz

-ss	-ll	-ff	-zz

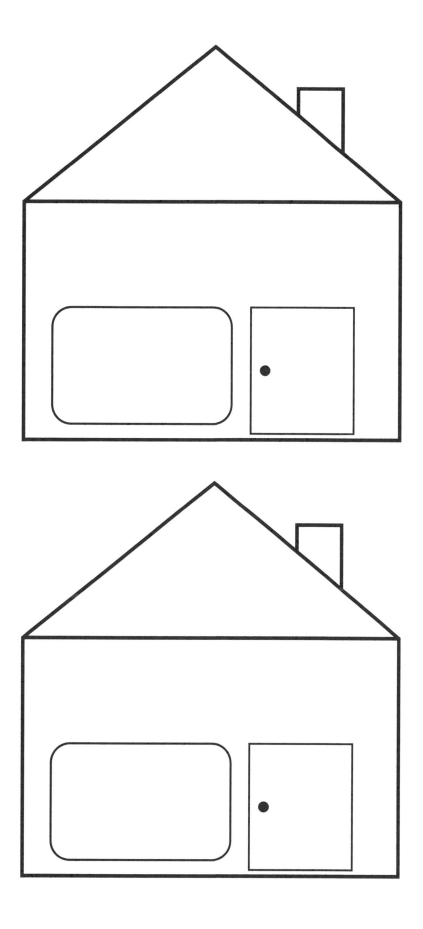

Closed or Open Syllable?

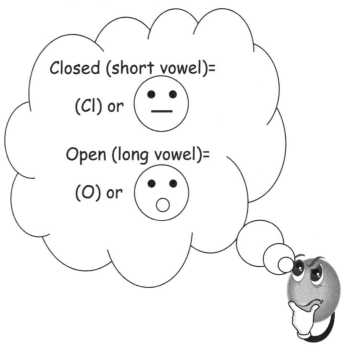

Closed (short vowel)=

(Cl) or

Open (long vowel)=

(O) or

| hi |
| bet |
| sop |
| lan |
| ba |
| vet |
| po |
| dut |
| up |
| bit |
| de |
| sho |
| tum |
| guz |
| va |
| ri |
| lam |

SYLLABLE DIVISION PATTERNS

1. VC/CV
2. V/CV
3. VC/V
4. V/V

SYLLABLE TYPE

1. Closed Syllable   Cl
2. Open Syllable   O
3. Magic E   ME
4. Vowel Team   VT
5. Bossy R   BR
6. Consonant-le   C-le

SYLLABLE DIVISION PATTERNS

1. VC/CV
2. V/CV
3. VC/V
4. V/V

SYLLABLE TYPE

1. Closed Syllable   Cl
2. Open Syllable   O
3. Magic E   ME
4. Vowel Team   VT
5. Bossy R   BR
6. Consonant-le   C-le

SYLLABLE DIVISION PATTERNS

1. VC/CV
2. V/CV
3. VC/V
4. V/V

SYLLABLE TYPE

1. Closed Syllable   Cl
2. Open Syllable   O
3. Magic E   ME
4. Vowel Team   VT
5. Bossy R   BR
6. Consonant-le   C-le

SYLLABLE DIVISION PATTERNS

1. VC/CV
2. V/CV
3. VC/V
4. V/V

SYLLABLE TYPE

1. Closed Syllable   Cl
2. Open Syllable   O
3. Magic E   ME
4. Vowel Team   VT
5. Bossy R   BR
6. Consonant-le   C-le

/yo͞o/ vs. /o͞o/ spelled with the letter 'u'

When the following letter precedes the long u sound, it is pronounced:

/yo͞o/	/o͞o/
b: bugle	d: dude
c: cute	j: juvenile
f: fume	l: luminate
g: argue	n: numeral
h: huge	r: prune
m: mule	s: sue
p: putrid	t: tube
	y: yule
	th: enthused

Note: Usually, when long u begins a syllable, it is pronounced /yo͞o/ regardless of any preceding letter. For example: unicorn, volume, value, evaluate, menu, January, monument.

When a t is next to a long u, the t makes a /ch/ or /sh/ sound as in habitual or actual. When a d is next to a long u, the d will make a /j/ sound, as in graduate.

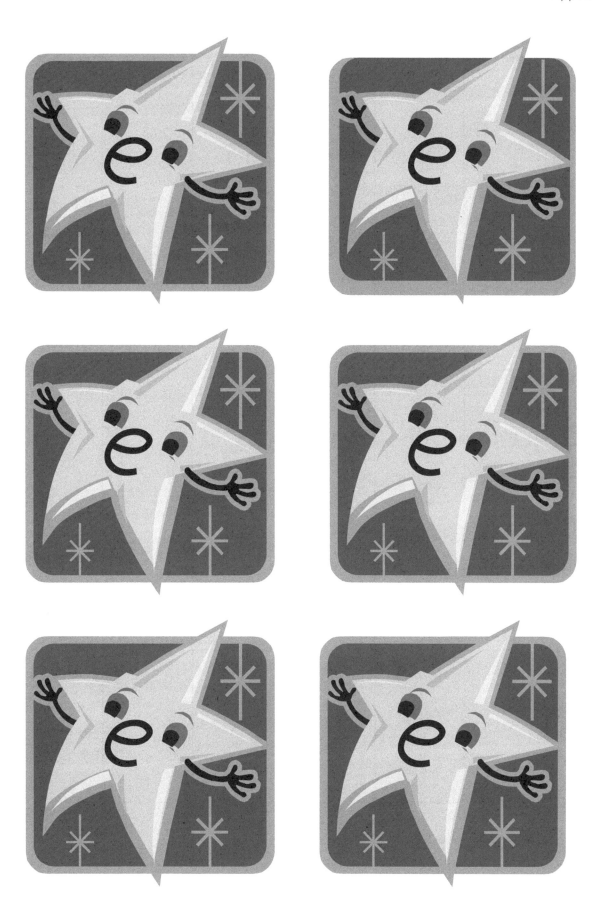

Vowel Team Placement Chart

	Beginning	Middle	End
ea			
ee			
ai			
ay			
oa			
oe			

Multiple Spellings for the Sound of /ē/

clen
clene
clyn
clean
cleen

	e	e - e	y	ea	ee
1.					
2.					
3.					
4.					
5.					
6.					

Multiple Spellings for the Sound of /ā/

snal
snale
snail
snayl

	a	a - e	ai	ay
1.				
2.				
3.				
4.				
5.				
6.				

© IMSE 2022

Multiple Spellings for the Sound of /ō/

bon
bone
boan
boen

	o	o - e	oa	oe
1.				
2.				
3.				
4.				
5.				
6.				

Page Intentionally Blank

Weekly Lesson Plan Template (Comprehensive OG Plus)

Day	Component	Checklist	Materials	Time:
Daily	**Phonological Awareness** *PA by Zgonc p.* — — — — — — *Equipped by Kilpatrick* Level — — — — — — p. — — — — — — —	❑ Direct Teaching ❑ Training/Reinforcing	❑ Tokens ❑ Sound Boxes ❑ One-Minute Activities ❑ Zgonc PA Book Materials:	1-10 min.
Minimum M, W, F	**Three-Part Drill** Concepts: — — — — — — —	❑ Visual ❑ Auditory/Kinesthetic ❑ Blending ❑ Vowel Intensive	❑ Cards (review) ❑ P/G Chart ❑ Sand (or another medium) ❑ Blending Board ❑ Sticks or Tents	10-15 min.
Monday	**New Concept(s):** — — — — — — — — — — — **Multi-Sensory Experience** *Comprehensive OG Plus Teacher's Guide p.* — — — — — —	**Multi-Sensory Experience** ❑ Alliteration (m-wh) ❑ Card ❑ Object/Picture Connection ❑ Letter Formation if Needed ❑ Practice Sound/Letter ❑ Connect with Literature ❑ Decodable Reader ❑ Mark P/G chart	❑ Screen ❑ Green Crayon ❑ Handwriting Paper ❑ Sand	20-30 min.
M-F	**New Concept(s): Application/Dictation** *Comprehensive OG Plus Teacher's Guide p.* — — — — — —	❑ Words: Visual Cues ❑ Sentences: Visual Cues, CUPS	❑ Fingertapping Hand ❑ Dictation Paper ❑ Differentiation Needed ❑ CUPS Poster	5-15 min.
T-F	**Red Word(s)** *Comprehensive OG Plus Teacher's Guide p.* — — — — — —	❑ Spell & Read ❑ Read Only ❑ Etymology needed	❑ Tokens ❑ Red Crayon ❑ Screen ❑ Red Word Paper ❑ Other:	10-30 min.
W-TH	**Syllabication** *Comprehensive OG Plus Teacher's Guide p.* — — — — — — *SDWB p.* — — — — — — —	❑ Choose 6+ Words	❑ Strips of Paper ❑ Written Words ❑ Highlighter ❑ Syllable Division Posters	10 min.

Day	Component	Checklist	Materials	Time:
Daily	**Fluency**	❑ Read Green Words ❑ Read Red Words ❑ Read Clean Copy	❑ Decodable Readers ❑ Rapid Word Chart ❑ Other:	10-20 min.
Weekly	**Vocabulary**	❑ Specific Word Instruction ❑ Word Learning Strategies ❑ Word Consciousness ❑ Tier II Words: _	❑ Vocabulary Maps ❑ Decodable Readers ❑ Other:	Minimum 50 min.
Weekly	**Comprehension**	❑ Comprehension Planning Checklist	❑ Decodable Reader ❑ Rich Literature ❑ Other:	Approx. 100 min.
Weekly	**Writing and Grammar**	❑ Incorporated Grammar with Writing ❑ Writing Activity	❑ Decodable Reader ❑ Journal Entry ❑ Other:	10-30 min.
TH: Pretest **F: Test**	**Weekly Assessment**	❑ Green Words ❑ Red Words	❑ Paper ❑ Pencil	10-20 min.

References

Archer, A. L., & Hughes, C. A. (2011). *Explicit instruction: Effective and efficient teaching.* The Guilford Press.

Chall, J. S. (1967). *Learning to read: The great debate.* McGraw-Hill.

Chall, J. S. (1996). *Stages of reading development* (2nd ed.). Cengage Learning.

Core Knowledge. (2013). *Core knowledge sequence: Content and skill guidelines for grades K-8.* Core Knowledge Foundation. https://www.coreknowledge.org/free-resource/core-knowledge-sequence/

Ehri, L. C., Cardoso-Martins, C., & Carroll, J. M. (2014). Developmental variation in reading words. In C. A. Stone, E. R. Silliman, B. J. Ehren, & G. P. Wallach (Eds.), *Handbook of language and literacy: Development and disorders* (2nd ed., pp. 285-407). Guilford Press.

Gough, P. B., & Tunmer, W. E. (1986). Decoding, reading, and reading disability. *Remedial and Special Education, 7*(1), 6-10. https://doi.org/10.1177/074193258600700104

Hirsch, E. D. (2020). *How to educate a citizen: The power of shared knowledge to unify a nation.* HarperCollins.

International Dyslexia Association. (2018, March). *Knowledge and practice standards for teachers of reading.* https://dyslexiaida.org/knowledge-and-practices/

Joshi, R. M., Dahlgren, M., & Boulware-Gooden, R. (2002). Teaching reading in an inner-city school through a multisensory teaching approach. *Annals of Dyslexia, 52*(1), 229-242. https://doi.org/10.1007/s11881-002-0014-9

Kilpatrick, D. A. (2016). *Equipped for reading success.* Casey & Kirsch Publishers.

Kohler-Curtis, J. (2022). *The IMSE Comprehensive Orton-Gillingham Plus teacher training manual.* The Institute for Multi-Sensory Education.

Moats, L. C., & Tolman, C. A. (2019). *LETRS* (3rd ed., Vol. 1). Voyager Sopris Learning.

The Reading League. (2021, Feb. 3). The Reading League Winter Symposium.

Scarborough, H. S. (2001). Connecting early language and literacy to later reading (dis)abilities: Evidence, theory, and practice. In S. Neuman & D. Dickinson (Eds.), *Handbook for research in early literacy* (Vol. 1, pp. 97-110). Guilford Press.

Seidenberg, M. S., & McClelland, J. L. (1989). A distributed, developmental model of word recognition and naming. *Psychological Review, 96*(4), 523–568. https://doi.apa.org/doiLanding?doi= 10.1037%2F0033-295X.96.4.523

Spear-Swerling, L. (2018). Structured literacy and typical literacy practices: Understanding differences to create instructional opportunities. *Teaching Exceptional Children, 51*(3), 201-211.

Zgonc, Y. (2010). *Interventions for all: Phonological awareness.* Crystal Springs Books.